Contents at a Glance

▓ **Contents** iv

▓ **About the Author** viii

▓ **About the Technical Reviewers** ix

▓ **Acknowledgments** x

▓ **Preface** xi

▓ **Chapter 1: Introduction to Android Imaging** 1

▓ **Chapter 2: Building Custom Camera Applications** 23

▓ **Chapter 3: Image Editing and Processing** 47

▓ **Chapter 4: Graphics and Touch Events** 79

▓ **Chapter 5: Introduction to Audio on Android** 105

▓ **Chapter 6: Background and Networked Audio** 125

▓ **Chapter 7: Audio Capture** 151

▓ **Chapter 8: Audio Synthesis and Analysis** 179

▓ **Chapter 9: Introduction to Video** 195

▓ **Chapter 10: Advanced Video** 211

▓ **Chapter 11: Video Capture** 229

▓ **Chapter 12: Media Consumption and Publishing Using Web Services** 251

▓ **Index** 291

Contents

▇Contents at a Glance iii

▇About the Author viii

▇About the Technical Reviewers ix

▇Acknowledgments x

▇Preface xi

▇**Chapter 1: Introduction to Android Imaging** 1

Image Capture Using the Built-In Camera Application 1

    Returning Data from the Camera App 3

    Capturing Larger Images 5

    Displaying Large Images 6

Image Storage and Metadata 10

    Obtaining an URI for the Image 11

    Updating Our CameraActivity to Use MediaStore for Image Storage and to Associate Metadata 12

    Retrieving Images Using the MediaStore 16

    Creating an Image Viewing Application 18

    Internal Metadata 21

Summary 21

▇**Chapter 2: Building Custom Camera Applications** 23

Using the Camera Class 23

    Camera Permissions 24

    Preview Surface 24

    Implementing the Camera 25

    Putting It All Together 35

Extending the Custom Camera Application 38

    Building a Timer-Based Camera App 38

    Building a Time-Lapse Photography App 43

Summary 45

Pro Android Media

Developing Graphics, Music, Video and Rich Media Apps for Smartphones and Tablets

Shawn Van Every

Apress®

Pro Android Media: Developing Graphics, Music, Video and Rich Media Apps for Smartphones and Tablets

Distributed to the book trade worldwide by Springer Science+Business Media, LLC., 233 Spring Street, 6th Floor, New York, NY 10013. Phone 1-800-SPRINGER, fax (201) 348-4505, e-mail orders-ny@springer-sbm.com, or visit www.springeronline.com.

For information on translations, please e-mail rights@apress.com, or visit www.apress.com.

Apress and friends of ED books may be purchased in bulk for academic, corporate, or promotional use. eBook versions and licenses are also available for most titles. For more information, reference our Special Bulk Sales–eBook Licensing web page at www.apress.com/info/bulksales.

The information in this book is distributed on an "as is" basis, without warranty. Although every precaution has been taken in the preparation of this work, neither the author(s) nor Apress shall have any liability to any person or entity with respect to any loss or damage caused or alleged to be caused directly or indirectly by the information contained in this work.

The source code for this book is available to readers at www.apress.com.

■Chapter 3: Image Editing and Processing 47

Selecting Images Using the Built-In Gallery Application...47
Drawing a Bitmap onto a Bitmap...52
Basic Image Scaling and Rotating 54
    Enter the Matrix 55
    Matrix Methods..58
    Alternative to Drawing 64
Image Processing 65
    ColorMatrix 65
    Altering Contrast and Brightness...67
    Changing Saturation 69
Image Compositing 69
Summary 78

■Chapter 4: Graphics and Touch Events.. 79

Canvas Drawing..79
    Bitmap Creation 79
    Bitmap Configuration 80
    Creating the Canvas 81
    Working with Paint..82
    Drawing Shapes...83
    Drawing Text...87
Finger Painting...93
    Touch Events 93
    Drawing on Existing Images 97
    Saving a Bitmap-Based Canvas Drawing..101
Summary 104

■Chapter 5: Introduction to Audio on Android.. 105

Audio Playback 105
    Supported Audio Formats 106
    Using the Built-In Audio Player via an Intent 107
    Creating a Custom Audio-Playing Application 109
    MediaStore for Audio...115
Summary 123

■Chapter 6: Background and Networked Audio 125

Background Audio Playback 125
    Services 125
    Local Service plus MediaPlayer..129
    Controlling a MediaPlayer in a Service...132
Networked Audio 137
    HTTP Audio Playback 137
    Streaming Audio via HTTP...143
    RTSP Audio Streaming 150
Summary 150

■Chapter 7: Audio Capture 151

Audio Capture with an Intent 151
Custom Audio Capture 154

MediaRecorder Audio Sources..155

MediaRecorder Output Formats..155

MediaRecorder Audio Encoders..156

MediaRecorder Output and Recording...156

MediaRecorder State Machine..156

MediaRecorder Example..157

Other MediaRecorder Methods...162

Inserting Audio into the MediaStore...167

Raw Audio Recording with AudioRecord 167

Raw Audio Playback with AudioTrack 170

Raw Audio Capture and Playback Example 172

Summary 177

Chapter 8: Audio Synthesis and Analysis 179

Digital Audio Synthesis 179

Playing a Synthesized Sound...180

Generating Samples...182

Audio Analysis...187

Capturing Sound for Analysis...188

Visualizing Frequencies 189

Summary 193

Chapter 9: Introduction to Video 195

Video Playback..195

Supported Formats 195

Playback Using an Intent..196

Playback Using VideoView...197

Adding Controls with MediaController 199

Playback Using a MediaPlayer...200

Summary 210

Chapter 10: Advanced Video 211

MediaStore for Retrieving Video 211

Video Thumbnails from the MediaStore...212

Full MediaStore Video Example 212

Networked Video..218

Supported Network Video Types...218

Network Video Playback 221

Summary 228

Chapter 11: Video Capture... 229

Recording Video Using an Intent...229

Adding Video Metadata..232

Custom Video Capture..235

MediaRecorder for Video 235

Full Custom Video Capture Example 246

Summary 250

Chapter 12: Media Consumption and Publishing Using Web Services 251

Web Services 251

HTTP Requests...252

JSON 254
   Pulling Flickr Images Using JSON..257
   Location 263
   Pulling Flickr Images Using JSON and Location 266
REST 273
   Representing Data in XML 273
   SAX Parsing 274
HTTP File Uploads 278
   Making an HTTP Request..278
   Uploading Video to Blip.TV 280
Summary 290

■Index.. 291

About the Author

Shawn Van Every runs a mobile and streaming media consultancy to help companies better utilize emerging technologies related to audio and video with a focus on mobile and streaming applications. His clients have ranged from 19 Entertainment, MoMA, and Disney to Morgan Stanley, Lehman Brothers, and NYU Medical School, along with countless start-ups and other small clients.

Additionally, Shawn is an Adjunct Assistant Professor of Communication in NYU's Interactive Telecommunications Program. His teaching is varied and includes courses on participatory and social media, programming, mobile technologies, and interactive telephony. In 2008 he was honored with the David Payne Carter award for excellence in teaching.

He has demonstrated, exhibited, and presented work at many conferences and technology demonstrations, including O'Reilly's Emerging Telephony, O'Reilly's Emerging Technology, ACM Multimedia, Vloggercon, and Strong Angel II. He was a co-organizer of the Open Media Developers Summit, Beyond Broadcast (2006), and iPhoneDevCamp NYC.

Shawn holds a Master's degree in Interactive Telecommunications from NYU and a Bachelor's degree in Media Study from SUNY at Buffalo.

About the Technical Reviewers

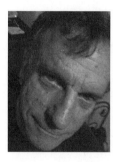 **Steve Bull** has been coding and manipulating mobile devices since his days at Paul Allen's Interval Research in Palo Alto. As a mixed-media technology artist and entrepreneur, for the last nine years Bull has created location-specific narratives and games that explore the social, technological and creative possibilities of cell phones. He can be reached at www.stevebull.org.

Wallace Jackson is a seasoned multimedia producer and i3D programmer for Acrobat3D PDF, Android mobile apps, iTV Design, JavaFX, and JavaTV. He has been designing rich media since the Atari ST1040 and AMIGA 3000 and has been writing for leading multimedia publications on new media content development since the advent of *Multimedia Producer* magazine nearly two decades ago. He can be reached at www.wallacejackson.com.

Acknowledgments

The idea for this book came out of my work teaching at NYU. A huge debt of gratitude is owed to the ever encouraging faculty, staff, and students who comprise NYU's Interactive Telecommunications Program and who provide an endless source of inspiration. Thank you to Red Burns for creating, fostering, and ever improving ITP. Thank you to Dan O'Sullivan for constantly challenging me. Thank you to Tom Igoe and Dan Shiffman for showing me that it can be done. Thank you to Rob Ryan and Marianne Petite for all of your support. Thank you to all of the rest of the faculty, staff, and residents that I have worked with. And thank you to all of my current and former students who have made me realize how rewarding it can be to teach and see projects come alive; particularly Nisma Zaman, who provided very valuable early feedback.

This book would not have come close to being in existence if it weren't for the dedicated and very talented staff at Apress. Thank you Steve Anglin, Matthew Moodie, Corbin Collins, Mary Ann Fugate, Adam Heath, Anne Collette, and the rest of the Apress staff for your extraordinary effort.

A huge thank you to Steve Bull and Wallace Jackson, the technical reviewers for testing every piece of code and for filling in the blanks when I missed something. Your contributions were invaluable!

It goes without saying but this book could not have been written if it weren't for the folks responsible for bringing Android into existence. Thank you to them, particularly Dave Sparks from Google who made himself available for some very valuable fact checking and question answering.

To all of my friends and family who were so encouraging, thank you.

Finally, of course, this book would not have happened without the support of my wonderful wife, Karen Van Every. Thank you!

Preface

Among all the things that mobile phones are and have become, one definite trend is the increase in the media production and consumption capabilities they offer. This trend began with the advent of the camera phone in the late 1990s, and over the last few years has dramatically taken off with the surging popularity of smart phones. In terms of media capabilities, today's mobile handsets are simultaneously cameras, photo albums, camcorders, movie players, music players, dictation machines, and potentially much more.

In particular, Android has rich capabilities available within the SDK that this book seeks to illuminate with discussion and examples so that you can get a jump-start on developing the next generation media applications. It walks you through examples that not only show how to display and play media but also allow you to take advantage of the camera, microphone, and video capture capabilities. It is organized more or less into four sections: The first four chapters deal with imaging; the second four handle audio; and the final four are about video and harnessing web services for finding and sharing media.

The examples presented within get a bit more challenging as the book progresses, as the amount of work that needs to be done to develop applications that harness the capabilities increases. Regardless, with some familiarity with Android application development you, the reader should be able to jump to any section and utilize the discussion and example code to create an application that utilizes the capabilities presented.

The examples are generally in the form of a full class that extends an Activity targeted to run with the SDK version 4 (Android 1.6) or later. The examples also include the contents of an XML layout file and in many cases the contents of the `AndroidManifest.xml` file. It is assumed that you will be using Eclipse (Galileo or later) with the ADT plugin (0.9.9 or later) and using the Android SDK (r7 or later). Since much of the book is geared toward audio and video, I advise that you run the examples on a handset (running Android 1.6 or later) rather than on the emulator, because in many cases the examples do not function on the emulator.

I am excited to see what the future of media applications on mobile devices is. It is my hope that through this book I can help you to create and define that future. I look forward to seeing your Android media applications in action.

With all that out of the way, let's get started!

Chapter 1

Introduction to Android Imaging

In this chapter, we'll look at the basics of image capture and storage on Android. We'll explore the built-in capabilities that Android provides first and in later chapters move into more custom software. The built-in capabilities for image capture and storage provide a good introduction to the overall media capabilities on Android and pave the way toward what we'll be doing in later chapters with audio and video.

With that in mind, we'll start with how to harness the built-in Camera application and move on to utilizing the MediaStore, the built-in media and metadata storage mechanism. Along the way, we'll look at ways to reduce memory usage and leverage EXIF, the standard in the consumer electronics and image processing software worlds for sharing metadata.

Image Capture Using the Built-In Camera Application

With mobile phones quickly becoming mobile computers, they have in many ways replaced a whole variety of consumer electronics. One of the earliest non-phone related hardware capabilities added to mobile phones was a camera. Currently, it seems someone would be hard pressed to buy a mobile phone that doesn't include a camera. Of course, Android-based phones are no exception; from the beginning, the Android SDK has supported accessing the built-in hardware camera on phones to capture images.

The easiest and most straightforward way to do many things on Android is to leverage an existing piece of software on the device by using an **intent**. An intent is a core component of Android that is described in the documentation as a "description of an action to be performed." In practice, intents are used to trigger other applications to do something or to switch between activities in a single application.

All stock Android devices with the appropriate hardware (camera) come with the Camera application. The Camera application includes an intent filter, which allows developers to offer image capture capabilities on a par with the Camera application without having to build their own custom capture routines.

An intent filter is a means for a programmer of an application to specify that their application offers a specific capability. Specifying an intent filter in the AndroidManifest.xml file of an application tells Android that this application and, in particular, the activity that contains the intent filter will perform the specified task, on command.

The Camera application has the following intent filter specified in its manifest file. The intent filter shown here is contained within the "Camera" activity tags.

```
<intent-filter>
    <action android:name="android.media.action.IMAGE_CAPTURE" />
    <category android:name="android.intent.category.DEFAULT" />
</intent-filter>
```

In order to utilize the Camera application via an intent, we simply have to construct an intent that will be caught by the foregoing filter.

```
Intent i = new Intent("android.media.action.IMAGE_CAPTURE");
```

In practice, we probably don't want to create the intent with that action string directly. In this case, a constant is specified in the MediaStore class, ACTION_IMAGE_CAPTURE. The reason we should use the constant rather than the string itself is that if the string happens to change, it is likely that the constant will change as well, thereby making our call a bit more future-proof than it would otherwise be.

```
Intent i = new Intent(android.provider.MediaStore.ACTION_IMAGE_CAPTURE);
startActivity(i);
```

Using this intent in a basic Android activity will cause the default Camera application to launch in still picture mode, as shown in Figure 1–1.

Figure 1–1. *The built-in Camera application as called from an intent shown running in an emulator*

Returning Data from the Camera App

Of course, simply capturing an image using the built-in camera application won't actually be useful without having the Camera application return the picture to the calling activity when one is captured. This can be accomplished by substituting the startActivity method in our activity with the startActivityForResult method. Using this method allows us the ability to access the data returned from the Camera application, which happens to be the image that was captured by the user as a Bitmap.

Here is a basic example:

```
package com.apress.proandroidmedia.ch1.cameraintent;

import android.app.Activity;
import android.content.Intent;
import android.graphics.Bitmap;
import android.os.Bundle;
import android.widget.ImageView;

public class CameraIntent extends Activity {

    final static int CAMERA_RESULT = 0;

    ImageView imv;

    @Override
    public void onCreate(Bundle savedInstanceState) {
        super.onCreate(savedInstanceState);
        setContentView(R.layout.main);
        Intent i = new Intent(android.provider.MediaStore.ACTION_IMAGE_CAPTURE);
        startActivityForResult(i, CAMERA_RESULT);
    }

    protected void onActivityResult(int requestCode, int resultCode, Intent intent) {
        super.onActivityResult(requestCode, resultCode, intent);

        if (resultCode == RESULT_OK)
        {
            Get Bundle extras = intent.getExtras();
            Bitmap bmp = (Bitmap) extras.get("data");


            imv = (ImageView) findViewById(R.id.ReturnedImageView);
            imv.setImageBitmap(bmp);
        }
    }
}
```

It requires the following in the project's layout/main.xml file:

```
<?xml version="1.0" encoding="utf-8"?>
<LinearLayout xmlns:android="http://schemas.android.com/apk/res/android"
    android:orientation="vertical"
    android:layout_width="fill_parent"
    android:layout_height="fill_parent"
    >
```

```
    <ImageView android:id="@+id/ReturnedImageView" android:layout_width="wrap_content"↵
android:layout_height="wrap_content"></ImageView>
</LinearLayout>
```

To complete the foregoing example, here are the contents of AndroidManifest.xml.

```
<?xml version="1.0" encoding="utf-8"?>
<manifest xmlns:android="http://schemas.android.com/apk/res/android"
      android:versionCode="1"
      android:versionName="1.0" package="com.apress.proandroidmedia.ch1.cameraintent">
    <application android:icon="@drawable/icon" android:label="@string/app_name">
        <activity android:name=".CameraIntent"
                  android:label="@string/app_name">
            <intent-filter>
                <action android:name="android.intent.action.MAIN" />
                <category android:name="android.intent.category.LAUNCHER" />
            </intent-filter>
        </activity>
    </application>
    <uses-sdk android:minSdkVersion="4" />
</manifest>
```

In this example, the image is returned from the Camera application in an **extra** passed through the intent that is sent to our calling activity in the onActivityResult method. The name of the extra is "data" and it contains a Bitmap object, which needs to be cast from a generic Object.

```
// Get Extras from the intent
Bundle extras = intent.getExtras();

// Get the returned image from that extra
Bitmap bmp = (Bitmap) extras.get("data");
```

In our layout XML (layout/main.xml) file, we have an ImageView. An ImageView is an extension of a generic View, which supports the display of images. Since we have an ImageView with the id ReturnedImageView specified, in our activity we need to obtain a reference to that and set its Bitmap through its setImageBitmap method to be our returned image. This enables the user of our application to view the image that was captured.

To get a reference to the ImageView object, we use the standard findViewById method specified in the Activity class. This method allows us to programmatically reference elements specified in the layout XML file that we are using via setContentView by passing in the id of the element. In the foregoing example, the ImageView object is specified in the XML as follows:

```
<ImageView android:id="@+id/ReturnedImageView" android:layout_width="wrap_content"↵
android:layout_height="wrap_content"></ImageView>
```

To reference the ImageView and tell it to display the Bitmap from the Camera, we use the following code.

```
imv = (ImageView) findViewById(R.id.ReturnedImageView);imv.setImageBitmap(bmp);
```

When you run this example, you'll probably notice that the resulting image is small. (On my phone, it is 121 pixels wide by 162 pixels tall. Other devices have different default sizes.) This is not a bug—rather, it is by design. The Camera application, when triggered via an intent, does not return the full-size image back to the calling activity. In general, doing so would require quite a bit of memory, and the mobile device is generally constrained in this respect. Instead the Camera application returns a small thumbnail image in the returned intent, as shown in Figure 1–2.

Figure 1–2. *The resulting 121x162 pixel image displayed in our ImageView*

Capturing Larger Images

To get around the size limitation, starting with Android 1.5, on most devices we can pass an extra into the intent that is used to trigger the Camera application. The name for this extra is specified in the MediaStore class as a constant called EXTRA_OUTPUT. The value (extras take the form of name-value pairs) for this extra indicates to the Camera application where you would like the captured image saved in the form of an URI.

The following code snippet specifies to the Camera application that the image should be saved to the SD card on a device with a file name of myfavoritepicture.jpg.

```
String imageFilePath = Environment.getExternalStorageDirectory().getAbsolutePath()
        + "/myfavoritepicture.jpg";
File imageFile = new File(imageFilePath);
Uri imageFileUri = Uri.fromFile(imageFile);

Intent i = new Intent(android.provider.MediaStore.ACTION_IMAGE_CAPTURE);
i.putExtra(android.provider.MediaStore.EXTRA_OUTPUT, imageFileUri);
startActivityForResult(i, CAMERA_RESULT);
```

> **NOTE:** The foregoing code snippet for creating the URI to the image file could be simplified to the following: `imageFileUri =`
> `Uri.parse("file:///sdcard/myfavoritepicture.jpg");`
>
> In practice, though, using the method shown will be more device-independent and future-proof should the SD card–naming conventions or the URI syntax for the local filesystem change.

Displaying Large Images

Loading and displaying an image has significant memory usage implications. For instance, the HTC G1 phone has a 3.2-megapixel camera. A 3.2-megapixel camera typically captures images at 2048 pixels by 1536 pixels. Displaying a 32-bit image of that size would take more than100663kb or approximately 13MB of memory. While this may not guarantee that our application will run out of memory, it will certainly make it more likely.

Android offers us a utility class called `BitmapFactory`, which provides a series of static methods that allow the loading of `Bitmap` images from a variety of sources. For our needs, we'll be loading it from a file to display in our original activity. Fortunately, the methods available in `BitmapFactory` take in a `BitmapFactory.Options` class, which allows us to define how the Bitmap is read into memory. Specifically, we can set the sample size that the `BitmapFactory` should use when loading an image. Indicating the `inSampleSize` parameter in `BitmapFactory.Options` indicates that the resulting `Bitmap` image will be that fraction of the size once loaded. For instance, setting the `inSampleSize` to 8 as I do here would yield an image that is 1/8 the size of the original image.

```
BitmapFactory.Options bmpFactoryOptions = new BitmapFactory.Options();
bmpFactoryOptions.inSampleSize = 8;
Bitmap bmp = BitmapFactory.decodeFile(imageFilePath, bmpFactoryOptions);
imv.setImageBitmap(bmp);
```

This is a quick way to load up a large image but doesn't really take into account the image's original size nor the size of the screen. It would be better if we scaled the image to something that would fit nicely on our screen.

The segments of code that follow illustrate how to use the dimensions of the display to determine the amount of down sampling that should occur when loading the image. When we use these methods, the image is assured of filling the bounds of the display as much as possible. If, however, the image is only going to be shown at 100 pixels in any one dimension, that value should be used instead of the display dimensions, which we obtain as follows.

```
Display currentDisplay = getWindowManager().getDefaultDisplay();
int dw = currentDisplay.getWidth();
int dh = currentDisplay.getHeight();
```

To determine the overall dimensions of the image, which are needed for the calculation, we use the `BitmapFactory` and `BitmapFactory.Options` with the `BitmapFactory.Options.inJustDecodeBounds` variable set to true. This tells the `BitmapFactory` class to just give us the bounds of the image rather than attempting to decode the image itself. When we use this method, the `BitmapFactory.Options.outHeight` and `BitmapFactory.Options.outWidth` variables are filled in.

```
// Load up the image's dimensions not the image itself
BitmapFactory.Options bmpFactoryOptions = new BitmapFactory.Options();
bmpFactoryOptions.inJustDecodeBounds = true;
Bitmap bmp = BitmapFactory.decodeFile(imageFilePath, bmpFactoryOptions);

int heightRatio = (int)Math.ceil(bmpFactoryOptions.outHeight/(float)dh);
int widthRatio = (int)Math.ceil(bmpFactoryOptions.outWidth/(float)dw);

Log.v("HEIGHTRATIO",""+heightRatio);
Log.v("WIDTHRATIO",""+widthRatio);
```

Simple division of the dimensions of the image by the dimensions of the display tells us the ratio. We can then choose whether to use the height ratio or the width ratio, depending on which is greater. Simply using that ratio as the `BitmapFactory.Options.inSampleSize` variable will yield an image that should be loaded into memory with dimensions close to the same dimensions that we need—in this case, close to the dimensions of the display itself.

```
// If both of the ratios are greater than 1,
// one of the sides of the image is greater than the screen
if (heightRatio > 1 && widthRatio > 1)
{
    if (heightRatio > widthRatio)
    {
        // Height ratio is larger, scale according to it
        bmpFactoryOptions.inSampleSize = heightRatio;
    }
    else
    {
        // Width ratio is larger, scale according to it
        bmpFactoryOptions.inSampleSize = widthRatio;
    }
}

// Decode it for real
bmpFactoryOptions.inJustDecodeBounds = false;
bmp = BitmapFactory.decodeFile(imageFilePath, bmpFactoryOptions);
```

Here is the code for a full example that uses the built-in camera via an intent and displays the resulting picture. Figure 1–3 shows a resulting screen sized image as generated by this example.

```java
package com.apress.proandroidmedia.ch1.sizedcameraintent;

import java.io.File;

import android.app.Activity;
import android.content.Intent;
import android.graphics.Bitmap;
import android.graphics.BitmapFactory;
import android.net.Uri;
import android.os.Bundle;
import android.os.Environment;
import android.util.Log;
import android.view.Display;
import android.widget.ImageView;

public class SizedCameraIntent extends Activity {

    final static int CAMERA_RESULT = 0;

    ImageView imv;
    String imageFilePath;

    @Override
    public void onCreate(Bundle savedInstanceState) {
        super.onCreate(savedInstanceState);
        setContentView(R.layout.main);

        imageFilePath = Environment.getExternalStorageDirectory().getAbsolutePath() +
            "/myfavoritepicture.jpg";
        File imageFile = new File(imageFilePath);
        Uri imageFileUri = Uri.fromFile(imageFile);

        Intent i = new Intent(android.provider.MediaStore.ACTION_IMAGE_CAPTURE);
        i.putExtra(android.provider.MediaStore.EXTRA_OUTPUT, imageFileUri);
        startActivityForResult(i, CAMERA_RESULT);
    }

    protected void onActivityResult(int requestCode, int resultCode, Intent intent) {
        super.onActivityResult(requestCode, resultCode, intent);

        if (resultCode == RESULT_OK)
        {
            // Get a reference to the ImageView
            imv = (ImageView) findViewById(R.id.ReturnedImageView);

            Display currentDisplay = getWindowManager().getDefaultDisplay();
            int dw = currentDisplay.getWidth();
            int dh = currentDisplay.getHeight();

            // Load up the image's dimensions not the image itself
            BitmapFactory.Options bmpFactoryOptions = new BitmapFactory.Options();
            bmpFactoryOptions.inJustDecodeBounds = true;
            Bitmap bmp = BitmapFactory.decodeFile(imageFilePath, bmpFactoryOptions);

            int heightRatio = (int)Math.ceil(bmpFactoryOptions.outHeight/(float)dh);
            int widthRatio = (int)Math.ceil(bmpFactoryOptions.outWidth/(float)dw);
```

```java
            Log.v("HEIGHTRATIO",""+heightRatio);
            Log.v("WIDTHRATIO",""+widthRatio);

            // If both of the ratios are greater than 1,
            // one of the sides of the image is greater than the screen
            if (heightRatio > 1 && widthRatio > 1)
            {
                if (heightRatio > widthRatio)
                {
                    // Height ratio is larger, scale according to it
                    bmpFactoryOptions.inSampleSize = heightRatio;
                }
                else
                {
                    // Width ratio is larger, scale according to it
                    bmpFactoryOptions.inSampleSize = widthRatio;
                }
            }

            // Decode it for real
            bmpFactoryOptions.inJustDecodeBounds = false;
            bmp = BitmapFactory.decodeFile(imageFilePath, bmpFactoryOptions);

            // Display it
            imv.setImageBitmap(bmp);
        }
    }
}
```

The foregoing code requires the following layout/main.xml file:

```xml
<?xml version="1.0" encoding="utf-8"?>
<LinearLayout xmlns:android="http://schemas.android.com/apk/res/android"
    android:orientation="vertical"
    android:layout_width="fill_parent"
    android:layout_height="fill_parent"
    >
  <ImageView android:id="@+id/ReturnedImageView" android:layout_width="wrap_content"↵
android:layout_height="wrap_content"></ImageView>
</LinearLayout>
```

Figure 1–3. *The resulting screen-sized image displayed in our ImageView*

Image Storage and Metadata

Android has a standard way to share data across applications. The classes responsible for this are called **content providers**. Content providers offer a standard interface for the storage and retrieval of various types of data.

The standard content provider for images (as well as audio and video) is the `MediaStore`. The `MediaStore` allows the setting of the file in a standard location on the device and has facilities for storing and retrieving metadata about that file. Metadata is data about data; it could include information about the data in the file itself, such as its size and name, but the `MediaStore` also allows setting for a wide variety of additional data, such as title, description, latitude, and longitude.

To start utilizing the `MediaStore`, let's change our `SizedCameraIntent` activity so that it uses it for image storage and metadata association instead of storing the image in an arbitrary file on the SD card.

Obtaining an URI for the Image

To obtain the standard location for storage of images, we first need to get a reference to the MediaStore. To do this, we use a **content resolver**. A content resolver is the means to access a content provider, which the MediaStore is.

By passing a specific URI, the content resolver knows to provide an interface to the MediaStore as the content provider. Since we are inserting a new image, the method we are using is insert and the URI that we should use is contained in a constant in the android.provider.MediaStore.Images.Media class called EXTERNAL_CONTENT_URI. This means that we want to store the image on the primary external volume of the device, generally the SD card. If we wanted to store it instead in the internal memory of the device, we could use INTERNAL_CONTENT_URI. Generally, though, for media storage, as images, audio, and video can be rather large in size, you'll want to use the EXTERNAL_CONTENT_URI.

The insert call shown previously returns an URI, which we can use to write the image file's binary data to. In our case, as we are doing in the CameraActivity, we want to simply pass that as an extra in the intent that triggers the Camera application.

```
Uri imageFileUri = getContentResolver().insert(
    Media.EXTERNAL_CONTENT_URI, new ContentValues());

Intent i = new Intent(android.provider.MediaStore.ACTION_IMAGE_CAPTURE);
i.putExtra(android.provider.MediaStore.EXTRA_OUTPUT, imageFileUri);
startActivityForResult(i, CAMERA_RESULT);
```

You'll notice that we are also passing in a new ContentValues object. The ContentValues object is the metadata that we want to associate with the record when it is created. In the preceding example, we are passing in an empty ContentValues object.

Prepopulating Associated Metadata

If we wanted to pre-fill the metadata, we would use the put method to add some data into it. ContentValues takes data as name-value pairs. The names are standard and defined as constants in the android.provider.MediaStore.Images.Media class. (Some of the constants are actually located in the android.provider.MediaStore.MediaColumns interface, which the Media class implements.)

```
// Save the name and description of an image in a ContentValues map.
ContentValues contentValues = new ContentValues(3);
contentValues.put(Media.DISPLAY_NAME, "This is a test title");
contentValues.put(Media.DESCRIPTION, "This is a test description");
contentValues.put(Media.MIME_TYPE, "image/jpeg");

// Add a new record without the bitmap, but with some values set.
// insert() returns the URI of the new record.
Uri imageFileUri = getContentResolver().insert(Media.EXTERNAL_CONTENT_URI,⏎
contentValues);
```

Again, what is returned by this call is a URI that can be passed to the Camera application via the intent to specify the location that the image should be saved in.

If you output this URI via a Log command, it should look something like this:

content://media/external/images/media/16

The first thing you might notice is that it looks like a regular URL, such as you would use in a web browser; but instead of starting with something like http, which is the protocol that delivers web pages, it starts with content. In Android, when a URI starts with content, it is one that is used with a content provider (such as MediaStore).

Retrieving the Saved Image

The same URI obtained previously for saving the image can be used as the means to access the image as well. Instead of passing in the full path to the file to our BitmapFactory, we can instead open an InputStream for the image via the content resolver and pass that to BitmapFactory.

```
Bitmap bmp = BitmapFactory.decodeStream(↵
getContentResolver().openInputStream(imageFileUri), null, bmpFactoryOptions);
```

Adding Metadata Later

If we want to associate more metadata with the image after we have captured it into the MediaStore, we can use the update method of our content resolver. This is very similar to the insert method we used previously, except we are accessing the image file directly with the URI to the image file.

```
// Update the record with Title and Description
ContentValues contentValues = new ContentValues(3);
contentValues.put(Media.DISPLAY_NAME, "This is a test title");
contentValues.put(Media.DESCRIPTION, "This is a test description");
getContentResolver().update(imageFileUri,contentValues,null,null);
```

Updating Our CameraActivity to Use MediaStore for Image Storage and to Associate Metadata

The following is an update to our previous example, which saves our image in the MediaStore and then presents us with an opportunity to add a title and description. In addition, this version has several UI elements whose visibility is managed based upon the progress of the user in the application.

```
package com.apress.proandroidmedia.ch1.mediastorecameraintent;

import java.io.FileNotFoundException;
import android.app.Activity;
import android.content.Intent;
import android.graphics.Bitmap;
import android.graphics.BitmapFactory;
import android.net.Uri;
```

```
import android.os.Bundle;
import android.util.Log;
import android.view.View;
import android.view.View.OnClickListener;
import android.widget.Button;
import android.widget.EditText;
import android.widget.ImageView;
import android.widget.TextView;
import android.widget.Toast;
import android.provider.MediaStore.Images.Media;
import android.content.ContentValues;

public class MediaStoreCameraIntent extends Activity {

    final static int CAMERA_RESULT = 0;

    Uri imageFileUri;

    // User interface elements, specified in res/layout/main.xml
    ImageView returnedImageView;
    Button takePictureButton;
    Button saveDataButton;
    TextView titleTextView;
    TextView descriptionTextView;
    EditText titleEditText;
    EditText descriptionEditText;
```

We are including a couple of user interface elements. They are specified as normal in layout/main.xml and their objects are declared in the foregoing code.

```
    @Override
    public void onCreate(Bundle savedInstanceState)
    {
        super.onCreate(savedInstanceState);

        // Set the content view to be what is defined in the res/layout/main.xml file
        setContentView(R.layout.main);

        // Get references to UI elements
        returnedImageView = (ImageView) findViewById(R.id.ReturnedImageView);
        takePictureButton = (Button) findViewById(R.id.TakePictureButton);
        saveDataButton = (Button) findViewById(R.id.SaveDataButton);
        titleTextView = (TextView) findViewById(R.id.TitleTextView);
        descriptionTextView = (TextView) findViewById(R.id.DescriptionTextView);
        titleEditText = (EditText) findViewById(R.id.TitleEditText);
        descriptionEditText = (EditText) findViewById(R.id.DescriptionEditText);
```

In the standard activity onCreate method, after we call setContentView, we instantiate the user interface elements that we'll need control over in code. We have to cast each one to the appropriate type after obtaining it via the findViewById method.

```
        // Set all except takePictureButton to not be visible initially
        // View.GONE is invisible and doesn't take up space in the layout
        returnedImageView.setVisibility(View.GONE);
        saveDataButton.setVisibility(View.GONE);
        titleTextView.setVisibility(View.GONE);
        descriptionTextView.setVisibility(View.GONE);
        titleEditText.setVisibility(View.GONE);
        descriptionEditText.setVisibility(View.GONE);
```

Continuing on, we set all of the user interface elements to not be visible and not to take up space in the layout. View.GONE is the constant that can be used in the setVisibility method to do this. The other option, View.INVISIBLE, hides them but they still take up space in the layout.

```
        // When the Take Picture Button is clicked
        takePictureButton.setOnClickListener(new OnClickListener() {
            public void onClick(View v)
            {
                // Add a new record without the bitmap
                // returns the URI of the new record
                imageFileUri = getContentResolver().insert(Media.EXTERNAL_CONTENT_URI,↵
new ContentValues());

                // Start the Camera App
                Intent i = new Intent(android.provider.MediaStore.ACTION_IMAGE_CAPTURE);
                i.putExtra(android.provider.MediaStore.EXTRA_OUTPUT, imageFileUri);
                startActivityForResult(i, CAMERA_RESULT);
            }
        });
```

In the OnClickListener for the takePictureButton, we create the standard intent for the built-in camera and call startActivityForResult. Doing it here rather than directly in the onCreate method makes for a slightly nicer user experience.

```
        saveDataButton.setOnClickListener(new OnClickListener() {
            public void onClick(View v)
            {
                // Update the MediaStore record with Title and Description
                ContentValues contentValues = new ContentValues(3);
                contentValues.put(Media.DISPLAY_NAME,↵
titleEditText.getText().toString());
                contentValues.put(Media.DESCRIPTION,↵
descriptionEditText.getText().toString());
                getContentResolver().update(imageFileUri,contentValues,null,null);

                // Tell the user
                Toast bread = Toast.makeText(MediaStoreCameraIntent.this, "Record↵
Updated", Toast.LENGTH_SHORT);
                bread.show();

                // Go back to the initial state, set Take Picture Button Visible
                // hide other UI elements
                takePictureButton.setVisibility(View.VISIBLE);

                returnedImageView.setVisibility(View.GONE);
                saveDataButton.setVisibility(View.GONE);
                titleTextView.setVisibility(View.GONE);
                descriptionTextView.setVisibility(View.GONE);
                titleEditText.setVisibility(View.GONE);
                descriptionEditText.setVisibility(View.GONE);
            }
        });
    }
```

The OnClickListener for the saveDataButton, which is visible once the Camera application has returned an image, does the work of associating the metadata with the image. It takes the values that the user has typed into the various EditText elements and creates a ContentValues object that is used to update the record for this image in the MediaStore.

```
protected void onActivityResult(int requestCode, int resultCode, Intent intent)
{
    super.onActivityResult(requestCode, resultCode, intent);

    if (resultCode == RESULT_OK)
    {
        // The Camera App has returned

        // Hide the Take Picture Button
        takePictureButton.setVisibility(View.GONE);

        // Show the other UI Elements
        saveDataButton.setVisibility(View.VISIBLE);
        returnedImageView.setVisibility(View.VISIBLE);
        titleTextView.setVisibility(View.VISIBLE);
        descriptionTextView.setVisibility(View.VISIBLE);
        titleEditText.setVisibility(View.VISIBLE);
        descriptionEditText.setVisibility(View.VISIBLE);

        // Scale the image
        int dw = 200; // Make it at most 200 pixels wide
        int dh = 200; // Make it at most 200 pixels tall

        try
        {
            // Load up the image's dimensions not the image itself
            BitmapFactory.Options bmpFactoryOptions = new BitmapFactory.Options();
            bmpFactoryOptions.inJustDecodeBounds = true;
            Bitmap bmp = BitmapFactory.decodeStream(getContentResolver().↵
openInputStream(imageFileUri), null, bmpFactoryOptions);

            int heightRatio = (int)Math.ceil(bmpFactoryOptions.outHeight/(float)dh);
            int widthRatio = (int)Math.ceil(bmpFactoryOptions.outWidth/(float)dw);

            Log.v("HEIGHTRATIO",""+heightRatio);
            Log.v("WIDTHRATIO",""+widthRatio);

            // If both of the ratios are greater than 1,
            // one of the sides of the image is greater than the screen
            if (heightRatio > 1 && widthRatio > 1)
            {
                if (heightRatio > widthRatio)
                {
                    // Height ratio is larger, scale according to it
                    bmpFactoryOptions.inSampleSize = heightRatio;
                }
                else
                {
                    // Width ratio is larger, scale according to it
                    bmpFactoryOptions.inSampleSize = widthRatio;
                }
```

```
                }

                // Decode it for real
                bmpFactoryOptions.inJustDecodeBounds = false;
                bmp = BitmapFactory.decodeStream(getContentResolver().↩
openInputStream(imageFileUri), null, bmpFactoryOptions);

                // Display it
                returnedImageView.setImageBitmap(bmp);
            }
            catch (FileNotFoundException e)
            {
                Log.v("ERROR",e.toString());
            }
        }
    }
}
```

Here is the layout XML file, "main.xml" that is used in the above example.

```
<?xml version="1.0" encoding="utf-8"?>
<LinearLayout xmlns:android="http://schemas.android.com/apk/res/android"
    android:orientation="vertical"
    android:layout_width="fill_parent"
    android:layout_height="fill_parent"
    >
    <ImageView android:id="@+id/ReturnedImageView" android:layout_width="wrap_content"↩
android:layout_height="wrap_content"></ImageView>
    <TextView android:layout_width="wrap_content" android:layout_height="wrap_content"↩
android:text="Title:" android:id="@+id/TitleTextView"></TextView>
    <EditText android:layout_height="wrap_content" android:id="@+id/TitleEditText"↩
android:layout_width="fill_parent"></EditText>
    <TextView android:layout_width="wrap_content" android:layout_height="wrap_content"↩
android:text="Description" android:id="@+id/DescriptionTextView"></TextView>
    <EditText android:layout_height="wrap_content" android:layout_width="fill_parent"↩
android:id="@+id/DescriptionEditText"></EditText>
    <Button android:layout_width="wrap_content" android:layout_height="wrap_content"↩
android:id="@+id/TakePictureButton" android:text="Take Picture"></Button>
    <Button android:layout_width="wrap_content" android:layout_height="wrap_content"↩
android:id="@+id/SaveDataButton" android:text="Save Data"></Button>
</LinearLayout>
```

As in previous examples, the onActivityResult method is triggered when the Camera application returns. The newly created image is decoded into a Bitmap and displayed. In this version, the relevant user interface elements are also managed.

Retrieving Images Using the MediaStore

One example that shows the power of using shared content providers on Android is the ease with which we can use them to create something like a gallery application. Because the content provider, in this case the MediaStore, is shared between applications, we don't need to actually create a camera application and a means to store images in order to make our own application to view images. Since most applications will use the default `MediaStore`, we can leverage that to build our own gallery application.

Selecting from the `MediaStore` is very straightforward. We use the same URI that we used to create a new record, to select records from it.

```
Media.EXTERNAL_CONTENT_URI
```

The `MediaStore` and, in fact, all content providers operate in a similar manner to a database. We select records from them and are given a `Cursor` object, which we can use to iterate over the results.

In order to do the selection in the first place, we need to create a string array of the columns we would like returned. The standard columns for images in the `MediaStore` are represented in the `MediaStore.Images.Media` class.

```
String[] columns = { Media.DATA, Media._ID, Media.TITLE, Media.DISPLAY_NAME };
```

To perform the actual query, we can use the activity `managedQuery` method. The first argument is the URI, followed by the array of column names, followed by a limiting `WHERE` clause, any arguments for the `WHERE` clause, and, lastly, an `ORDER BY` clause.

The following would select records that were created within the last hour and order them oldest to most recent.

First we create a variable called `oneHourAgo`, which holds the number of seconds elapsed from January 1, 1970 as of one hour ago. `System.currenTimeMillis()` returns the number of milliseconds from the same date, so dividing by 1000 gives us the number of seconds. If we subtract 60 minutes * 60 seconds, we'll get the value as of one hour ago.

```
long oneHourAgo =  System.currentTimeMillis()/1000 - (60 * 60);
```

We then place that value in an array of strings that we can use as the arguments for the `WHERE` clause.

```
String[] whereValues = {""+oneHourAgo};
```

Then we choose the columns we want returned.

```
String[] columns = { Media.DATA, Media._ID, Media.TITLE, Media.DISPLAY_NAME,↵
Media.DATE_ADDED };
```

And finally we perform the query. The `WHERE` clause has a `?`, which will get substituted with the value in the next parameter. If there are multiple `?`, there must be multiple values in the array passed in. The `ORDER BY` clause used here specifies that the data returned will be ordered by the date added in ascending order.

```
cursor = managedQuery(Media.EXTERNAL_CONTENT_URI, columns, Media.DATE_ADDED + " > ?",↵
whereValues, Media.DATE_ADDED + " ASC");
```

You can, of course, pass in `null` for the last three arguments if you want all records returned.

```
Cursor cursor = managedQuery(Media.EXTERNAL_CONTENT_URI, columns, null, null, null);
```

The cursor returned can tell us the index of each of the columns as selected.

```
displayColumnIndex = cursor.getColumnIndexOrThrow(MediaStore.Images.Media.DATA);
```

We need the index in order to select that field out of the cursor. First we make sure that the cursor is valid and has some results by calling the moveToFirst method. This method will be false if the cursor isn't holding any results. We use one of several methods in the Cursor class to select the actual data. The method we choose is dependent on what type the data is, getString for strings, getInt for integers, and so on.

```
if (cursor.moveToFirst()) {
    String displayName = cursor.getString(displayColumnIndex);
}
```

Creating an Image Viewing Application

What follows is a full example that queries the MediaStore to find images and presents them to the user one after the other in the form of a slideshow.

```
package com.apress.proandroidmedia.ch1.mediastoregallery;

import android.app.Activity;
import android.database.Cursor;
import android.graphics.Bitmap;
import android.graphics.BitmapFactory;
import android.os.Bundle;
import android.provider.MediaStore;
import android.provider.MediaStore.Images.Media;
import android.util.Log;
import android.view.View;
import android.view.View.OnClickListener;
import android.widget.ImageButton;
import android.widget.TextView;

public class MediaStoreGallery extends Activity {

    public final static int DISPLAYWIDTH = 200;
    public final static int DISPLAYHEIGHT = 200;
```

Instead of using the size of the screen to load and display the images, we'll use the foregoing constants to decide how large to display them.

```
    TextView titleTextView;
    ImageButton imageButton;
```

In this example, we are using an ImageButton instead of an ImageView. This gives us both the functionality of a Button (which can be clicked) and an ImageView (which can display an image).

```
    Cursor cursor;
    Bitmap bmp;
    String imageFilePath;
    int fileColumn;
    int titleColumn;
    int displayColumn;

    @Override
    public void onCreate(Bundle savedInstanceState) {
```

```
        super.onCreate(savedInstanceState);
        setContentView(R.layout.main);

        titleTextView = (TextView) this.findViewById(R.id.TitleTextView);
        imageButton = (ImageButton) this.findViewById(R.id.ImageButton);
```

Here we specify which columns we want returned. This must be in the form of an array of strings. We pass that array into the managedQuery method on the next line.

```
        String[] columns = { Media.DATA, Media._ID, Media.TITLE, Media.DISPLAY_NAME };
        cursor = managedQuery(Media.EXTERNAL_CONTENT_URI, columns, null, null, null);
```

We'll need to know the index for each of the columns we are looking to get data out of from the Cursor object. In this example, we are switching from Media.DATA to MediaStore.Images.Media.DATA. This is just to illustrate that they are the same. Media.DATA is just shorthand that we can use since we have an import statement that encompasses it: android.provider.MediaStore.Images.Media.

```
        fileColumn = cursor.getColumnIndexOrThrow(MediaStore.Images.Media.DATA);
        titleColumn = cursor.getColumnIndexOrThrow(MediaStore.Images.Media.TITLE);
        displayColumn = ↵
cursor.getColumnIndexOrThrow(MediaStore.Images.Media.DISPLAY_NAME);
```

After we run the query and have a resulting Cursor object, we call moveToFirst on it to make sure that it contains results.

```
        if (cursor.moveToFirst()) {
            //titleTextView.setText(cursor.getString(titleColumn));
            titleTextView.setText(cursor.getString(displayColumn));

            imageFilePath = cursor.getString(fileColumn);
            bmp = getBitmap(imageFilePath);

            // Display it
            imageButton.setImageBitmap(bmp);
        }
```

We then specify a new OnClickListener for imageButton, which calls the moveToNext method on the Cursor object. This iterates through the result set, pulling up and displaying each image that was returned.

```
        imageButton.setOnClickListener(
            new OnClickListener() {
                public void onClick(View v) {
                    if (cursor.moveToNext())
                    {
                        //titleTextView.setText(cursor.getString(titleColumn));
                        titleTextView.setText(cursor.getString(displayColumn));

                        imageFilePath = cursor.getString(fileColumn);
                        bmp = getBitmap(imageFilePath);
                        imageButton.setImageBitmap(bmp);
                    }
                }
            }
        );
    }
```

Here is a method called getBitmap, which encapsulates the image scaling and loading that we need to do in order to display these images without running into memory problems as discussed earlier in the chapter.

```java
private Bitmap getBitmap(String imageFilePath)
{
    // Load up the image's dimensions not the image itself
    BitmapFactory.Options bmpFactoryOptions = new BitmapFactory.Options();
    bmpFactoryOptions.inJustDecodeBounds = true;
    Bitmap bmp = BitmapFactory.decodeFile(imageFilePath, bmpFactoryOptions);

    int heightRatio = (int) Math.ceil(bmpFactoryOptions.outHeight↵
            / (float) DISPLAYHEIGHT);
    int widthRatio = (int) Math.ceil(bmpFactoryOptions.outWidth↵
            / (float) DISPLAYWIDTH);

    Log.v("HEIGHTRATIO", "" + heightRatio);
    Log.v("WIDTHRATIO", "" + widthRatio);

    // If both of the ratios are greater than 1, one of the sides of
    // the image is greater than the screen
    if (heightRatio > 1 && widthRatio > 1) {
        if (heightRatio > widthRatio) {
            // Height ratio is larger, scale according to it
            bmpFactoryOptions.inSampleSize = heightRatio;
        } else {
            // Width ratio is larger, scale according to it
            bmpFactoryOptions.inSampleSize = widthRatio;
        }
    }

    // Decode it for real
    bmpFactoryOptions.inJustDecodeBounds = false;
    bmp = BitmapFactory.decodeFile(imageFilePath, bmpFactoryOptions);

    return bmp;
}
}
```

The following is the layout XML that goes along with the foregoing activity. It should be put in the res/layout/main.xml file.

```xml
<?xml version="1.0" encoding="utf-8"?>
<LinearLayout xmlns:android="http://schemas.android.com/apk/res/android"
    android:orientation="vertical"
    android:layout_width="fill_parent"
    android:layout_height="fill_parent"
    >
<ImageButton android:layout_width="wrap_content" android:layout_height="wrap_content"↵
android:id="@+id/ImageButton"></ImageButton>
<TextView
    android:layout_width="fill_parent"
    android:layout_height="wrap_content"
    android:id="@+id/TitleTextView"
    android:text="Image Title"/>
</LinearLayout>
```

Internal Metadata

EXIF, which stands for exchangeable image file format, is a standard way of saving metadata within an image file. Many digital cameras and desktop applications support the use of EXIF data. Since EXIF data is actually a part of the file, it shouldn't get lost in the transfer of the file from one place to another. For instance, when copying a file from the SD card of the Android device to a home computer, this data would remain intact. If you open the file in an application such as iPhoto, the data will be present.

In general, EXIF data is very technically orientated; most of the tags in the standard relate to data about the capturing of the image itself, such as ExposureTime and ShutterSpeedValue.

There are some tags, though, that make sense for us to consider filling in or modifying. Some of these might include the following:

- *UserComment*: A comment generated by the user

- *ImageDescription*: The title

- *Artist*: Creator or taker of image

- *Copyright*: Copyright holder of image

- *Software*: Software used to create image

Fortunately, Android provides us a nice means to both read and write EXIF data. The main class for doing so is ExifInterface.

Here's how to use ExifInterface to read specific EXIF data from an image file:

```
ExifInterface ei = new ExifInterface(imageFilePath);
String imageDescription = ei.getAttribute("ImageDescription");
if (imageDescription != null)
{
    Log.v("EXIF", imageDescription);
}
```

Here is how to save EXIF data to an image file using ExifInterface:

```
ExifInterface ei = new ExifInterface(imageFilePath);
ei.setAttribute("ImageDescription","Something New");
```

ExifInterface includes a set of constants that define the typical set of data that is automatically included in captured images by the Camera application.

The latest version of the EXIF specification is version 2.3 from April 2010. It is available online here: www.cipa.jp/english/hyoujunka/kikaku/pdf/DC-008-2010_E.pdf.

Summary

Throughout this chapter, we looked at the basics of image capture and storage on Android. We saw how powerful using the built-in Camera application on Android could be and how to effectively leverage its capabilities through an intent. We saw that the

Camera application offers a nice and consistent interface for adding image capture capabilities into any Android application.

We also looked at the need to be conscious of memory usage when dealing with large images. We learned that the `BitmapFactory` class helps us load scaled versions of an image in order to conserve memory. The need to pay attention to memory reminds us that mobile phones are not desktop computers with seemingly limitless memory.

We went over using Android's built-in content provider for Images, the `MediaStore`. We learned how to use it to save images to a standard location on the device as well as how to query it to quickly build applications that leverage already captured images.

Finally we looked at how we can associate certain metadata with images with a standard called EXIF, which is transportable and used in a variety of devices and software applications.

This should give us a great starting point for exploring what more we can do with media on Android.

I am looking forward to it!

Chapter 2

Building Custom Camera Applications

In the last chapter, we looked at how we can leverage Android's built-in Camera application to provide a ready-made photo capture component in any other application. While this provides a standard interface to the end user and is straightforward for us the programmers, it doesn't provide us with much in the way of flexibility. For instance, if we wanted our photo capture application to support time-lapse photography, we couldn't easily do that using the built-in application.

Fortunately, Android doesn't limit us to just using the built-in applications for accessing the hardware camera. We have as much access to the underlying hardware and available methods as the Camera application itself, which allows us to use those capabilities in any type of application we would like.

In this chapter, we'll explore building a photo-taking application utilizing the underlying Camera class and learn how to exploit the capabilities we are given. We'll go through the steps required to build a few different applications:

- A straightforward point and shoot photo app

- A countdown-style timer

- A time-lapse photo-taking application

Using the Camera Class

The Camera class in Android is what we use to access the camera hardware on the device. It allows us to actually capture an image, and through its nested Camera.Parameters class, we can change set various attributes, such as whether the flash should be activated and what value the white balance should be set to.

http://developer.android.com/reference/android/hardware/Camera.html

Camera Permissions

In order to use the Camera class to capture an image, we need to specify in our AndroidManifest.xml file that we require the CAMERA permission.

```
<uses-permission android:name="android.permission.CAMERA" />
```

Preview Surface

Also before we can get started using the camera, we need to create some type of Surface for the Camera to draw viewfinder or preview images on. A Surface is an abstract class in Android representing a place to draw graphics or images. One straightforward way to provide a drawing Surface is to use the SurfaceView class. SurfaceView is a concrete class providing a Surface within a standard View.

To specify a SurfaceView in our layout, we simply use the <SurfaceView /> element within any normal layout XML. Here is a basic layout that just implements a SurfaceView within a LinearLayout for a camera preview.

```
<?xml version="1.0" encoding="utf-8"?>
<LinearLayout xmlns:android="http://schemas.android.com/apk/res/android"
    android:orientation="vertical"
    android:layout_width="fill_parent"
    android:layout_height="fill_parent"
    >
<SurfaceView android:id="@+id/CameraView" android:layout_width="fill_parent"
 android:layout_height="fill_parent"></SurfaceView>
</LinearLayout>
```

In our code, for the purposes of using this SurfaceView with the Camera class, we'll need to add a SurfaceHolder to the mix. The SurfaceHolder class can act as a monitor on our Surface, giving us an interface through callbacks to let us know when the Surface is created, destroyed, or changed. The SurfaceView class conveniently gives us a method, getHolder, to obtain a SurfaceHolder for its Surface.

Here is a snippet of code that accesses the SurfaceView as declared in the layout XML and obtains a SurfaceHolder from it. It also sets the Surface to be a "push" type of Surface, which means that the drawing buffers are maintained external to the Surface itself. In this case, the buffers are managed by the Camera class. A "push" type of Surface is required for the Camera preview.

```
SurfaceView cameraView = (CameraView) this.findViewById(R.id.CameraView);
SurfaceHolder surfaceHolder = cameraView.getHolder();
surfaceHolder.setType(SurfaceHolder.SURFACE_TYPE_PUSH_BUFFERS);
```

Additionally, we'll want to implement SurfaceHolder.Callback in our activity. This allows our activity to be notified when the Surface is created, when it changes and when it is destroyed. To implement the Callback, we'll add the following methods.

```
public void surfaceChanged(SurfaceHolder holder, int format, int w, int h) {}
public void surfaceCreated(SurfaceHolder holder) {}
public void surfaceDestroyed(SurfaceHolder holder) {}
```

To finish up, we'll need to tell our SurfaceHolder to use this activity as the Callback handler.

```
surfaceHolder.addCallback(this);
```

Our activity should now look something this.

```
package com.apress.proandroidmedia.ch2.snapshot;

import android.app.Activity;
import android.os.Bundle;
import android.view.SurfaceHolder;
import android.view.SurfaceView;

public class SnapShot extends Activity implements SurfaceHolder.Callback {

    SurfaceView cameraView;
    SurfaceHolder surfaceHolder;

    @Override
    public void onCreate(Bundle savedInstanceState)
    {
        super.onCreate(savedInstanceState);
        setContentView(R.layout.main);

        cameraView = (SurfaceView) this.findViewById(R.id.CameraView);
        surfaceHolder = cameraView.getHolder();
        surfaceHolder.setType(SurfaceHolder.SURFACE_TYPE_PUSH_BUFFERS);
        surfaceHolder.addCallback(this);
    }

    public void surfaceChanged(SurfaceHolder holder, int format, int w, int h) {
    }
    public void surfaceCreated(SurfaceHolder holder) {
    }
    public void surfaceDestroyed(SurfaceHolder holder) {
    }
}
```

Implementing the Camera

Now that we have the activity and preview Surface all set up, we are ready to start using the actual Camera object.

When the Surface is created, which will trigger calling the surfaceCreated method in our code due to the SurfaceHolder.Callback, we can obtain a Camera object by calling the static open method on the Camera class.

```
Camera camera;
public void surfaceCreated(SurfaceHolder holder) {
    camera = Camera.open();
```

We'll want to follow that up with setting the preview display to the SurfaceHolder we are using, which is provided to our method through the callback. This method needs to be wrapped in a try catch block as it can throw an IOException. If this happens, we'll want to release the camera as we could tie up the camera hardware resources for other applications if we don't.

```
try
{
   camera.setPreviewDisplay(holder);
}
catch (IOException exception)
{
   camera.release();
}
```

Finally, we'll want to start the camera preview.

```
   camera.startPreview();

}
```

Likewise, in surfaceDestroyed, we'll want to release the camera as well. We'll first call stopPreview, just to make sure everything cleans up as it should.

```
public void surfaceDestroyed(SurfaceHolder holder) {
   camera.stopPreview();
   camera.release();
}
```

Running this code, you'll probably notice something strange with the preview. It is rotating the preview image 90 degrees counter-clockwise as shown in Figure 2–1.

Figure 2–1. *The camera preview rotated 90 degrees*

The reason this rotation is happening is that the Camera assumes the orientation to be horizontal or landscape. The easiest way to correct the rotation is to make our activity appear in landscape mode. To do this, we can add the following code in our activity's onCreate method.

```
@Override
public void onCreate(Bundle savedInstanceState)
{
    super.onCreate(savedInstanceState);
    setRequestedOrientation(ActivityInfo.SCREEN_ORIENTATION_LANDSCAPE);
```

Now our Camera preview appears correctly as illustrated in Figure 2–2. Unfortunately, our application is now stuck in landscape mode.

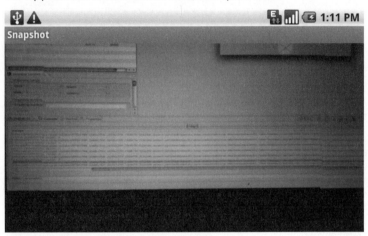

Figure 2–2. *The camera preview in landscape*

Setting Camera Parameters

As previously mentioned, the Camera class has a nested Camera.Parameters class. This class has a series of important attributes or settings that can be used to change how the Camera operates. One of these that would help us right now is a way to deal with the rotation/landscape issue we have in the preview.

The Parameters to be used by the Camera can be modified as follows:

```
Camera.Parameters parameters = camera.getParameters();

parameters.set("some parameter", "some value");
// or
parameters.set("some parameter", some_int);

camera.setParameters(parameters);
```

There are two different generic Parameters.set methods. The first takes a string for the parameter name and value, and the second takes a string for the name but the value is an integer.

Setting the Parameters should be done in the surfaceCreated method right after the Camera is created and its preview Surface specified.

Here is how we can use Parameters to request that the Camera be used with a portrait orientation rather than landscape.

```
public void surfaceCreated(SurfaceHolder holder) {
        camera = Camera.open();
        try {
            Camera.Parameters parameters = camera.getParameters();
            if (this.getResources().getConfiguration().orientation !=
                Configuration.ORIENTATION_LANDSCAPE) {
                // This is an undocumented although widely known feature
                parameters.set("orientation", "portrait");

                // For Android 2.2 and above
                //camera.setDisplayOrientation(90);

                // Uncomment for Android 2.0 and above
                //parameters.setRotation(90);
            } else {
                // This is an undocumented although widely known feature
                parameters.set("orientation", "landscape");

                // For Android 2.2 and above
                //camera.setDisplayOrientation(0);

                // Uncomment for Android 2.0 and above
                //parameters.setRotation(0);
            }
            camera.setParameters(parameters);
            camera.setPreviewDisplay(holder);
        } catch (IOException exception) {
            camera.release();
            Log.v(LOGTAG,exception.getMessage());
        }
        camera.startPreview();
    }
```

The foregoing code first checks the device configuration (through a call to Context.getResources().getConfiguration()) to see what the current orientation is. If the orientation is not landscape, it sets the Camera.Parameters "orientation" to be "portrait." Additionally, the Camera.Parameters setRotation method is called, and 90 degrees is passed in. This method, which is available in API level 5 (version 2.0) and higher, does not actually do any rotation; rather, it tells the Camera to specify in the EXIF data that the image should be rotated 90 degrees on display. If this isn't included, when you view this image in other applications, it would likely be displayed sideways.

NOTE: The method shown for modifying the Camera's rotation by using `Camera.Parameters` is for use with Android version 2.1 and earlier. In Android 2.2, a new method on the `Camera` class, `setDisplayOrientation(int degrees)`, was introduced. This method takes in an integer representing the degrees the image should be rotated. The only valid degrees are 0, 90, 180, 270.

Most parameters that can or should be modified have specific methods associated with them. As we can see with the `setRotation` method, they follow the Java getter and setter design pattern. For instance, the flash mode of the Camera can be set with `setFlashMode(Camera.Parameters.FLASH_MODE_AUTO)` and the current value can be gotten with `getFlashMode()` rather than having to be done through the generic `Parameters.set` method.

Starting with Android 2.0, one fun parameter that we can use for demonstration allows us to change effects. The getter and setter are `getColorEffect` and `setColorEffect`. There is also a `getSupportedColorEffects` method, which returns a `List` of `String` objects with the various effects that are supported on the specific device. In fact, this method exists for all of the parameters that have getter and setter methods and should be used to ensure that the capability requested is available before being used.

```
Camera.Parameters parameters = camera.getParameters();
List<String> colorEffects = parameters.getSupportedColorEffects();
Iterator<String> cei = colorEffects.iterator();
while (cei.hasNext()) {
    String currentEffect = cei.next();
    Log.v("SNAPSHOT","Checking " + currentEffect);
    if (currentEffect.equals(Camera.Parameters.EFFECT_SOLARIZE)) {
        Log.v("SNAPSHOT","Using SOLARIZE");
        parameters.setColorEffect(Camera.Parameters.EFFECT_SOLARIZE);
        break;
    }
}
Log.v("SNAPSHOT","Using Effect: " + parameters.getColorEffect());
camera.setParameters(parameters);
```

In the foregoing code, we first query the `Camera.Parameters` object to see what effects are supported through the `getSupportedColorEffect` method. We then use an `Iterator` to go through the `List` of effects and see if any of them match the one we want, in this case `Camera.Parameters.EFFECT_SOLARIZE`. If it appears in the list, it is supported and we can go ahead and call `setColorEffect` on the `Camera.Parameters` object, passing in the solarize constant. Figure 2–3 shows the `Camera.Parameters.EFFECT_SOLARIZE` in action.

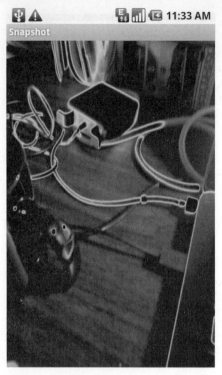

Figure 2–3. *Solarized preview image from the camera*

The other possibilities are also listed as constants within the Camera.Parameters class:

- EFFECT_NONE
- EFFECT_MONO
- EFFECT_NEGATIVE
- EFFECT_SOLARIZE
- EFFECT_SEPIA
- EFFECT_POSTERIZE
- EFFECT_WHITEBOARD
- EFFECT_BLACKBOARD
- EFFECT_AQUA

Similar constants exist for antibanding, flash mode, focus mode, scene mode, and white balance.

Changing the Camera Preview Size

Another particularly useful setting available in Camera.Parameters is the ability to set a preview size. As with other settings, we'll first want to query the parameters object and get the supported values. Having gotten this list of sizes, we can go through it to make sure the size we want is supported before we set it.

In this example, we aren't specifying an exact size that we want, rather choosing a size that is close to but no larger than a couple of constants. Figure 2–4 shows the output of this example.

```
...
public static final int LARGEST_WIDTH  =  200;
public static final int LARGEST_HEIGHT= 200;
...
```

As with all `Camera.Parameters`, we'll want to get and set them in `surfaceCreated` after we have opened the camera and set its preview display `Surface`.

```
public void surfaceCreated(SurfaceHolder holder) {
    camera = Camera.open();
    try {
      camera.setPreviewDisplay(holder);
      Camera.Parameters parameters = camera.getParameters();
```

We'll keep track of the closest values that are under our constant in these two variables:

```
    int bestWidth = 0;
    int bestHeight = 0;
```

Then we'll get the list of all of the supported sizes on our device. This returns a list of `Camera.Size` objects that we can loop through.

```
    List<Camera.Size> previewSizes = parameters.getSupportedPreviewSizes();
    if (previewSizes.size() > 1)
    {
        Iterator<Camera.Size> cei = previewSizes.iterator();
        while (cei.hasNext())
        {
            Camera.Size aSize = cei.next();
```

If the current size in the list is larger than our saved best sizes and smaller than or equal to our `LARGEST_WIDTH` and `LARGEST_HEIGHT` constants, then we save that height and width in our `bestWidth` and `bestHeight` variables and continue checking.

```
            Log.v("SNAPSHOT","Checking " + aSize.width + " x " + aSize.height);
            if (aSize.width > bestWidth && aSize.width <= LARGEST_WIDTH
                && aSize.height > bestHeight && aSize.height <= LARGEST_HEIGHT) {
                // So far it is the biggest without going over the screen dimensions
                    bestWidth = aSize.width;
                    bestHeight = aSize.height;
            }
        }
    }
```

After we have finished going through the supported sizes, we make sure we got something out. If our `bestHeight` and `bestWidth` variables are equal to 0, then we didn't find anything that matched our needs, or there is only one supported size and we shouldn't take any action. If, on the other-hand, they have values, we'll call `setPreviewSize` with the `bestWidth` and `bestHeight` variables on the `Camera.Parameters` object.

Additionally, we want to tell our camera preview SurfaceView object, cameraView, to display at that size as well. If we don't do this, SurfaceView won't change sizes and the preview image from the camera will be either distorted or very low quality.

```
        if (bestHeight != 0 && bestWidth != 0) {
          Log.v("SNAPSHOT", "Using " + bestWidth + " x " + bestHeight);
          parameters.setPreviewSize(bestWidth, bestHeight);
          cameraView.setLayoutParams(new LinearLayout.LayoutParams( bestWidth, ↵
bestHeight));
        }
    }
    camera.setParameters(parameters);
```

After we set the parameters, all that remains is to close out the surfaceCreated method.

```
    } catch (IOException exception) {
        camera.release();
    }
}
```

Figure 2–4. *Camera preview with small preview size*

Capturing and Saving an Image

To capture an image with the Camera class, we have to call the takePicture method. This method takes in three or four arguments, all of which are Callback methods. The simplest form of the takePicture method is to have all of the arguments be null. Unfortunately, while a picture would be captured, no reference to it will be available. At the very least, one of the callback methods should be implemented. The safest one is Camera.PictureCallback.onPictureTaken. This is guaranteed to be called and is called when the compressed image is available. To utilize this, we'll make our activity implement Camera.PictureCallback and add an onPictureTaken method.

```
public class SnapShot extends Activity implements
  SurfaceHolder.Callback, Camera.PictureCallback {

  public void onPictureTaken(byte[] data, Camera camera) {
  }
```

The onPictureTaken method has two arguments; the first is a byte array of the actual JPEG image data. The second is a reference to the Camera object that captured the image.

Since we are handed the actual JPEG data, we simply need to write it to disk somewhere in order to save it. As we already know, it is a good idea to leverage the MediaStore for specifying its location and metadata.

When our onPictureTaken method is called, we can call startPreview on the Camera object. The preview had been automatically paused when the takePicture method was called, and this method tells us that it is now safe to be restarted.

```
public void onPictureTaken(byte[] data, Camera camera) {
    Uri imageFileUri = getContentResolver().insert(Media.EXTERNAL_CONTENT_URI, new↵
ContentValues());
    try {
       OutputStream imageFileOS = getContentResolver().openOutputStream(imageFileUri);
       imageFileOS.write(data);
       imageFileOS.flush();
       imageFileOS.close();

    } catch (FileNotFoundException e) {
    } catch (IOException e) {
    }

    camera.startPreview();
}
```

In the foregoing snippet, we are inserting a new record into the MediaStore and given a URI in return. This URI is what we can subsequently use to obtain an OutputStream to write the JPEG data to. This creates a file in the location specified by the MediaStore and links it to the new record.

If we wanted to update the metadata stored in the MediaStore record later, we can update the record with a new ContentValues object as described in Chapter 1.

```
ContentValues contentValues = new ContentValues(3);
contentValues.put(Media.DISPLAY_NAME, "This is a test title");
contentValues.put(Media.DESCRIPTION, "This is a test description");
getContentResolver().update(imageFileUri,contentValues,null,null);
```

Last, we'll have to actually call Camera.takePicture. To do this, let's make the preview screen be "clickable," and in the onClick method, we'll take the picture.

We'll make our activity implement an OnClickListener and set our SurfaceView's onClickListener to be the activity itself. We'll then make our SurfaceView be "clickable" with setClickable(true). Additionally we'll need to make the SurfaceView be "focusable." A SurfaceView by default isn't focusable, so we'll have to explicitly set that with setFocusable(true). Also, when we are in "touch mode," focus is generally disabled, so we'll have to explicitly set that not to happen with setFocusInTouchMode(true).

```
public class SnapShot extends Activity implements OnClickListener,↵
 SurfaceHolder.Callback, Camera.PictureCallback {
...
```

```
    public void onCreate(Bundle savedInstanceState)  {
...
        cameraView.setFocusable(true);
        cameraView.setFocusableInTouchMode(true);
        cameraView.setClickable(true);
        cameraView.setOnClickListener(this);
    }

    public void onClick(View v) {
        camera.takePicture(null, null, null, this);
    }
```

Other Camera Callback Methods

Aside from Camera.PictureCallback, there are a few others that are worth mentioning.

- *Camera.PreviewCallback*: Defines a method, onPreviewFrame(byte[] data, Camera camera) , which is called when preview frames are available. A byte array that holds the current pixels of the image may be passed in. There are three different ways that this callback can be used on a Camera object.

  - *setPreviewCallback(Camera.PreviewCallback)*: Registering a Camera.PreviewCallback with this method ensures that the onPreviewFrame method is called whenever a new preview frame is available and displayed on the screen. The data byte array that is passed into the onPreviewFrame method will most likely be in YUV format. Unfortunately Android 2.2 is the first version to have a YUV format decoder (YuvImage); in previous versions, decoding has to be done by hand.

  - *setOneShotPreviewCallback(Camera.PreviewCallback)*: Registering a Camera.PreviewCallback with this method on the Camera object causes the onPreviewFrame to be called once, when the next preview image is available. Again, the preview image data passed to the onPreviewFrame method will most likely be in the YUV format. This can be determined by checking the result of Camera. getParameters().getPreviewFormat() with the constants in ImageFormat.

  - *setPreviewCallbackWithBuffer(Camera.PreviewCallback)*: Introduced in Android 2.2, this method works in the same manner as the normal setPreviewCallback but requires us to specify a byte array that will be used as a buffer for the preview image data. This is done to allow us the ability to better manage the memory that will be used when dealing with preview images.

- *Camera.AutoFocusCallback*: Defines a method, onAutoFocus, which is called when an auto-focus activity has completed. Auto-focus may be triggered by calling the autoFocus method on the Camera object, passing in an instance of this callback interface.

- *Camera.ErrorCallback*: Defines an onError method, which is called when a Camera error occurs. There are two constants that can be compared with the passed-in error code: CAMERA_ERROR_UNKNOWN and CAMERA_ERROR_SERVER_DIED.

- *Camera.OnZoomChangeListener*: Defines a method, onZoomChange, which is called when a "smooth zoom" (slow zoom in or out) is in progress or completed. This class and method were introduced in Android 2.2 (API level 8).

- *Camera.ShutterCallback*: Defines a method, onShutter, which is called at the moment an image is captured.

Putting It All Together

Let's go through the entire example. The following code is written to run on Android 2.2 and higher, but with minor changes, it should run on versions 1.6 and higher. The sections that require higher than 1.6 are noted with comments.

```java
package com.apress.proandroidmedia.ch2.snapshot;

import java.io.FileNotFoundException;
import java.io.IOException;
import java.io.OutputStream;
import java.util.Iterator;
import java.util.List;

import android.app.Activity;
import android.content.ContentValues;
import android.content.res.Configuration;
import android.hardware.Camera;
import android.net.Uri;
import android.os.Bundle;
import android.provider.MediaStore.Images.Media;
import android.util.Log;
import android.view.SurfaceHolder;
import android.view.SurfaceView;
import android.view.View;
import android.view.View.OnClickListener;
import android.widget.Toast;

public class SnapShot extends Activity implements OnClickListener,↵
 SurfaceHolder.Callback, Camera.PictureCallback {

    SurfaceView cameraView;
    SurfaceHolder surfaceHolder;
    Camera camera;

    @Override
    public void onCreate(Bundle savedInstanceState)  {
        super.onCreate(savedInstanceState);

        setContentView(R.layout.main);

        cameraView = (SurfaceView) this.findViewById(R.id.CameraView);
```

```
        surfaceHolder = cameraView.getHolder();
        surfaceHolder.setType(SurfaceHolder.SURFACE_TYPE_PUSH_BUFFERS);
        surfaceHolder.addCallback(this);

        cameraView.setFocusable(true);
        cameraView.setFocusableInTouchMode(true);
        cameraView.setClickable(true);

        cameraView.setOnClickListener(this);
    }

    public void onClick(View v) {
        camera.takePicture(null, null, this);
    }
```

We follow this up with the onPictureTaken method as described earlier.

```
    public void onPictureTaken(byte[] data, Camera camera) {
        Uri imageFileUri =
        getContentResolver().insert(Media.EXTERNAL_CONTENT_URI, new ContentValues());
        try {
            OutputStream imageFileOS =
                getContentResolver().openOutputStream(imageFileUri);
            imageFileOS.write(data);
            imageFileOS.flush();
            imageFileOS.close();
        } catch (FileNotFoundException e) {
            Toast t = Toast.makeText(this,e.getMessage(), Toast.LENGTH_SHORT);
            t.show();
        } catch (IOException e) {
            Toast t = Toast.makeText(this,e.getMessage(), Toast.LENGTH_SHORT);
            t.show();
        }
        camera.startPreview();
    }
```

Last, we need the various SurfaceHolder.Callback methods in which we set up the
Camera object.

```
    public void surfaceChanged(SurfaceHolder holder, int format, int w, int h) {
        camera.startPreview();
    }

    public void surfaceCreated(SurfaceHolder holder) {
        camera = Camera.open();
        try {
            camera.setPreviewDisplay(holder);
            Camera.Parameters parameters = camera.getParameters();
            if (this.getResources().getConfiguration().orientation !=
              Configuration.ORIENTATION_LANDSCAPE)
            {
                parameters.set("orientation", "portrait");
                // For Android Version 2.2 and above
                camera.setDisplayOrientation(90);

                // For Android Version 2.0 and above
                parameters.setRotation(90);
            }
```

```java
            // Effects are for Android Version 2.0 and higher
            List<String> colorEffects = parameters.getSupportedColorEffects();
            Iterator<String> cei = colorEffects.iterator();
            while (cei.hasNext())
            {
                String currentEffect = cei.next();
                if (currentEffect.equals(Camera.Parameters.EFFECT_SOLARIZE))
                {
                parameters.setColorEffect(Camera.Parameters.EFFECT_SOLARIZE);
                    break;
                }
            }
            // End Effects for Android Version 2.0 and higher

                camera.setParameters(parameters);
        }
        catch (IOException exception)
        {
                camera.release();
        }
    }

    public void surfaceDestroyed(SurfaceHolder holder) {
        camera.stopPreview();
        camera.release();
    }
} // End the Activity
```

That takes care of our Snapshot activity. Here is the layout XML that is in use by it. It belongs in res/layout/main.xml.

```xml
<?xml version="1.0" encoding="utf-8"?>
<LinearLayout xmlns:android="http://schemas.android.com/apk/res/android"
    android:orientation="vertical"
    android:layout_width="fill_parent"
    android:layout_height="fill_parent"
    >
    <SurfaceView android:id="@+id/CameraView" android:layout_width="fill_parent"↵
 android:layout_height="fill_parent"></SurfaceView>
</LinearLayout>
```

Last, we need to add the CAMERA permission to our AndroidManifest.xml file. Here is the entire manifest.

```xml
<?xml version="1.0" encoding="utf-8"?>
<manifest xmlns:android="http://schemas.android.com/apk/res/android"
      package="com.apress.proandroidmedia.ch2.snapshot"
      android:versionCode="1"
      android:versionName="1.0">
    <application android:icon="@drawable/icon" android:label="@string/app_name">
        <activity android:name=".SnapShot"
                  android:label="@string/app_name">
            <intent-filter>
                <action android:name="android.intent.action.MAIN" />
                <category android:name="android.intent.category.LAUNCHER" />
            </intent-filter>
        </activity>
```

```
    </application>
    <uses-sdk android:minSdkVersion="8" />
    <uses-permission android:name="android.permission.CAMERA"></uses-permission>
</manifest>
```

That should cover the basics of building a custom camera-based application. Next, let's look at how we can extend this application, implementing features that don't exist in the built-in camera application.

Extending the Custom Camera Application

In my opinion, the built-in camera application on Android is missing a few essential features. One of those is the ability to take a picture after a small amount of time, say 10 or 30 seconds. This feature is generally useful with a camera that can be mounted on a tripod. One thing it enables is the ability for a photographer to set up a shot, set the timer, and then run into the shot.

While this isn't something you would often do with a mobile phone, I do think it would be useful in certain situations. For example, I would love to have this feature when want to take a picture of both someone I am with and myself. Currently when I try to do so, I have a difficult time, as I cannot see the touchscreen interface because it is facing away from me. I fumble around, pushing the screen in various spots, hoping that I hit the shutter button.

Building a Timer-Based Camera App

To rectify the situation just described, we can add a time delay to the taking of the picture. Let's update our SnapShot example so that picture is taken ten seconds after pushing a button.

In order to accomplish this, we'll need to use something like a java.util.Timer. Unfortunately, in Android, using a Timer creates some complications as it introduces a separate thread. To have separate threads interact with the UI, we need to use a Handler to cause an action to occur on the main thread.

The other use of a Handler is to schedule something to happen in the future. This capability of a Handler makes using the Timer unnecessary.

To create a Handler that will execute something in the future, we simply construct a generic one:

```
Handler timerHandler = new Handler();
```

We then have to create a Runnable. This Runnable will contain within its run method the action to happen later. In our case, we want this action to occur ten seconds later and trigger the taking of the picture:

```
Runnable timerTask = new Runnable() {
    public void run() {
        camera.takePicture(null,null,null,TimerSnapShot.this);
```

```
        }
};
```

That should cover it. Now when we push a button, we simply need to schedule it:

```
timerHandler.postDelayed(timerTask, 10000);
```

This tells the `timerHandler` to call our `timerTask` method 10 seconds (10000 milliseconds) in the future.

In the following example, we are creating a `Handler` and having it call a method every second. In this way, we can provide a countdown on the screen to the user.

```
package com.apress.proandroidmedia.ch2.timersnapshot;

import java.io.FileNotFoundException;
import java.io.IOException;
import java.io.OutputStream;
import java.util.Iterator;
import java.util.List;
import android.app.Activity;
import android.content.ContentValues;
import android.content.res.Configuration;
import android.hardware.Camera;
import android.net.Uri;
import android.os.Bundle;
import android.os.Handler;
import android.provider.MediaStore.Images.Media;
import android.util.Log;
import android.view.SurfaceHolder;
import android.view.SurfaceView;
import android.view.View;
import android.view.View.OnClickListener;
import android.widget.Button;
import android.widget.TextView;
import android.widget.Toast;

public class TimerSnapShot extends Activity implements OnClickListener,⏎
    SurfaceHolder.Callback, Camera.PictureCallback {

    SurfaceView cameraView;
    SurfaceHolder surfaceHolder;
    Camera camera;
```

This activity is very similar to our SnapShot activity. We are going to add a `Button` to trigger the start of countdown and a `TextView` to display the countdown.

```
    Button startButton;
    TextView countdownTextView;
```

We'll also need a `Handler`, in this case `timerUpdateHandler`, a Boolean to help us keep track of whether the timer has started (`timerRunning`), and we'll have an integer (`currentTime`) that will keep track of the countdown.

```
    Handler timerUpdateHandler;
    boolean timerRunning = false;
    int currentTime = 10;
```

```
@Override
public void onCreate(Bundle savedInstanceState) {
    super.onCreate(savedInstanceState);
    setContentView(R.layout.main);

    cameraView = (SurfaceView) this.findViewById(R.id.CameraView);
    surfaceHolder = cameraView.getHolder();
    surfaceHolder.setType(SurfaceHolder.SURFACE_TYPE_PUSH_BUFFERS);
    surfaceHolder.addCallback(this);
```

Next, we'll obtain references to the new UI elements (defined in the layout XML) and make our activity be the OnClickListener for the Button. We can do this because our activity implements OnClickListener.

```
countdownTextView = (TextView) findViewById(R.id.CountDownTextView);
startButton = (Button) findViewById(R.id.CountDownButton);
startButton.setOnClickListener(this);
```

The last thing we'll do in our onCreate method is instantiate our Handler object.

```
    timerUpdateHandler = new Handler();
}
```

Our onClick method will be called when the startButton Button is pressed. We'll make sure the timer routine isn't already running by checking our timerRunning Boolean, and if it isn't, we'll call timerUpdateTask Runnable (described here) without delay through our Handler object, timerUpdateHandler.

```
public void onClick(View v) {
    if (!timerRunning)
    {
        timerRunning = true;
        timerUpdateHandler.post(timerUpdateTask);
    }
}
```

Here is our Runnable called timerUpdateTask. This is the object that contains the run method that will be triggered by our timerUpdateHandler object.

```
private Runnable timerUpdateTask = new Runnable() {
    public void run()
    {
```

If the currentTime, the integer holding our countdown, is greater than 1, we'll decrement it and schedule the Handler call again in 1 second.

```
        if (currentTime > 1)
        {
            currentTime--;
            timerUpdateHandler.postDelayed(timerUpdateTask, 1000);
        }
        else
        {
```

If currentTime isn't greater than 1, we'll actually trigger the camera to take the picture and reset all of our tracking variables.

```
            camera.takePicture(null,null ,TimerSnapShot.this);
            timerRunning = false;
```

```
            currentTime = 10;
        }
```

No matter what, we'll update the TextView to display the current time remaining before the picture is taken.

```
        countdownTextView.setText(""+currentTime);
    }
};
```

The rest of the activity is essentially the same as the foregoing SnapShot example.

```
public void surfaceChanged(SurfaceHolder holder, int format, int w, int h) {
    camera.startPreview();
}

public void surfaceCreated(SurfaceHolder holder) {
    camera = Camera.open();
    try {
        camera.setPreviewDisplay(holder);
        Camera.Parameters parameters = camera.getParameters();
        if (this.getResources().getConfiguration().orientation !=
          Configuration.ORIENTATION_LANDSCAPE)
        {
            parameters.set("orientation", "portrait");

            // For Android Version 2.2 and above
            camera.setDisplayOrientation(90);

            // For Android Version 2.0 and above
            parameters.setRotation(90);
        }
        camera.setParameters(parameters);
    }
    catch (IOException exception)
    {
        camera.release();
    }
}
public void surfaceDestroyed(SurfaceHolder holder) {
  camera.stopPreview();
    camera.release();
}

public void onPictureTaken(byte[] data, Camera camera) {
    Uri imageFileUri =
    getContentResolver().insert(Media.EXTERNAL_CONTENT_URI, new ContentValues());
    try {
        OutputStream imageFileOS =
            getContentResolver().openOutputStream(imageFileUri);
        imageFileOS.write(data);
        imageFileOS.flush();
        imageFileOS.close();

        Toast t = Toast.makeText(this,"Saved JPEG!", Toast.LENGTH_SHORT);
        t.show();

    } catch (FileNotFoundException e) {
```

```
            Toast t = Toast.makeText(this,e.getMessage(), Toast.LENGTH_SHORT);
            t.show();
        } catch (IOException e) {
          Toast t = Toast.makeText(this,e.getMessage(), Toast.LENGTH_SHORT);
            t.show();
        }
          camera.startPreview();
      }
}
```

The layout XML is a bit different. In this application, we are displaying the Camera preview `SurfaceView` within a `FrameLayout` along with a `LinearLayout` that contains the `TextView` for displaying the countdown and the Button for triggering the countdown. The `FrameLayout` aligns all of its children to the top left and on top of each other. This way the `TextView` and `Button` appear over top of the Camera preview.

```xml
<?xml version="1.0" encoding="utf-8"?>
<LinearLayout xmlns:android="http://schemas.android.com/apk/res/android"
    android:orientation="vertical"
    android:layout_width="fill_parent"
    android:layout_height="fill_parent"
    >
  <FrameLayout android:id="@+id/FrameLayout01" android:layout_width="wrap_content"↵
 android:layout_height="wrap_content">
    <SurfaceView android:id="@+id/CameraView" android:layout_width="fill_parent"↵
 android:layout_height="fill_parent"></SurfaceView>
    <LinearLayout android:id="@+id/LinearLayout01"
 android:layout_width="wrap_content"↵
 android:layout_height="wrap_content">
        <TextView android:id="@+id/CountDownTextView" android:text="10"↵
 android:textSize="100dip" android:layout_width="fill_parent"↵
 android:layout_height="wrap_content"↵
 android:layout_gravity="center_vertical|center_horizontal|center"></TextView>
        <Button android:layout_width="wrap_content"
 android:layout_height="wrap_content"↵
 android:id="@+id/CountDownButton" android:text="Start Timer"></Button>
    </LinearLayout>
  </FrameLayout>
</LinearLayout>
```

Last, we need to make sure our `AndroidManifest.xml` file contains the `CAMERA` permission.

```xml
<uses-permission android:name="android.permission.CAMERA"></uses-permission>
```

Figure 2–5. *Camera with countdown timer*

Building a Time-Lapse Photography App

We have all seen beautiful examples of time-lapse photography. It is the process of taking several pictures over an even course of time. It could be one per minute, one per hour, or even one per week. Looking through a series of time-lapse photographs, we can see how something changes over time. One example might be watching a building being constructed, another might be documenting how a flower grows and blooms.

Now that we have built a timer-based camera app, updating it to be a time-lapse app is fairly straightforward.

First we'll change up some of the instance variables and add in a constant.

```
...
public class TimelapseSnapShot extends Activity implements OnClickListener,↵
  SurfaceHolder.Callback, Camera.PictureCallback {
    SurfaceView cameraView;
    SurfaceHolder surfaceHolder;
    Camera camera;
```

We'll rename the Button to be startStopButton as it will now handle both actions and perform a few minor naming updates to the rest of the variables.

```
    Button startStopButton;
    TextView countdownTextView;
```

```
Handler timerUpdateHandler;
boolean timelapseRunning = false;
```

The currentTime integer will be used to count up to the amount of time between photos in seconds instead of down from the total delay, as in the previous example. A constant called SECONDS_BETWEEN_PHOTOS is set to 60. As its name implies, this will be used to determine the time to wait between photos.

```
int currentTime = 0;
public static final int SECONDS_BETWEEN_PHOTOS = 60;  // one minute
```

The onCreate method will largely remain the same—only the new variable names will be referenced.

```
@Override
public void onCreate(Bundle savedInstanceState) {
    super.onCreate(savedInstanceState);
    setContentView(R.layout.main);
    cameraView = (SurfaceView) this.findViewById(R.id.CameraView);
    surfaceHolder = cameraView.getHolder();
    surfaceHolder.setType(SurfaceHolder.SURFACE_TYPE_PUSH_BUFFERS);
    surfaceHolder.addCallback(this);

    countdownTextView = (TextView) findViewById(R.id.CountDownTextView);
    startStopButton = (Button) findViewById(R.id.CountDownButton);
    startStopButton.setOnClickListener(this);
    timerUpdateHandler = new Handler();
}
```

The bulk of the changes to make this into a time-lapse application from a single timer-based application will come in the onClick method, which is what happens when the button is pressed and in the Runnable method that is scheduled by the Handler.

The onClick method first checks to see if the time-lapse processes are currently going (the Button has previously been pressed), and if not, it sets it to running and calls the Handler's post method with the Runnable (described here) as the argument.

If the time-lapse process is going, the button press is meant to stop it, so the removeCallbacks method on the Handler, timerUpdateHandler, is called. This will clear any pending calls to the Runnable that are passed in as an argument.

```
public void onClick(View v) {
    if (!timelapseRunning) {
        startStopButton.setText("Stop");
        timelapseRunning = true;
        timerUpdateHandler.post(timerUpdateTask);
    } else {
        startStopButton.setText("Start");
        timelapseRunning = false;
        timerUpdateHandler.removeCallbacks(timerUpdateTask);
    }
}
```

As we are dealing with a Handler to do the scheduling, we have a Runnable that the Handler calls upon when the time comes. In the run method of our Handler, we first check to see if the currentTime integer is less than the number of seconds we want to wait between photos (SECONDS_BETWEEN_PHOTOS). If it is, we simply increment currentTime. If the currentTime isn't less than the period to wait, we tell the Camera to take a picture and set currentTime back to 0 so it continues counting up.

After each of these cases, we simply update our TextView with the currentTime and schedule a call back to ourselves in another second.

```
private Runnable timerUpdateTask = new Runnable() {
    public void run() {
        if (currentTime < SECONDS_BETWEEN_PHOTOS)
        {
            currentTime++;
        }
        else
        {
            camera.takePicture(null,null,null,TimelapseSnapShot.this);
            currentTime = 0;
        }

        timerUpdateHandler.postDelayed(timerUpdateTask, 1000);
        countdownTextView.setText(""+currentTime);
    }
};
```

The res/layout/main.xml interface and, of course, AndroidManifest.xml for this example are the same as the single countdown timer version.

Summary

As you can see, there are myriad reasons that we might want to build our own camera-based application rather than just utilizing the built-in application in our own app. The sky is the limit with what you can accomplish, from simply creating an application that takes a picture after a countdown to building your own time-lapse system and more.

Moving forward, we'll look at what we can do with these images now that they are captured.

Chapter 3

Image Editing and Processing

As handheld devices become more and more powerful, many of the features that could exist only on a desktop computer are now possible on a mobile device. Once the purview of desktop apps such a Photoshop and the like, image editing and processing can now be accomplished on a phone.

In this chapter, we'll look at what we can do with images after they are captured. We'll go through how to alter them through rotation and scaling, how to adjust brightness and contrast, as well as how we can composite two or more images together.

Selecting Images Using the Built-In Gallery Application

As we know, using an intent is often the quickest way to harness a capability that already exists in a pre-installed Android application. For the purposes of the examples in this chapter, let's look at how we can harness the built-in Gallery application to select an image that we might want to work with.

The intent that we'll want to use is a generic `Intent.ACTION_PICK` that signals to Android that we want to select a piece of data. We also supply a URI for the data that we want to pick from. In this case, we are using `android.provier.MediaStore.Images.Media.EXTERNAL_CONTENT_URI`, which means that we'll be selecting images that are stored using the MediaStore on the SD card.

```
Intent choosePictureIntent = new Intent(Intent.ACTION_PICK,↵
 android.provider.MediaStore.Images.Media.EXTERNAL_CONTENT_URI);
```

When this intent is triggered, it launches the Gallery application in a mode where the user is able to select an image.

As is usual with the return from an intent, after the user has selected the image, our
onActivityResult method is triggered. The selected image's URI is returned in the data
of the returned intent.

```
onActivityResult(int requestCode, int resultCode, Intent intent) {
    super.onActivityResult(requestCode, resultCode, intent);

    if (resultCode == RESULT_OK) {
        Uri imageFileUri = intent.getData();
    }
}
```

Here is a full example:

```
package com.apress.proandroidmedia.ch3.choosepicture;

import java.io.FileNotFoundException;
import android.app.Activity;
import android.content.Intent;
import android.graphics.Bitmap;
import android.graphics.BitmapFactory;
import android.net.Uri;
import android.os.Bundle;
import android.util.Log;
import android.view.Display;
import android.view.View;
import android.view.View.OnClickListener;
import android.widget.Button;
import android.widget.ImageView;
```

Our activity will be responding to click events fired by a button; we'll therefore
implement OnClickListener. In the onCreate method, we use the normal findViewById
method to access the necessary UI elements that are defined in the Layout XML.

```
public class ChoosePicture extends Activity implements OnClickListener {

    ImageView chosenImageView;
    Button choosePicture;

    @Override
    public void onCreate(Bundle savedInstanceState) {
        super.onCreate(savedInstanceState);
        setContentView(R.layout.main);

        chosenImageView = (ImageView) this.findViewById(R.id.ChosenImageView);
        choosePicture = (Button) this.findViewById(R.id.ChoosePictureButton);

        choosePicture.setOnClickListener(this);
    }
```

Figure 3–1. *The* choosePicture *button, displayed when the app first launches*

What follows is the onClick method, which will respond to the pressing of the choosePicture button which is displayed when the app starts as illustrated in Figure 3–1. In this method, we create the intent that will trigger the Gallery application to launch in a mode that allows the user to select a picture as shown in Figure 3–2.

```
public void onClick(View v) {
    Intent choosePictureIntent = new Intent(Intent.ACTION_PICK,
android.provider.MediaStore.Images.Media.EXTERNAL_CONTENT_URI);
    startActivityForResult(choosePictureIntent, 0);
}
```

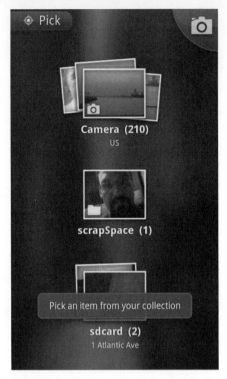

Figure 3–2. *The view of the Gallery application when triggered by the* ACTION_PICK *intent prompting the user to choose an image; the UI of the Gallery application may vary per device.*

When the Gallery application returns after the user has selected an image, our onActivityResult method is called. We get the URI to the selected image in the passed-in intent's data.

```
        protected void onActivityResult(int requestCode, int resultCode, ↵
  Intent intent) {
        super.onActivityResult(requestCode, resultCode, intent);

        if (resultCode == RESULT_OK) {
            Uri imageFileUri = intent.getData();
```

Since the returned image is likely too big to load completely in memory, we'll use the technique we went over in Chapter 1 to resize it as it is loaded. The dw int and the dh int will be the maximum width and height respectively. The maximum height will be less than half the screen height, as we will eventually be displaying two images, aligned vertically.

```
        Display currentDisplay = getWindowManager().getDefaultDisplay();
        int dw = currentDisplay.getWidth();
        int dh = currentDisplay.getHeight()/2 - 100;

        try {
            // Load up the image's dimensions not the image itself
            BitmapFactory.Options bmpFactoryOptions = new BitmapFactory.Options();
            bmpFactoryOptions.inJustDecodeBounds = true;
```

```
                    Bitmap bmp = BitmapFactory.decodeStream(getContentResolver().↵
openInputStream(imageFileUri), null, bmpFactoryOptions);

                int heightRatio = (int)Math.ceil(bmpFactoryOptions.outHeight/(float)dh);
                int widthRatio = (int)Math.ceil(bmpFactoryOptions.outWidth/(float)dw);

                if (heightRatio > 1 && widthRatio > 1)
                {
                    if (heightRatio > widthRatio) {
                        bmpFactoryOptions.inSampleSize = heightRatio;
                    }
                    else {
                        bmpFactoryOptions.inSampleSize = widthRatio;
                    }
                }

                bmpFactoryOptions.inJustDecodeBounds = false;
                bmp = BitmapFactory.decodeStream(getContentResolver().↵
openInputStream(imageFileUri), null, bmpFactoryOptions);

                choosenImageView.setImageBitmap(bmp);

            } catch (FileNotFoundException e) {
                Log.v("ERROR",e.toString());
            }
        }
    }
}
```

It requires the following in the project's layout/main.xml file:

```
<?xml version="1.0" encoding="utf-8"?>
<LinearLayout xmlns:android="http://schemas.android.com/apk/res/android"
    android:orientation="vertical"
    android:layout_width="fill_parent"
    android:layout_height="fill_parent"
    >
    <Button
        android:layout_width="fill_parent"
        android:layout_height="wrap_content"
        android:text="Choose Picture" android:id="@+id/ChoosePictureButton"/>
    <ImageView android:layout_width="wrap_content" android:layout_height=↵
    "wrap_content" android:id="@+id/ChosenImageView"></ImageView>
</LinearLayout>
```

Figure 3–3. *The application after the user has chosen a picture*

That's it; we now have a user-chosen image as a `Bitmap` object displayed to the user as illustrated in Figure 3–3. Let's look at how we can use this `Bitmap` as a starting point for other operations.

Drawing a Bitmap onto a Bitmap

Before we get into the specific mechanisms used to alter the images, let's look at how we can create a new, empty `Bitmap` object and draw an existing `Bitmap` into that. This is the process that we will be using to create altered versions of our images.

In the foregoing example, we have a `Bitmap` object instantiated with an image that has been selected by the user. It has been instantiated by a call to `BitmapFactory`'s `decodeStream` method, as we learned how to do in Chapter 1.

```
Bitmap bmp = BitmapFactory.decodeStream(getContentResolver().↵
openInputStream(imageFileUri), null, bmpFactoryOptions);
```

In order to use this `Bitmap` as the source for our image editing experiments, we need to be able to draw this `Bitmap` onto the screen with the effects applied. Additionally, it would be great to draw it to an object that we can use to save the resulting image from. It makes sense that we'll want to create an empty `Bitmap` object with the same dimensions as this one and use that as the destination for our altered `Bitmap`.

```
Bitmap alteredBitmap = Bitmap.createBitmap(bmp.getWidth(),↵
```

```
bmp.getHeight(),bmp.getConfig());
```

This object, alteredBitmap, is created with the same width, height, and color depth as the source Bitmap, bmp. Since we used the Bitmap class's createBitmap method with the width, height, and Bitmap.Config object as parameters, we are obtaining a mutable Bitmap object in return. Mutable means that we can change the pixel values represented by this Bitmap. If we had an immutable Bitmap, we would be unable to draw into it. This method call is one of the only ways to instantiate a mutable Bitmap object.

The next thing we'll need is a Canvas object. In Android a Canvas is, as you would expect, something used to draw on. A Canvas can be created by passing in a Bitmap object in its constructor, and subsequently it can be used to draw.

```
Canvas canvas = new Canvas(alteredBitmap);
```

Last, we'll need a Paint object. When we do the actual drawing, the Paint object comes into play. Specifically, it allows us to alter things such as color and contrast, but we'll get to that later. For now, we are going to use a default Paint object.

```
Paint paint = new Paint();
```

Now we have all of the required components to draw the source Bitmap into an empty mutable Bitmap object. Here is all of the code just described put together.

```
Bitmap bmp = BitmapFactory.decodeStream(getContentResolver().↩
openInputStream(imageFileUri), null, bmpFactoryOptions);
Bitmap alteredBitmap = Bitmap.createBitmap(bmp.getWidth(),bmp.getHeight(),↩
bmp.getConfig());
Canvas canvas = new Canvas(alteredBitmap);
Paint paint = new Paint();
```

```
canvas.drawBitmap(bmp, 0, 0, paint);
```

```
ImageView alteredImageView = (ImageView) this.findViewById(R.id.AlteredImageView);
alteredImageView.setImageBitmap(alteredBitmap);
```

The drawBitmap method on the Canvas object we are using takes the source Bitmap and an x, y offset along with our Paint object. This causes our alteredBitmap object to contain the exact same information as our original bitmap.

We can plug all of this code into our Choose Picture example. It would come near the end of the onActivityResult method, directly after the bmp = BitmapFactory.decodeStream line. Be careful not to duplicate that line, as is shown in the foregoing code snippet as well. Also don't forget to add the appropriate import statements.

Following that, we want to display our alteredBitmap object. To do that, we are using a standard ImageView and calling setImageBitmap with our alteredBitmap. This assumes that we have an ImageView with the id AlteredImageView declared in our Layout XML.

Here is the updated Layout XML for our full Choose Picture example, which contains the original ImageView as well as our new ImageView for the alteredBitmap as shown in Figure 3–4.

```xml
<?xml version="1.0" encoding="utf-8"?>
<LinearLayout xmlns:android="http://schemas.android.com/apk/res/android"
    android:orientation="vertical"
    android:layout_width="fill_parent"
    android:layout_height="fill_parent"
    >
    <Button
        android:layout_width="fill_parent"
        android:layout_height="wrap_content"
        android:text="Choose Picture" android:id="@+id/ChoosePictureButton"/>

    <ImageView android:layout_width="wrap_content" android:layout_height="wrap_content"↵
        android:id="@+id/ChosenImageView"></ImageView>
    <ImageView android:layout_width="wrap_content" android:layout_height="wrap_content"↵
        android:id="@+id/AlteredImageView"></ImageView>
</LinearLayout>
```

Figure 3–4. *The application after the user has selected an image with the second bitmap object displayed*

Basic Image Scaling and Rotating

We'll start our exploration of image editing and processing with learning how we can perform spatial transformations such as changing scale and rotating images.

Enter the Matrix

The Android API has a Matrix class, which can be used when drawing on existing Bitmap objects or creating a Bitmap object from another Bitmap object. This class allows us to apply a spatial transformation to an image. A transformation of this type would be rotating, cropping, scaling, or otherwise altering the coordinate space of the image.

The Matrix class represents transformations with an array of nine numbers. In many cases, these can be generated by a formula that mathematically represents the transformation that should occur. For instance, the formula for rotation involves using sine and cosine to generate the number in the matrix.

The numbers in the Matrix can also be input manually. In order to understand how the Matrix works, we'll start by doing some manual transforms.

Each number in the Matrix applies to one of the three (x, y, or z) coordinates for each point in the image.

For instance, here is a Matrix of nine floats:

```
1 0 0
0 1 0
0 0 1
```

The top row (1, 0, 0) specifies that the source x coordinate will be transformed according the following formula: $x = 1x + 0y + 0z$. As you can see, the placement of the values in the matrix determines how that number will affect the outcome. The top row will always affect the x coordinate but can operate with the source x, y, and z coordinate.

The second row (0, 1, 0) means that the y coordinate will be determined as $y = 0x + 1y + 0z$, and the third row (0, 0, 1) means that the z coordinate will be determined by $z = 0x + 0y + 1z$.

In other words, this Matrix won't do any transformation; everything will be placed as it is in the source image.

To implement this in code, we would create the Matrix object and then explicitly set the values through its setValues method.

```
Matrix matrix = new Matrix();
matrix.setValues(new float[] {
    1, 0, 0,
    0, 1, 0,
    0, 0, 1
});
```

We can use the Matrix object when drawing a bitmap onto a canvas.

```
canvas.drawBitmap(bmp, matrix, paint);
```

This would be in place of the drawBitmap method that we are using in our previous example.

To have this Matrix change the image in some manner, we can replace any of the existing numbers with a different value. If we change the first number from a 1 to a .5, we would squish the image on the x axis by 50% as illustrated in Figure 3–5. This first number operates on the x coordinate in the source to influence the x coordinate in the resulting image.

```
.5 0 0
0 1 0
0 0 1
```

```
Matrix matrix = new Matrix();
matrix.setValues(new float[] {
    .5f, 0, 0,
    0, 1, 0,
    0, 0, 1
});
canvas.drawBitmap(bmp, matrix, paint);
```

Figure 3–5. *The second image displayed with the custom matrix applied, scaling the x axis by 50%*

If we altered the matrix to have the x coordinate also be affected by the source y coordinate, we can alter the second number.

```
Matrix matrix = new Matrix();
matrix.setValues(new float[] {
    1, .5f, 0,
    0, 1, 0,
    0, 0, 1
});
canvas.drawBitmap(bmp, matrix, paint);
```

Figure 3–6. *The second image displayed with the custom matrix applied, skewing the image*

As you can see in Figure 3–6, it causes the image to skew. It skews because the first row, which operates on the x value of each pixel, is being altered by the y value of each pixel. As the y value increases, as we move down the image, the x value increases, causing the image to skew. If we used a negative value, it would skew in the opposite direction. You'll also notice that the image gets cut off due to the coordinates changing. We need to increase the size of the resulting bitmap as shown in Figure 3–7 if we are going to perform operations like this.

```
alteredBitmap = Bitmap.createBitmap(bmp.getWidth()*2,bmp.getHeight(),bmp.getConfig());
```

Figure 3–7. *The second image displayed with the same custom matrix but with a larger width so the image isn't cropped*

As you can see, these Matrix transformations are very powerful. Also, you can see that doing them by hand can be cumbersome. Unfortunately, the formulas to accomplish much of what you would want to do with the Matrix by hand require math that is out of the scope of this book. There are plenty of resources online, though, if you are interested in learning more. A good place to start is the Wikipedia Transformation Matrix article: http://en.wikipedia.org/wiki/Transformation_matrix.

Matrix Methods

What we will do now, though, is explore the other methods of the Matrix class, as they help us accomplish much of what we would want without having to resort to relearning our high school and college math lessons.

Instead of creating our own Matrix numbers, we can simply call corresponding methods for the transformations that we would like to use.

Each of the snippets presented next can take the place of the canvas.drawBitmap line in the "Drawing a Bitmap onto a Bitmap" example.

Rotate

One of the built-in methods is the setRotation method. It takes in a float representing the degrees of rotation. Positive values rotate the image clockwise and negative values rotate it counter-clockwise around the default point (0,0), which is the top left corner of the image as illustrated in Figure 3–8.

```
Matrix matrix = new Matrix();
matrix.setRotate(15);
canvas.drawBitmap(bmp, matrix, paint);
```

Figure 3–8. *Rotation around the default point (0,0)*

Alternatively, the setRotation method can be called with the degrees of rotation and the points around which to rotate. Choosing the center point on the image might yield results more in line with what we are looking for as shown in Figure 3–9.

```
matrix.setRotate(15,bmp.getWidth()/2,bmp.getHeight()/2);
```

Figure 3–9. *Rotation around the mid-point of the image*

Scale

Another useful method of Matrix is the setScale method. It takes in two floats representing the amount of scaling to occur on each axis. The first argument is the x-axis scale, and the second is the y-axis scaling. Figure 3–10 shows the result of the following setScale method call.

```
matrix.setScale(1.5f,1);
```

Figure 3–10. *1.5 scale applied on the x axis*

Translate

One of the most useful methods of Matrix is the setTranslate method. A translate simply moves the image on the x and y axes. The setTranslate method takes in two floats representing the amount to move on each axis. The first argument is the amount the image will move on the x axis, and the second argument is the amount the image will move on the y axis. Translating with positive values on the x axis will move the image to the right, while using negative values will move the image to the left. Translating with positive values on the y –axis will move the image downward and using negative values will move the image upward.matrix.

```
setTranslate(1.5f,-10);.
```

Pre and Post

Of course, these are just the tip of the iceberg. There are several more that may prove to be useful to you. Each of them also has a pre and a post version. These enable you to do more than one transformation at a time in sequence. For instance, you could do a preScale and then setRotate or a setScale and then postRotate. Changing the order of when they occur could yield vastly different results depending on the operations performed. Figure 3–11 shows the results of the following two method calls.

```
matrix.setScale(1.5f, 1);
matrix.postRotate(15,bmp.getWidth()/2,bmp.getHeight()/2);
```

Figure 3–11. *Scaled and rotated*

Mirroring

One particularly useful pair is `setScale` and `postTranslate`, which allow you to flip the image across a single axis (or both if you desire). If you scale by a negative number, the image will draw in the negative space of the coordinate system. Since the 0, 0 point is the top left, using a negative number on the x axis would cause the image to draw to the left. Therefore we need to use the `postTranslate` method to move it over to the right as displayed in Figure 3–12.

```
matrix.setScale(-1, 1);
matrix.postTranslate(bmp.getWidth(),0);
```

Figure 3–12. *Mirrored*

Flipping

We could do the same thing, but on the y axis, to flip the image upside-down. We could have achieved the same effect by rotating the image 180 degrees around the midpoint on both axes as shown in Figure 3–13.

```
matrix.setScale(1, -1);
matrix.postTranslate(0, bmp.getHeight());
```

Figure 3–13. *Flipped*

Alternative to Drawing

One of the drawbacks to the methods we are using in the foregoing sections is that the images get cut off, as we aren't calculating the resulting size after the transformation and just drawing into a `Bitmap` with a predetermined size.

One way that we can overcome this issue is to apply the `Matrix` as we are creating the `Bitmap` in the first place, rather than drawing into an empty `Bitmap`.

Going about things this way removes the need for us to have a `Canvas` and a `Paint` object. The drawback is that we cannot continually change the `Bitmap` object and have to recreate it if we want to do any more transformations on it.

The static `createBitmap` method available in the `Bitmap` class allows this. The first argument is the source `Bitmap`, the next arguments are the start x, y, width, and height values to use from the source, followed by the `Matrix` to apply, and last a Boolean representing whether to apply any filtering to the image. Since we are not applying a matrix that contains a filter, which we'll discuss later in the chapter, we set that to be false.

```
Matrix matrix = new Matrix();
matrix.setRotate(15,bmp.getWidth()/2,bmp.getHeight()/2);
alteredBitmap = Bitmap.createBitmap(bmp, 0, 0, bmp.getWidth(), bmp.getHeight(),↵
 matrix, false);
alteredImageView.setImageBitmap(alteredBitmap);
```

As you can see, we deal with the matrix in the same way, but we instantiate our second `Bitmap` (alteredBitmap) using the original (bmp) as the source and pass in the `Matrix` object. This creates a `Bitmap` from the source with the translation and scaled to the size of the `Bitmap` object as shown in Figure 3–14.

Figure 3–14. *Matrix applied when* `Bitmap` *created; the dimensions of the* `Bitmap` *are adjusted to match the actual image data.*

Image Processing

Another form of image editing or processing has to do with changing the color values of the pixels themselves. Being able to do this allows us the ability to change contrast levels, brightness, overall hue, and so on.

ColorMatrix

In a way similar to how we use the `Matrix` object when drawing on a `Canvas`, we can use a `ColorMatrix` object to alter the `Paint` that is used to draw on a `Canvas`.

The `ColorMatrix` works in a similar manner as well. It is an array of numbers that operate on the pixels of the image. Instead of operating on the x, y, and z coordinates, though, it operates on the color values—Red, Green, Blue, and Alpha of each pixel.

We can construct a default `ColorMatrix` object by calling its constructor without any arguments.

```
ColorMatrix cm = new ColorMatrix();
```

This `ColorMatrix` can be used to alter how things are drawn to a `Canvas` by being applied to the `Paint` object through a `ColorMatrixColorFilter` object that is constructed using our `ColorMatrix` object.

```
paint.setColorFilter(new ColorMatrixColorFilter(cm));
```

This can simply be plugged into the drawing portion of our Choose Picture example to allow us the ability to experiment with the `ColorMatrix`.

```
Bitmap bmp = BitmapFactory.decodeStream(getContentResolver().↵
openInputStream(imageFileUri), null, bmpFactoryOptions);
Bitmap alteredBitmap = Bitmap.createBitmap(bmp.getWidth(),↵
bmp.getHeight(),bmp.getConfig());
Canvas canvas = new Canvas(alteredBitmap);
Paint paint = new Paint();


ColorMatrix cm = new ColorMatrix();

paint.setColorFilter(new ColorMatrixColorFilter(cm));

Matrix matrix = new Matrix();
canvas.drawBitmap(bmp, matrix, paint);
alteredImageView.setImageBitmap(alteredBitmap);
chosenImageView.setImageBitmap(bmp);
```

The default `ColorMatrix` is what is called the identity, just like the default `Matrix` object, in that when it is applied, it doesn't alter the image. Looking at what the array contains will help us understand how it works.

```
1 0 0 0 0
0 1 0 0 0
0 0 1 0 0
0 0 0 1 0
```

As you can see, it is an array of 20 floats. The first row of five comprises the operation to occur on the red portion of an individual pixel, the second row affects the green portion, the third operates on the blue portion, and the last row operates on the alpha value of the pixel.

Within each row, the first number is the multiplier that is used along with the red value of the pixel, the second is the multiplier used with the green, the third with the blue, the fourth with the alpha, and the last number is not multiplied with anything. These values are all added up to alter the pixel they are operating on.

If we have a single pixel that is a middle gray, its red value is 128, its blue value 128, its green value 128, and its alpha value 0 (it is opaque). If we run that pixel through this color matrix, the math would look like this:

```
New Red Value = 1*128 + 0*128 + 0*128 + 0*0 + 0
New Blue Value = 0*128 + 1*128 + 0*128 + 0*0 + 0
New Green Value = 0*128 + 0*128 + 1*128 + 0*0 + 0
```

New Alpha Value = 0*128 + 0*128 + 0*128 + 1*0 + 0

As you can see, all of the values will remain the same, set to 128. This would be the case for any color variant that we used for the pixel, as each row has a 1 in the position meant to operate on its color but a 0 everywhere else.

If we simply wanted to make an image appear twice as red as it was previously, we could increase the number that operates on the red value of all of the pixels to be a 2 instead of a 1. This would double the red value across the board.

```
2 0 0 0 0
0 1 0 0 0
0 0 1 0 0
0 0 0 1 0
```

To implement this in code, we would do the following:

```
ColorMatrix cm = new ColorMatrix();
cm.set(new float[] {
    2, 0, 0, 0, 0,
    0, 1, 0, 0, 0,
    0, 0, 1, 0, 0,
    0, 0, 0, 1, 0
});
paint.setColorFilter(new ColorMatrixColorFilter(cm));
```

By hand, we could do similar things with any color across the board.

Altering Contrast and Brightness

Adjusting the brightness and contrast of an image can be done by increasing or decreasing the color values.

This code will double the intensity of each color channel, which affects both the brightness and contrast in an image as illustrated in Figure 3–15

```
ColorMatrix cm = new ColorMatrix();
float contrast = 2;
cm.set(new float[] {
    contrast, 0, 0, 0, 0,
    0, contrast, 0, 0, 0,
    0, 0, contrast, 0, 0,
    0, 0, 0, 1, 0 });
paint.setColorFilter(new ColorMatrixColorFilter(cm));
```

Figure 3–15. *ColorMatrix with each color's intensity doubled, increasing brightness and contrast*

In this example, both effects are linked. If we simply want to increase contrast without increasing brightness, we actually have to reduce brightness to compensate for the increase in color intensity.

Generally, when adjusting brightness, it is easier to just use the final column in the matrix for each color. This is the amount that is simply added to the value of the color without any multiplication of the existing color values.

Therefore, to reduce the brightness, we would use code for a matrix as follows.

```
ColorMatrix cm = new ColorMatrix();
float brightness = -25;
cm.set(new float[] {
    1, 0, 0, 0, brightness,
    0, 1, 0, 0, brightness,
    0, 0, 1, 0, brightness,
    0, 0, 0, 1, 0 });
paint.setColorFilter(new ColorMatrixColorFilter(cm));
```

Putting these two transformations together would yield the following.

```
ColorMatrix cm = new ColorMatrix();

float contrast = 2;
float brightness = -25;
cm.set(new float[] {
    contrast, 0, 0, 0, brightness,
```

```
   0, contrast, 0, 0, brightness,
   0, 0, contrast, 0, brightness,
   0, 0, 0, contrast, 0 });
paint.setColorFilter(new ColorMatrixColorFilter(cm));
```

The result of this operation is shown in Figure 3–16.

Figure 3–16. *ColorMatrix with each color's intensity doubled but brightness decreased to affect contrast without changing brightness*

Changing Saturation

Fortunately, we don't need to know the formula for each operation we might want to accomplish. For instance, the ColorMatrix has a method for changing saturation built in.

```
ColorMatrix cm = new ColorMatrix();
cm.setSaturation(.5f);
paint.setColorFilter(new ColorMatrixColorFilter(cm));
```

Passing in a number greater than 1 will increase saturation, and a number between 0 and 1 decreases saturation. A value of 0 will yield a grayscale image.

Image Compositing

Compositing is the act of putting together two images, allowing features of both images to be seen.

In the Android SDK, we can accomplish compositing by first drawing one `Bitmap` to a `Canvas` and then drawing a second `Bitmap` to the same `Canvas`. The only difference is that we specify a transfermode (`Xfermode`) on the `Paint` when drawing the second image.

The set of classes that can be used as a transfermode all derive from the `Xfermode` base class and include one called `PorterDuffXfermode`. The `PorterDuffXfermode` class is named for Thomas Porter and Tom Duff, who published a paper entitled "Compositing digital images" in the ACM SIGGRAPH Computer Graphics publication in 1984, detailing a series of different rules for drawing images on top of one another. These rules define which portions of which images will appear in the resulting output.

The rules devised by Porter and Duff and more are enumerated in the `PorterDuff.Mode` class in Android.

They include the following:

- *android.graphics.PorterDuff.Mode.SRC*: This rule means that only the **source**, in our case, the paint that we are applying this to, will be drawn.

- *android.graphics.PorterDuff.Mode.DST*: This rule means that only the **destination**, the original image, already on the canvas, will be shown.

Following the SRC and DST rules, there is a set that works with them to determine which parts of each image will be drawn in the end. These generally apply when the images are different sizes or when they have transparent portions.

- *android.graphics.PorterDuff.Mode.DST_OVER*: The destination image will be drawn over the top of the source image.

- *android.graphics.PorterDuff.Mode.DST_IN*: The destination image will be drawn only where the source and destination images intersect.

- *android.graphics.PorterDuff.Mode.DST_OUT*: The destination image will be drawn only where the source and destination images do not intersect.

- *android.graphics.PorterDuff.Mode.DST_ATOP*: The destination image will be drawn where it intersects with the source; elsewhere the source will be drawn.

- *android.graphics.PorterDuff.Mode.SRC_OVER*: The source image will be drawn over the top of the destination image.

- *android.graphics.PorterDuff.Mode.SRC_IN*: The source image will be drawn only where the destination and source images intersect.

- *android.graphics.PorterDuff.Mode.SRC_OUT*: The source image will be drawn only where the destination and source images do not intersect.

- *android.graphics.PorterDuff.Mode.SRC_ATOP*: The source image will be drawn where it intersects with the destination; elsewhere the destination will be drawn.

- *android.graphics.PorterDuff.Mode.XOR*: The source and destination images will be drawn everywhere except where they overlap, where neither will be drawn.

Four additional rules are defined that define how two images can be blended together when one is placed above the other.

- *android.graphics.PorterDuff.Mode.LIGHTEN*: Takes the lightest pixel of the two images from each position and shows that.

- *android.graphics.PorterDuff.Mode.DARKEN*: Takes the darkest pixel from the two images in each position and shows that.

- *android.graphics.PorterDuff.Mode.MULTIPLY*: Multiplies the two pixels from each position, divides by 255, and uses that value to create a new pixel for display. Result Color = Top Color * Bottom Color / 255

- *android.graphics.PorterDuff.Mode.SCREEN*: Inverts each of the colors, performs the same operation (multiplies them together and divides by 255), and then inverts once again. Result Color = 255 - (((255 - Top Color) * (255 - Bottom Color)) / 255)

Let's illustrate how these rules may be used with an example application.

```
package com.apress.proandroidmedia.ch3.choosepicturecomposite;

import java.io.FileNotFoundException;

import android.app.Activity;
import android.content.Intent;
import android.graphics.Bitmap;
import android.graphics.BitmapFactory;
import android.graphics.Canvas;
import android.graphics.Paint;
import android.graphics.PorterDuffXfermode;
import android.net.Uri;
import android.os.Bundle;
import android.util.Log;
import android.view.Display;
import android.view.View;
import android.view.View.OnClickListener;
import android.widget.Button;
import android.widget.ImageView;

public class ChoosePictureComposite extends Activity implements OnClickListener {
```

We are creating a standard activity-based application, which we'll call Choose Picture Composite. The activity will implement OnClickListener so it can respond to Button clicks.

Since we are going to be compositing two images, we'll need to make sure the user picks two images before we attempt to draw the composited version. To do this, we'll make two constants, one for each Button press and then two Booleans to track whether a Button has been pressed. Of course, we'll have two Button objects as well.

```
static final int PICKED_ONE = 0;
static final int PICKED_TWO = 1;

boolean onePicked = false;
boolean twoPicked = false;

Button choosePicture1, choosePicture2;
```

We'll have one `ImageView` to display the final composited image. Also, we'll need to have two `Bitmap` objects, one for each of the chosen images.

```
ImageView compositeImageView;

Bitmap bmp1, bmp2;
```

As in our previous examples, we'll need a `Canvas` to draw on and a `Paint` object to draw with.

```
Canvas canvas;
Paint paint;

@Override
public void onCreate(Bundle savedInstanceState) {
    super.onCreate(savedInstanceState);
    setContentView(R.layout.main);

    compositeImageView = (ImageView) this.findViewById(R.id.CompositeImageView);

    choosePicture1 = (Button) this.findViewById(R.id.ChoosePictureButton1);
    choosePicture2 = (Button) this.findViewById(R.id.ChoosePictureButton2);

    choosePicture1.setOnClickListener(this);
    choosePicture2.setOnClickListener(this);
}
```

Since we set the `OnClickListener` for each `Button` to be this class, we need to implement an `onClick` method that will respond. To tell which one was clicked, we compare the `View` object that is passed in with each of the `Button` objects. If they are equal, that is the button that was clicked.

We are setting a variable called `which` to the value of one of the constants defined previously to keep track of which `Button` was pressed. This variable is then passed through to our Gallery Application, which is being instantiated with the `ACTION_PICK` intent. As shown in our previous examples, this will launch that application in a mode that allows the user to pick an image.

```
public void onClick(View v) {

    int which = -1;

    if (v == choosePicture1){
        which = PICKED_ONE;
    }
    else if (v == choosePicture2){
        which = PICKED_TWO;
    }

    Intent choosePictureIntent = new Intent(Intent.ACTION_PICK,android.provider.↵
MediaStore.Images.Media.EXTERNAL_CONTENT_URI);
    startActivityForResult(choosePictureIntent, which);
}
```

After the user has selected an image, our onActivityResult method is called. The variable that we passed in via the startActivityForResult method is passed back to us in the first parameter, which we are calling requestCode. Using this we know which image, the first or second, the user just chose. We use this value to decide which Bitmap object to load the chosen image into.

```
protected void onActivityResult(int requestCode, int resultCode, Intent intent)
{
    super.onActivityResult(requestCode, resultCode, intent);

    if (resultCode == RESULT_OK){
        Uri imageFileUri = intent.getData();

        if (requestCode == PICKED_ONE){
            bmp1 = loadBitmap(imageFileUri);
            onePicked = true;
        }
        else if (requestCode == PICKED_TWO){
            bmp2 = loadBitmap(imageFileUri);
            twoPicked = true;
        }
```

When both images have been selected and both Bitmap objects have been instantiated, we can then move forward with our compositing operations. This will be a very similar process to our previous examples in this chapter. First we'll create an empty mutable Bitmap that is the same size and configuration as our first Bitmap, bmp1. Following that we'll construct a Canvas from that and a Paint object. We'll simply draw our first Bitmap (bmp1) into that canvas. This will cause that to be our destination for the compositing operations.

Now we can set the transfer mode on the Paint object. We instantiate a new PorterDuffXfermode object by passing in one of the constants that defines the mode that it will operate in. After we do that, we draw the second Bitmap on the Canvas and set the ImageView to be our new Bitmap. In the following version, we are using the MULTIPLY mode.

```
        if (onePicked && twoPicked){
            Bitmap drawingBitmap = Bitmap.createBitmap(bmp1.getWidth(),↵
bmp1.getHeight(), bmp1.getConfig());
```

```
            canvas = new Canvas(drawingBitmap);
            paint = new Paint();
            canvas.drawBitmap(bmp1, 0, 0, paint);
            paint.setXfermode(new PorterDuffXfermode(android.graphics.↵
PorterDuff.Mode.MULTIPLY));
            canvas.drawBitmap(bmp2, 0, 0, paint);

            compositeImageView.setImageBitmap(drawingBitmap);
        }
    }
}
```

Here is a helper class such as we defined in Chapter 1 to load a `Bitmap` from a URI scaled to be no larger than the size of the screen.

```
    private Bitmap loadBitmap(Uri imageFileUri){
        Display currentDisplay = getWindowManager().getDefaultDisplay();

        float dw = currentDisplay.getWidth();
        float dh = currentDisplay.getHeight();
        // ARGB_4444 is desired

        Bitmap returnBmp = Bitmap.createBitmap((int)dw, (int)dh,↵
    Bitmap.Config.ARGB_4444);

        try {
            // Load up the image's dimensions not the image itself
            BitmapFactory.Options bmpFactoryOptions = new BitmapFactory.Options();
            bmpFactoryOptions.inJustDecodeBounds = true;
            returnBmp = BitmapFactory.decodeStream(getContentResolver().↵
openInputStream(imageFileUri), null, bmpFactoryOptions);

            int heightRatio = (int)Math.ceil(bmpFactoryOptions.outHeight/dh);
            int widthRatio = (int)Math.ceil(bmpFactoryOptions.outWidth/dw);

            Log.v("HEIGHTRATIO",""+heightRatio);
            Log.v("WIDTHRATIO",""+widthRatio);

            // If both of the ratios are greater than 1, one of the sides of the↵
        image is greater than the screen
            if (heightRatio > 1 && widthRatio > 1){
                if (heightRatio > widthRatio){
                    // Height ratio is larger, scale according to it
                    bmpFactoryOptions.inSampleSize = heightRatio;
                }
                else{
                    // Width ratio is larger, scale according to it
                    bmpFactoryOptions.inSampleSize = widthRatio;
                }
            }

            // Decode it for real
            bmpFactoryOptions.inJustDecodeBounds = false;
            returnBmp = BitmapFactory.decodeStream(getContentResolver().↵
openInputStream(imageFileUri), null, bmpFactoryOptions);
        }
        catch (FileNotFoundException e) {
```

```
        Log.v("ERROR",e.toString());
    }

    return returnBmp;
    }
}
```

Here is the Layout XML to be used with the foregoing activity.

```xml
<?xml version="1.0" encoding="utf-8"?>
<LinearLayout xmlns:android="http://schemas.android.com/apk/res/android"
    android:orientation="vertical"
    android:layout_width="fill_parent"
    android:layout_height="fill_parent">
    <Button
        android:layout_width="fill_parent"
        android:layout_height="wrap_content"
        android:id="@+id/ChoosePictureButton1" android:text="Choose Picture 1"/>
    <Button
        android:layout_width="fill_parent"
        android:layout_height="wrap_content"
        android:id="@+id/ChoosePictureButton2" android:text="Choose Picture 2"/>
    <ImageView android:layout_width="wrap_content" android:layout_height=
"wrap_content" android:id="@+id/CompositeImageView"></ImageView>
</LinearLayout>
```

The result of the foregoing example with different transfer modes is illustrated in Figures 3–17 through 3–22

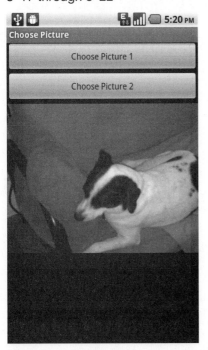

Figure 3–17. *The output from the foregoing example using* `android.graphics.PorterDuff.Mode.DST` *as the PorterDuffXfermode; as you can see, only the image selected as Picture 1 is displayed.*

Figure 3–18. *The output from the foregoing example using* `android.graphics.PorterDuff.Mode.SRC` *as the PorterDuffXfermode; as you can see, only the image selected as Picture 2 is displayed.*

Figure 3–19. *The output from the foregoing example using* `android.graphics.PorterDuff.Mode.MULTIPLY` *as the PorterDuffXfermode; as you can see, the two images are combined.*

Figure 3–20. *The output from the foregoing example using* `android.graphics.PorterDuff.Mode.LIGHTEN` *as the PorterDuffXfermode*

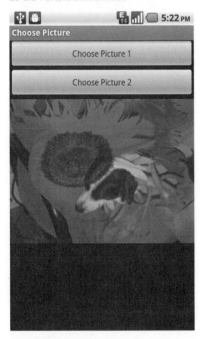

Figure 3–21. *The output from the foregoing example using* `android.graphics.PorterDuff.Mode.DARKEN` *as the PorterDuffXfermode*

Figure 3–22. *The output from the foregoing example using* `android.graphics.PorterDuff.Mode.SCREEN` *as the PorterDuffXfermode*

Summary

Throughout this chapter, we have learned that even though Android is primarily an operating system for devices that are constrained by size, memory, and processor power, it provides support for fairly sophisticated image processing. We covered many of the capabilities for processing existing images, but our exploration of imaging capabilities doesn't end here. In the next chapter, we'll look at some of the APIs that allow us to create images from scratch and do further manipulation while harnessing other sensors such as touchscreens.

Chapter 4

Graphics and Touch Events

Thus far we have explored how we can capture and manipulate photographic images. Of course, that isn't all that Android has to offer in terms of images. In this chapter, we'll change up a bit and look at how we can create images by drawing graphical elements and textual elements on a Canvas. Related to this, we'll explore the capabilities provided by Android for working with touchscreens. In particular we'll build a touchscreen drawing application.

Canvas Drawing

We know from the last chapter that we can draw Bitmap images on a Canvas object. That's not it for the Canvas class in Android, though. It also supports vector and text drawing. We can use a Canvas object either with Bitmap objects, as we did in the last chapter, or with Views. To start, we'll use a Canvas to create or alter a Bitmap and then move on to doing some very simple Canvas-based animation using a View.

Bitmap Creation

In the same manner we used previously, we can construct a Canvas object from a mutable Bitmap. To create a mutable Bitmap, a Bitmap that can be modified, we have to supply a width, a height, and a configuration. The configuration is generally a constant value defined in the Bitmap.Config class.

The following snippet of code creates a mutable Bitmap object with the dimensions of the display for the width and height and the Bitmap.Config.ARGB_8888 constant as the configuration.

```
Bitmap bitmap = Bitmap.createBitmap((int)↵
  getWindowManager().getDefaultDisplay().getWidth(), (int)↵
  getWindowManager().getDefaultDisplay().getHeight(), Bitmap.Config.ARGB_8888);
```

Bitmap Configuration

The ARGB_8888 configuration constant defines that the bitmap will be created with 8 bits of memory per color, 8 bits for the "A" or alpha channel, 8 bits for the "R" or red channel, 8 bits for the "G" or green channel, and 8 bits for the "B" or blue channel. This means that each pixel of the image will be represented by values between 0 and 255 for each color, including alpha. This means that each pixel will be represented by 32 bits and the total number of distinct colors that can be represented is more than 16.7 million.

Other configuration constants are available that use less memory and are therefore faster to process at the expense of image quality.

- *ALPHA_8*: Used for Bitmaps that function as alpha masks, 8 bits on alpha channel only. No other colors.

- *ARGB_4444*: 4 bits per color channel including alpha. Allows for 4096 unique colors with 16 alpha values. Figure 4–1 illustrates this setting using a rainbow gradient.

- *ARGB_8888*: 8 bits per color channel including alpha. Allows for 16.7 million unique colors with 256 alpha values. Figure 4–2 illustrates this setting using a rainbow gradient.

- *RGB_565*: 5 bits for the red channel, 6 bits for green, and 5 for blue (no alpha). Allows for 65,535 distinct colors. As Figure 4–3 illustrates, this setting is almost as high-quality as ARGB_8888 but takes up much less memory space.

Figure 4–1. *Rainbow gradient displayed on Bitmap in ARGB_4444 mode; notice the banding in the dark blue to light blue and yellow to orange portions. ARGB_4444 can't represent the required colors to make those transitions smooth.*

Figure 4–2. *Rainbow gradient displayed on Bitmap in* ARGB_8888 *mode*

Figure 4–3. *Rainbow gradient displayed on Bitmap in* RGB_565 *mode*

Creating the Canvas

Now that we have the Bitmap image that we'll be drawing into created, we need to create the Canvas object that we'll be using to actually draw.

To do this, we simply construct a Canvas object by passing in our new Bitmap object.

```
Bitmap bitmap = Bitmap.createBitmap((int)↵
 getWindowManager().getDefaultDisplay().getWidth(), (int)↵
 getWindowManager().getDefaultDisplay().getHeight(), Bitmap.Config.ARGB_8888);
Canvas canvas = new Canvas(bitmap);
```

Working with Paint

Before we can do any drawing, we need to construct a `Paint` object. The `Paint` object will allow us to define the color, size of the stroke, and style of the stroke used when drawing. We can therefore think of the `Paint` as both paint and brush.

```
Paint paint = new Paint();
paint.setColor(Color.GREEN);
paint.setStyle(Paint.Style.STROKE);
paint.setStrokeWidth(10);
```

The foregoing snippet of code creates a `Paint` object, sets its color to be green, defines that we want to draw the outline of shapes rather than fill them in, and sets the width of that stroke to be 10 pixels.

Let's examine each of these methods individually.

Color

Using the `setColor` method on the `Paint` object, we can pass in a `Color` object. The `Color` class defines a series of colors represented as 32bit integers as constants:

- `Color.BLACK`

- `Color.BLUE`

- `Color.RED`

For the complete list, you can refer to the online reference for the Color class at `http://developer.android.com/reference/android/graphics/Color.html`.

```
Paint paint = new Paint();
paint.setColor(Color.GREEN);
```

We can also construct a specific color by calling the static method `Color.argb`, passing in a value between 0 and 255 for alpha, red, green, and blue. This method returns a 32bit integer representing that color that we then pass to `setColor`.

```
Paint paint = new Paint();
int myColor = Color.argb(255,128,64,32);
paint.setColor(myColor);
```

We can actually skip the color creation step completely if we are defining the exact values:

```
Paint paint = new Paint();
paint.setARGB(255,128,64,32);
```

Style

When defining the style of the paint through the setStyle method, we are determining whether the shapes drawn will be filled or simply outlined. The possible styles are defined as constants in the Paint.Style class.

- *Paint.Style.STROKE*: Only draw the outline of the shapes

- *Paint.Style.FILL*: Only fill the shapes

- *Paint.Style.FILL_AND_STROKE*: Fill and draw the outline of the shapes

Stroke Width

Last, we can use the setStrokeWidth method on the Paint object to specify the width of the stroke that will be used when outlining the shapes. Setting a value of 0 will still yield a 1-pixel stroke. To remove the stroke altogether, the setStyle method should be used, passing in Paint.Style.FILL.

Drawing Shapes

The Canvas class defines several drawing methods. Let's go through a couple of these.

Point

The simplest of these is simply drawing a point. To draw a point, we use the drawPoint method on the Canvas object, passing in the x and y position as well as a Paint object.

```
canvas.drawPoint(199,201,paint);
```

The size of the point that is drawn is dependent on the stroke width of the Paint object. The following code will render as shown in Figure 4–4.

```
Paint paint = new Paint();
paint.setColor(Color.GREEN);
paint.setStrokeWidth(100);
canvas.drawPoint(199,201,paint);
```

Figure 4–4. *Point drawn using a Paint object that has a stroke width set to 100; it doesn't look much like a point due to the exceptionally large stroke width. In many cases, a point would be a single pixel, having a stroke width of 1.*

Line

A line is, well, a line: a series of points extending in a single direction from a start point to an end point. You draw a line in using the `Canvas` method `drawLine`, passing in a start x and y coordinate, an end x and y coordinate, and a `Paint` object. Figure 4–5 illustrates how the following code will render.

```
Paint paint = new Paint();
paint.setColor(Color.GREEN);
paint.setStrokeWidth(10);
int startx = 50;
int starty = 100;
int endx = 150;
int endy = 210;
canvas.drawLine(startx,starty,endx,endy,paint);
```

Figure 4–5. *Line*

Rectangle

Rectangles can be drawn in a few different ways, the easiest being to specify the left y coordinate, the top x coordinate, the right y coordinate, and the bottom x coordinate along with a `Paint` object.

```
Paint paint = new Paint();
paint.setColor(Color.GREEN);
paint.setStyle(Paint.Style.FILL_AND_STROKE);
paint.setStrokeWidth(10);
float leftx = 20;
float topy = 20;
float rightx = 50;
float bottomy = 100;
canvas.drawRect(leftx, topy, rightx, bottomy, paint);
```

Another means to draw a rectangle is to pass in a `RectF` object. `RectF` is a class that defines a rectangle using float values representing the left, top, right, and bottom coordinates.

```
Paint paint = new Paint();
float leftx = 20;
float topy = 20;
float rightx = 50;
float bottomy = 100;
RectF rectangle = new RectF(leftx,topy,rightx,bottomy);
canvas.drawRect(rectangle, paint);
```

Oval

In the same way a rectangle may be drawn using `RectF`, we can draw an oval. The `RectF` defines the bounds of the oval. In other words, the oval will be drawn inside the rectangle with the longest point of the oval hitting the midpoint of the top and bottom bounds and the widest point of the oval hitting the midpoint of left and right bounds.

```
Paint paint = new Paint();
paint.setColor(Color.GREEN);
paint.setStyle(Paint.Style.STROKE);
float leftx = 20;
float topy = 20;
float rightx = 50;
float bottomy = 100;
RectF ovalBounds = new RectF(leftx,topy,rightx,bottomy);
canvas.drawOval(ovalBounds, paint);
```

Circle

A circle can be drawn by specifying a center point (x and y) and radius. The following code will be rendered as shown in Figure 4–6.

```
Paint paint = new Paint();
paint.setColor(Color.GREEN);
paint.setStyle(Paint.Style.STROKE);
float x = 50;
float y = 50;
float radius = 20;
canvas.drawCircle(x, y, radius, paint);
```

Figure 4–6. *Circle*

Path

A path is a series of lines that can be used to create an arbitrary shape. To draw a path, we first have to construct a Path object. The Path object can have any number of calls telling it to move to a point without drawing, using moveTo, or draw a line to a point using lineTo. Of course, there are methods for drawing arcs and so on. Documentation of these methods can be found in the documentation of the Path class at http://developer.android.com/reference/android/graphics/Path.html.

The Path can then be passed to the Canvas method drawPath.

```
Paint paint = new Paint();
paint.setStyle(Paint.Style.STROKE);
paint.setColor(Color.GREEN);
Path p = new Path();
// Without the first "moveTo", drawing will start at (0,0)
p.moveTo(20, 20);
p.lineTo(100, 200);
p.lineTo(200, 100);
p.lineTo(240, 155);
p.lineTo(250, 175);
p.lineTo(20, 20);
canvas.drawPath(p, paint);
```

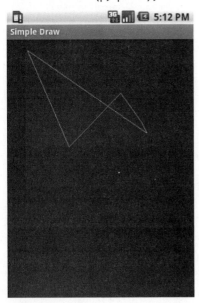

Figure 4–7. *Path*

Drawing Text

Of course, we aren't limited to just drawing lines, shapes, and points. We can draw text on the Canvas as well, using the method drawText; we simply pass in the text to draw as a String and the start x and y coordinates along with a Paint object. The Paint class has a method called setTextSize for setting the size of the text that we can use.

```
Paint paint = new Paint();
paint.setColor(Color.GREEN);
paint.setTextSize(40);
float text_x = 120;
float text_y = 120;
canvas.drawText("Hello", text_x, text_y, paint);
```

Figure 4–8. *Text drawn on a canvas*

Built-In Fonts

Drawing text without being able to specify a font or style would be pretty limiting. Fortunately, the Paint class allows us to specify which font should be used by calling the setTypeface method and passing in a Typeface object.

The Typeface class has a number of constants defined that represent the built-in fonts that come with the Android OS. These fonts were created by a company called Ascender (www.ascendercorp.com/) as part of their Droid suite of fonts.

They are defined in the Typeface class as follows:

- *Typeface.MONOSPACE*: This font has equal spacing for each letter.
- *Typeface.SANS_SERIF*: This is a font that doesn't have serifs.
- *Typeface.SERIF*: This is a font that contains serifs.

NOTE: Serifs are small lines at the ends of the lines that make up the letters. The font that you are reading right now is a sansserif font. This is an example of a serif font.

Figure 4–9. *Typeface.MONOSPACE example*

Figure 4–10. *Typeface.SANS_SERIF example*

Figure 4–11. *Typeface.SERIF example*

In addition to the main three fonts, there are two other Typeface constants:

- *Typeface.DEFAULT*: This is the same as the sanserif font and is the default font that is used if setTypeface is not called.

- *Typeface.DEFAULT_BOLD*: This is a bold version of the sanserif font.

Here is a short code example:

```
Paint paint = new Paint();
paint.setColor(Color.GREEN);
paint.setTextSize(40);
paint.setTypeface(Typeface.DEFAULT_BOLD);
float text_x = 120;
float text_y = 120;
canvas.drawText("Hello", text_x, text_y, paint);
```

Figure 4–12. *Typeface.DEFAULT_BOLD*

Font Styles

Along with the built-in fonts, there is a series of styles that are defined as constants in the Typeface class. These styles can be used to modify one of the built-in fonts through the create method available in the Typeface class. This method returns a new Typeface object that can be used.

Here is the list of styles that are defined in the Typeface class:

- Typeface.BOLD
- Typeface.ITALIC
- Typeface.NORMAL
- Typeface.BOLD_ITALIC

Using one of them is fairly straightforward. First we call Typeface.create, passing in the base font and the style we want to apply. We get back a Typeface that we pass into the Paint.setTypeface method, and that's it.

```
Paint paint = new Paint();
paint.setColor(Color.GREEN);
paint.setTextSize(40);

Typeface serif_italic = Typeface.create(Typeface.SERIF, Typeface.ITALIC);
paint.setTypeface(serif_italic);

float text_x = 120;
float text_y = 120;
canvas.drawText("Hello", text_x, text_y, paint);
```

Figure 4–13. *Serif font with* `Italic` *style applied*

External Fonts

We aren't limited in our Android applications to just the built-in fonts. Android supports the creation of `Typeface` objects from any TrueType font file. TrueType fonts are a standard and work on a variety of platforms. This opens up a wide range of possibilities for our applications.

Many sites on the Internet offer free fonts, and, of course, there are font foundries, companies that create fonts that will sell you a license to use their fonts.

One font that I found that was completely different from Android's built-in fonts is the Chopin Script font by Claude Pelletier. It is in the public domain and available as a free download from a variety of sources such as fontspace.com (`www.fontspace.com/diogene/chopinscript`). To use the font, I downloaded it and put the `.ttf` file (`ChopinScript.ttf`) into my project's "assets" folder.

The `Typeface.createFromAsset` method takes in an `AssetManager`, which can be gotten through a call to `getAssets` from the `Context` and the name of the file. It returns a `Typeface` object that can be passed into the `Paint.setTypeface` method.

```
Typeface chops = Typeface.createFromAsset(getAssets(), "ChopinScript.ttf");
paint.setTypeface(chops);
```

Figure 4–14. *Chopin Script font*

Text on a Path

Text isn't limited to being drawn on a horizontal line; it can be drawn on a Path as well.

Here is an example.

```
Paint paint = new Paint();
paint.setColor(Color.GREEN);
paint.setTextSize(20);
paint.setTypeface(Typeface.DEFAULT);

Path p = new Path();
p.moveTo(20, 20);
p.lineTo(100, 150);
p.lineTo(200, 220);

canvas.drawTextOnPath("Hello this is text on a path", p, 0, 0, paint);
```

Figure 4–15. *Text drawn on a path*

Finger Painting

Creating a static drawing on a `Bitmap` `Canvas` is all well and good, but let's take this a bit further and explore how we can make an application that allows the user to create a drawing.

Touch Events

To start this application, we'll need to understand how Android tells us when a user has touched the touchscreen. Being able to handle that, we can then allow the user create a drawing using his or her fingers on the touchscreen.

As we know, many of the UI elements that we use in Android derive from the `View` class. Since we have been working with the `Canvas` from a `Bitmap` that is displayed in an `ImageView`, it makes sense to see if that can help us out with detecting where the user touches.

As luck would have it, the `View` class is touch-capable. It has a method where we specify what class should receive any touch events that it gets. This method is `setOnTouchListener`, and it takes in an object that implements the `OnTouchListener` interface.

We can make our `activity` implement `OnTouchListener` by declaring it and creating a method called `onTouch`.

```
public class SimpleFingerDraw extends Activity implements OnTouchListener {

    ImageView imageView;
    Bitmap bitmap;
    Canvas canvas;
    Paint paint;

    @Override
    public void onCreate(Bundle savedInstanceState) {
        super.onCreate(savedInstanceState);
        setContentView(R.layout.main);

        imageView = (ImageView) this.findViewById(R.id.ImageView);

        Display currentDisplay = getWindowManager().getDefaultDisplay();
        float dw = currentDisplay.getWidth();
        float dh = currentDisplay.getHeight();

        bitmap = Bitmap.createBitmap((int)dw,(int)dh,Bitmap.Config.ARGB_8888);
        canvas = new Canvas(bitmap);
        paint = new Paint();
        paint.setColor(Color.GREEN);
        imageView.setImageBitmap(bitmap);

        imageView.setOnTouchListener(this);
    }

    public boolean onTouch(View v, MotionEvent event) {
        return false;
    }
}
```

Now whenever the ImageView is touched, the onTouch method in our activity will be called.

We can determine what kind of touch occurred by looking at the MotionEvent object that is passed into our onTouch method. To do so, we call the getAction on that object. The getAction method will return one of four values that are defined as constants in the MotionEvent class.

- *MotionEvent.ACTION_DOWN*: This indicates that the view has received a touch.

- *MotionEvent.ACTION_UP*: This indicates that the view has stopped receiving a touch.

- *MotionEvent.ACTION_MOVE*: This indicates that after a touch down has occurred, some movement has taken place before the ACTION_UP event.

- *MotionEvent.ACTION_CANCEL*: This indicates that the touch has been cancelled and should be ignored.

In addition, we can call the getX and getY methods on the MotionEvent object to determine where the touch event took place.

Here is an update to our onTouch method, taking into account the different event possibilities and drawing a line between the touch down and touch up events:

```
float downx = 0;
float downy = 0;
float upx = 0;
float upy = 0;

public boolean onTouch(View v, MotionEvent event) {
    int action = event.getAction();
    switch (action)
    {
        case MotionEvent.ACTION_DOWN:
            downx = event.getX();
            downy = event.getY();
            break;
        case MotionEvent.ACTION_MOVE:
            break;
        case MotionEvent.ACTION_UP:
            upx = event.getX();
            upy = event.getY();
            canvas.drawLine(downx, downy, upx, upy, paint);
            imageView.invalidate();
            break;
        case MotionEvent.ACTION_CANCEL:
            break;
        default:
            break;
    }
    return true;
}
```

You'll notice several things about this code. First, we aren't doing anything on ACTION_MOVE or ACTION_CANCEL. In ACTION_DOWN we are simply setting our downx and downy variables to be the X and Y position of the touch. In ACTION_UP we are setting upx and upy to be the X and Y position of the touch up event and then calling the drawLine function on our Canvas object. We also need to call the invalidate method on the ImageView so that it redraws to the screen. If we didn't do this, we wouldn't see the new line drawn on our Bitmap Canvas object. Last we are returning true instead of false. This tells Android that we want to continue receiving touch events once an event starts.

Figure 4–16. *Touch event–based drawing*

As you can see in Figure 4–16, this drawing application is great for doing straight lines from the point you touch down to the point you lift your finger up. If we wanted the ability to draw lines as the finger moves, we would have to implement the drawing code in the ACTION_MOVE case as well.

```
case MotionEvent.ACTION_MOVE:
    upx = event.getX();
    upy = event.getY();
    canvas.drawLine(downx, downy, upx, upy, paint);
    imageView.invalidate();
    downx = upx;
    downy = upy;
    break;
```

In this revised example, the upx and upy are captured in the ACTION_MOVE, the line is drawn, and then the downx and downy variables are set to be the same position (remember that the start of the line is defined by downx and downy in the ACTION_DOWN event). This allows for a line drawing application that is able to track a finger around the screen.

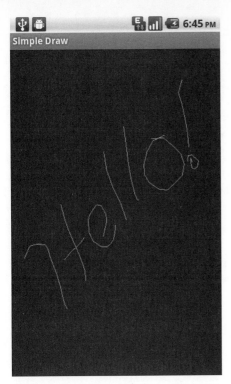

Figure 4–17. *Enhanced touch event–based drawing*

Drawing on Existing Images

Since we are drawing on a Canvas, we can use techniques described in the previous chapter to draw an image to the Canvas and then draw on top of that image.

Let's go through a full example.

```
package com.apress.proandroidmedia.ch4.choosepicturedraw;

import java.io.FileNotFoundException;

import android.app.Activity;
import android.content.Intent;
import android.graphics.Bitmap;
import android.graphics.BitmapFactory;
import android.graphics.Canvas;
import android.graphics.Color;
import android.graphics.Matrix;
import android.graphics.Paint;
import android.net.Uri;
import android.os.Bundle;
import android.util.Log;
import android.view.Display;
import android.view.MotionEvent;
import android.view.View;
```

```
import android.view.View.OnClickListener;
import android.view.View.OnTouchListener;
import android.widget.Button;
import android.widget.ImageView;
```

Our activity will implement both OnClickListener and OnTouchListener. The OnClickListener is so that our activity can respond to a Button press. The OnTouchListener is so that we can draw on the ImageView using the touchscreen.

```
public class ChoosePictureDraw extends Activity implements OnClickListener,↵
  OnTouchListener {
```

We have two main UI elements. The first one is the ImageView, which will display our Bitmap, which we'll draw onto. The second is a Button that the user will press to select an image from the Gallery application.

```
ImageView choosenImageView;
Button choosePicture;
```

We need to have two Bitmap objects. The first is the one that contains the scaled version of the selected image. The second is the mutable version that we'll draw the first one into and draw on top of.

```
Bitmap bmp;
Bitmap alteredBitmap;
Canvas canvas;
Paint paint;
Matrix matrix;

@Override
public void onCreate(Bundle savedInstanceState) {
    super.onCreate(savedInstanceState);
    setContentView(R.layout.main);

    choosenImageView = (ImageView) this.findViewById(R.id.ChoosenImageView);
    choosePicture = (Button) this.findViewById(R.id.ChoosePictureButton);
```

After we obtain references to the ImageView and Button, we set the listener for each of the events, OnClick and OnTouch, to be our activity.

```
    choosePicture.setOnClickListener(this);
    choosenImageView.setOnTouchListener(this);
}
```

Our onClick method follows. This uses the standard intent to allow the user to pick an image from the Gallery application.

```
public void onClick(View v) {
    Intent choosePictureIntent = new Intent(
      Intent.ACTION_PICK,
      android.provider.MediaStore.Images.Media.EXTERNAL_CONTENT_URI);
    startActivityForResult(choosePictureIntent, 0);
}
```

Our onActivityResult method is called after the user selects the image. It loads the image selected into a Bitmap that is scaled to the size of the screen.

```
protected void onActivityResult(int requestCode, int resultCode, Intent intent) {
```

```
        super.onActivityResult(requestCode, resultCode, intent);

    if (resultCode == RESULT_OK) {
        Uri imageFileUri = intent.getData();
        Display currentDisplay = getWindowManager().getDefaultDisplay();

        float dw = currentDisplay.getWidth();
        float dh = currentDisplay.getHeight();

        try {
            BitmapFactory.Options bmpFactoryOptions = new BitmapFactory.Options();
            bmpFactoryOptions.inJustDecodeBounds = true;
            bmp = BitmapFactory.decodeStream(
                getContentResolver().openInputStream(imageFileUri), null,
                bmpFactoryOptions);

            int heightRatio = (int)Math.ceil(bmpFactoryOptions.outHeight/dh);
            int widthRatio = (int)Math.ceil(bmpFactoryOptions.outWidth/dw);
            if (heightRatio > 1 && widthRatio > 1) {
                if (heightRatio > widthRatio) {
                    bmpFactoryOptions.inSampleSize = heightRatio;
                }
                else {
                    // Width ratio is larger, scale according to it
                    bmpFactoryOptions.inSampleSize = widthRatio;
                }
            }

            bmpFactoryOptions.inJustDecodeBounds = false;
            bmp = BitmapFactory.decodeStream(
                getContentResolver().openInputStream(imageFileUri), null,
                bmpFactoryOptions);
```

After the `Bitmap` is loaded, we create a mutable `Bitmap`, `alteredBitmap`, and draw our first Bitmap into it.

```
            alteredBitmap = Bitmap.createBitmap(
                bmp.getWidth(),bmp.getHeight(),bmp.getConfig());
            canvas = new Canvas(alteredBitmap);
            paint = new Paint();
            paint.setColor(Color.GREEN);
            paint.setStrokeWidth(5);
            matrix = new Matrix();
            canvas.drawBitmap(bmp, matrix, paint);

            choosenImageView.setImageBitmap(alteredBitmap);
            choosenImageView.setOnTouchListener(this);
        }
        catch (FileNotFoundException e) {
            Log.v("ERROR",e.toString());
        }
    }
}
```

Now we simply implement our onTouch method in the same manner as we did before. Instead of drawing on an empty `Bitmap` Canvas, we are now drawing over the top of an existing image.

```
    float downx = 0;
    float downy = 0;
    float upx = 0;
    float upy = 0;

    public boolean onTouch(View v, MotionEvent event) {
        int action = event.getAction();
        switch (action) {
            case MotionEvent.ACTION_DOWN:
                downx = event.getX();
                downy = event.getY();
                break;
            case MotionEvent.ACTION_MOVE:
                upx = event.getX();
                upy = event.getY();
                canvas.drawLine(downx, downy, upx, upy, paint);
                choosenImageView.invalidate();
                downx = upx;
                downy = upy;
                break;
            case MotionEvent.ACTION_UP:
                upx = event.getX();
                upy = event.getY();
                canvas.drawLine(downx, downy, upx, upy, paint);
                choosenImageView.invalidate();
                break;
            case MotionEvent.ACTION_CANCEL:
                break;
            default:
                break;
        }

        return true;
    }

}
```

What follows is the layout XML file for the foregoing activity. It specifies the ImageView and the Button in a standard LinearLayout.

```
<?xml version="1.0" encoding="utf-8"?>
<LinearLayout xmlns:android="http://schemas.android.com/apk/res/android"
    android:orientation="vertical"
    android:layout_width="fill_parent"
    android:layout_height="fill_parent"
    >
    <Button android:layout_width="fill_parent"
        android:layout_height="wrap_content"
        android:text="Choose Picture" android:id="@+id/ChoosePictureButton"/>
    <ImageView android:layout_width="wrap_content"
        android:layout_height="wrap_content"
        android:id="@+id/ChoosenImageView">
    </ImageView>
</LinearLayout>
```

Figure 4–18. *Drawing on an existing image*

Saving a Bitmap-Based Canvas Drawing

What good would it be to just draw on an image without being able to save it after the user has created a masterpiece? So far we have just drawn images—let's look at how we can commit these wonderful drawings to permanence. Well, at least let's look at how we can save them to the SD card.

Unsurprisingly, it will be a similar process to what we used in the second chapter to save images captured from our custom camera application. Let's go over the changes that we can make to our ChoosePictureDraw example to save the images.

First of all, we'll need to add the following imports.

```
import java.io.OutputStream;
import android.content.ContentValues;
import android.graphics.Bitmap.CompressFormat;
import android.provider.MediaStore.Images.Media;
import android.widget.Toast;
```

Then in the onCreate method, we'll get a reference to a new Button that we will add to the layout XML and declare in our activity.

We'll declare the savePicture button along with the rest of the instance variables right after the class definition.

```
Button savePicture;
```

In the onCreate after obtaining a reference to the choosePicture button we'll obtain a reference to the savePicture button:

```
savePicture = (Button) this.findViewById(R.id.SavePictureButton);
```

Following that, we'll set its onClickListener to be our activity, the same thing we are doing with the choosePicture Button.

```
savePicture.setOnClickListener(this);
```

Now we'll need to modify our onClick method to take into account that two different Buttons will be using it. The easiest way is to compare the View that is passed in with the Buttons. If the View is equal to one of the Buttons, that's the one that was clicked.

```
public void onClick(View v) {
    if (v == choosePicture)
    {
        Intent choosePictureIntent = new Intent(Intent.ACTION_PICK,
            android.provider.MediaStore.Images.Media.EXTERNAL_CONTENT_URI);
        startActivityForResult(choosePictureIntent, 0);
    }
    else if (v == savePicture)
    {
```

We know the savePicture button was clicked. Now we need to make sure the Bitmap we are drawing on has been defined.

```
        if (alteredBitmap != null)
        {
```

Once we do that, we're all set to go about saving it. Just like previous examples, we'll query the MediaStore to get a Uri for our new image and create an OutputStream from that Uri.

```
            Uri imageFileUri = getContentResolver().insert(
                Media.EXTERNAL_CONTENT_URI, new ContentValues());

            try {
                OutputStream imageFileOS =
                    getContentResolver().openOutputStream(imageFileUri);
```

In previous image saving examples, we actually already had the data in JPEG form, and we would simply write it out to the OutputStream. In this case, we have to use the compress method of the Bitmap object to convert it into a JPEG (or PNG if we choose).

The compress method compresses the Bitmap data and writes it out to an OutputStream for us. It takes in a constant defined in Bitmap.CompressFormat, which is either PNG or JPEG. PNG is great for line art and graphics. JPEG is great for full-color images with gradients, such as photographs. Since we are working with a photograph here, we'll use JPEG.

The next argument is the quality setting. The quality setting is useful only when compressing as a JPEG, as PNG images will always keep all of the data, making a quality setting useless. JPEG is what is considered a "lossy" codec, which means that data will be thrown away. The quality has an inverse relationship with the size. A quality setting of 0 will yield a small file size but not a great-looking file; a quality setting of 100 will yield a large file size, and the image will look pretty good. In this example and as illustrated in Figure 4–19, we are using 90, which is somewhat of a compromise. Figure 4–20 shows the same image with a quality setting of 10 for comparison.

The last argument we need to pass in is the actual OutputStream to write the file to.

```
alteredBitmap.compress(CompressFormat.JPEG, 90, imageFileOS);
```

That's it—now we just tell the user that the image has been saved through a Toast alert, and we continue on.

```
Toast t = Toast.makeText(this,"Saved!", Toast.LENGTH_SHORT);
t.show();

        } catch (FileNotFoundException e) {
            Log.v("EXCEPTION",e.getMessage());
        }
    }
  }
}
```

Here is the updated Layout XML, which contains the new Save Button.

```
<?xml version="1.0" encoding="utf-8"?>
<LinearLayout xmlns:android="http://schemas.android.com/apk/res/android"
    android:orientation="vertical"
    android:layout_width="fill_parent"
    android:layout_height="fill_parent"
    >
    <Button
        android:layout_width="fill_parent"
        android:layout_height="wrap_content"
        android:text="Choose Picture" android:id="@+id/ChoosePictureButton"/>
    <ImageView android:layout_width="wrap_content"
        android:layout_height="wrap_content"
        android:id="@+id/ChoosenImageView">
    </ImageView>
    <Button
        android:layout_width="fill_parent"
        android:layout_height="wrap_content"
        android:text="Save Picture" android:id="@+id/SavePictureButton"/>
</LinearLayout>
```

Figure 4–19. *Image saved as a JPEG using a quality setting of 90*

Figure 4–20. *Image saved as a JPEG using a quality setting of 10; it is less than 1/6 the file size of the one saved with a quality setting of 90.*

Summary

As we have explored, much can be done with canvas-based drawing on Android. This wraps up the first part of our exploration, which dealt with still images. Most of what we discussed merely scratched the surface of what can be done, but it provides a good starting point for making applications of your own that harness the camera, perform image processing, or have drawing features.

Next we'll set our sights on audio!

Chapter 5

Introduction to Audio on Android

Any smartphone worth its name these days has audio playback capabilities on par with dedicated portable media devices or MP3 players. Of course, Android-based devices are no different. These capabilities allow for the building of music player, audio book, podcast, or just about any other type of application that is centered around audio playback.

In this chapter, we'll explore what Android's capabilities are in terms of format and codec support, and we'll build a few different playback applications. Furthermore we'll look at what Android supports in the way of audio formats and metadata.

Audio Playback

As mentioned, Android supports audio playback capabilities on par with MP3 players. In fact, it probably goes a step further since it supports a fairly wide range of audio formats, more than most hardware players. This is one of the benefits of smartphones that perform functions previously relegated to dedicated hardware, since they have good faculties for running a variety of software; like a computer, they can offer a wide range of support for different and changing technologies that are simply not practical to build into the firmware of hardware-centric devices.

Supported Audio Formats

Android supports a variety of audio file formats and codecs for playback (it supports fewer for recording, which we'll discuss when we go over recording).

- *AAC*: Advanced Audio Coding codec (as well as both profiles of HE-AAC, High Efficiency AAC), .m4a (audio/m4a) or.3gp (audio/3gpp) files. AAC is a popular standard that is used by the iPod and other portable media players. Android supports this audio format inside of MPEG-4 audio files and inside of 3GP files (which are based on the MPEG-4 format). Recent additions to the AAC specification, High Efficiency AAC are also supported.

- *MP3*: MPEG-1 Audio Layer 3, .mp3 (audio/mp3) files. MP3, probably the most widely used audio codec, is supported. This allows Android to utilize the vast majority of audio available online through various web sites and music stores.

- *AMR*: Adaptive Multi-Rate codec (both AMR Narrowband, AMR-NB, and AMR Wideband, AMR-WB), .3gp (audio/3gpp) or .amr (audio/amr) files. AMR is the audio codec that has been standardized as the primary voice audio codec in use by the 3GPP (3rd Generation Partnership Project). The 3GPP is a telecommunications industry organization that creates specifications for the partner companies to use. In other words, the AMR codec is what is primarily used for voice calling applications on modern mobile phones and generally supported across mobile handset manufacturers and carriers. As such, this codec is generally useful for voice encoding but doesn't perform well for more complex types of audio such as music.

- *Ogg*: Ogg Vorbis, .ogg (application/ogg) files. Ogg Vorbis is an open source, patent-free audio codec with quality that is comparable to commercial and patent-encumbered codecs such as MP3 and AAC. It was developed by volunteers and is currently maintained by the Xiph.Org foundation.

- *PCM*: Pulse Code Modulation commonly used in WAVE or WAV files (Waveform Audio Format), .wav (audio/x-wav) files. PCM is the technique used for storing audio on computers and other digital audio devices. It is generally an uncompressed audio file with data that represents the amplitude of a piece of audio over time. The "sample rate" is how often an amplitude reading is stored. The "bit-depth" is how many bits are used to represent an individual sample. A piece of audio data with a sample rate of 16kHz and a bit-depth of 32 bits means that it will contain 32 bits of data representing the amplitude of the audio and it will have 16,000 of these per second. The higher the sample rate and the higher the bit-depth, the more accurate the digitization of the audio is. Sample rate and bit-depth also determine how large the audio file will be when its length is taken into account. Android supports PCM audio data within WAV files. WAV is a long-standing standard audio format on PCs.

Using the Built-In Audio Player via an Intent

As with using the camera, the easiest way to provide the ability to play an audio file within an application is to leverage the capabilities of the built-in "Music" application. This application plays all of the formats that Android supports, has a familiar interface to the user, and can be triggered to play a specific file via an intent.

The generic `android.content.Intent.ACTION_VIEW` intent with the data set to a Uri to the audio file and the MIME type specified allows Android to pick the appropriate application for playback. This should be the Music application, but the user may be presented with other options if he or she has other audio playback software installed.

```
Intent intent = new Intent(android.content.Intent.ACTION_VIEW);
intent.setDataAndType(audioFileUri, "audio/mp3");
startActivity(intent);
```

NOTE: MIME stands for Multipurpose Internet Mail Extensions. It was originally specified to help e-mail clients send and receive attachments. Its use, though, has extended greatly beyond e-mail to many other communication protocols, including HTTP or standard web serving. Android uses MIME types when resolving an intent, specifically to help determine which application should handle the intent.

Each file type has a specific (sometimes more than one) MIME type. This type is specified using at least two parts with slashes between them. The first is the more generic type, such as "audio." The second part is the more specific type, such as "mpeg." A generic type "audio" and a more specific type "mpeg" would yield a MIME type string of "audio/mpeg," which is the MIME type typically used for MP3 files.

Here is a full example of triggering the built-in audio player application through an intent:

```
package com.apress.proandroidmedia.ch5.intentaudioplayer;

import java.io.File;
import android.app.Activity;
import android.content.Intent;
import android.net.Uri;
import android.os.Bundle;
import android.os.Environment;
import android.view.View;
import android.view.View.OnClickListener;
import android.widget.Button;
```

Our activity will be listening for a Button to be pressed before it triggers the playback of the audio. It implements OnClickListener so that it can respond.

```
public class AudioPlayer extends Activity implements OnClickListener {

    Button playButton;

    @Override
    public void onCreate(Bundle savedInstanceState) {
        super.onCreate(savedInstanceState);
        setContentView(R.layout.main);
```

After we set the content view to our XML, we can get a reference to our Button in code and set our activity (this) to be the OnClickListener.

```
        playButton = (Button) this.findViewById(R.id.Button01);
        playButton.setOnClickListener(this);
    }
```

When our Button is clicked, the onClick method is called. In this method, we construct the intent with a generic android.content.Intent.ACTION_VIEW and then create a File object that is a reference to an audio file that exists on the SD card. In this case, the audio file is one that is manually placed on the SD card in the "Music" directory, which is the standard location for music-related audio files.

```
    public void onClick(View v) {
        Intent intent = new Intent(android.content.Intent.ACTION_VIEW);

        File sdcard = Environment.getExternalStorageDirectory();
        File audioFile = new File(sdcard.getPath() + "/Music/goodmorningandroid.mp3");
```

Next, we set the data of the intent to be a Uri derived from the audio file and the type to be its MIME type, audio/mp3. Finally, we trigger the built-in application to launch via the startActivity call passing in our intent. Figure 5–1 shows the built-in application playing the audio file.

```
        intent.setDataAndType(Uri.fromFile(audioFile), "audio/mp3");
        startActivity(intent);
    }
}
```

Here is a simple Layout XML file specifying the Button with the text "Play Audio" to be used with the foregoing activity.

```
<?xml version="1.0" encoding="utf-8"?>
<LinearLayout xmlns:android="http://schemas.android.com/apk/res/android"
    android:orientation="vertical"
    android:layout_width="fill_parent"
    android:layout_height="fill_parent"
    >
    <Button android:text="Play Audio" android:id="@+id/Button01"↵
    android:layout_width="wrap_content" android:layout_height="wrap_content"></Button>
</LinearLayout>
```

Figure 5–1. Android's built-in music player playing an audio file specified via an intent

Creating a Custom Audio-Playing Application

Of course, we aren't limited to using Android's built-in application for audio playback. We can write our own application that offers playback capabilities and more.

To enable this, Android includes a MediaPlayer class. This class is used for the playback and control of both audio and video. Right now we'll just be using the audio playback capabilities.

The simplest MediaPlayer example is to play back an audio file that is packaged with the application itself. In order to do that, an audio file should be placed within the application's raw resources. To do this using the Android Developer Tools on Eclipse, we need to create a new folder in our Project's res folder called raw as illustrated in

Figure 5–2. The Android Developer Tools will generate a resource id for this file in the R.java file (in the gen folder) with the syntax R.raw.file_name_without_extension.

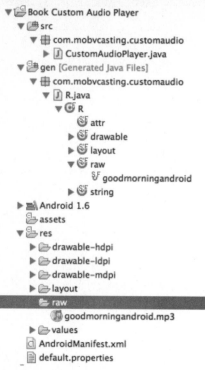

Figure 5–2. Custom audio player Eclipse Project layout showing audio file located in raw folder inside res folder.

Starting the Media Player

Creating a MediaPlayer for this audio file is straightforward. We instantiate a MediaPlayer object using the static method create, passing in this as a Context (which Activity is descended from) and the generated resource ID of the audio file.

```
MediaPlayer mediaPlayer = MediaPlayer.create(this, R.raw.goodmorningandroid);
```

Following that, we simply call the start method on the MediaPlayer object to play it.

```
mediaPlayer.start();
```

LOCAL ASSETS

When placing assets in the `res` folder of an Android Developer Tools/Eclipse project, a couple of things have to be considered: the file extension and using Uris.

File Extensions

The extension is removed, so files with the same base name but different extensions will cause issues. You wouldn't want to put a file named goodmorningandroid.mp3 and another file named goodmorningandroid.m4a in there. Instead, if you would like to provide the same audio in multiple formats, it would be better if you included the format as part of the file name so that you can differentiate between them and the Android Developer Tools doesn't have problems generating the resource ID. If you name them goodmorningandroid_mp3.mp3 and goodmorningandroid_m4a.m4a, you will be able to reference them as R.raw.goodmorningandroid_mp3 and R.raw.goodmorningandroid_m4a respectively.

Uris for Resource Files

While resource IDs are great for some purposes, they don't suit all. As we already know, many things in Android can be accomplished using a Uri. Fortunately, it is easy to construct a Uri for a file that has been placed in the resources. The resource ID can be appended to the end of a string, which can be used to construct the Uri. The string must start with `android.resource://`, followed by the package name of the application that the resources are local to, followed by the resource ID of the file.

Here is an example:

```
Uri fileUri = Uri.parse("android.resource://com.apress.proandroidmedia.ch5.customaudio/"
+ R.raw.goodmorningandroid);
```

To use the `MediaPlayer` with a Uri instead of a resource ID, which we will have to do if the file isn't part of the application, we can call a `create` method passing in the context and the Uri.

```
MediaPlayer mediaPlayer = MediaPlayer.create(this, fileUri);
```

Controlling Playback

The `MediaPlayer` class has several nested classes that are interfaces for listening to events that the `MediaPlayer` sends. These events relate to state changes.

For instance, the `MediaPlayer` will call the `onCompletion` method on a class that implements the `OnCompletionListener` and is registered via the `setOnCompletionListener`. This will be done when an audio file is done playing.

Here is a full example of an activity that infinitely repeats, playing the same audio file by using the `OnCompletionListener`. The `MediaPlayer` object is initialized and playback started in the `onStart` method, with playback stopped and the `MediaPlayer` object released in the `onStop` method. This prevents the audio from playing when the activity is no longer in the front but restarts it when the activity is brought to the front again.

```
package com.apress.proandroidmedia.ch5.customaudio;

import android.app.Activity;
import android.media.MediaPlayer;
import android.media.MediaPlayer.OnCompletionListener;
import android.os.Bundle;

public class CustomAudioPlayer extends Activity implements OnCompletionListener {

    MediaPlayer mediaPlayer;

    @Override
    public void onCreate(Bundle savedInstanceState) {
        super.onCreate(savedInstanceState);
        setContentView(R.layout.main);

    }

    public void onStart() {
        super.onStart();
        mediaPlayer = MediaPlayer.create(this, R.raw.goodmorningandroid);
        mediaPlayer.setOnCompletionListener(this);
        mediaPlayer.start();
    }

    public void onStop() {
        super.onStop();
        mediaPlayer.stop();
        mediaPlayer.release();
    }

    public void onCompletion(MediaPlayer mp) {
        mediaPlayer.start();
    }
}
```

Of course, this could be done without the OnCompletionListener by simply setting the MediaPlayer to loop using the setLooping(true) method.

Let's take this a step further and make it so that the playback is controlled by touch events. This code might be a good starting point for making a DJ audio scratching application.

```
package com.apress.proandroidmedia.ch5.customaudio;

import android.app.Activity;
import android.media.MediaPlayer;
import android.media.MediaPlayer.OnCompletionListener;
import android.os.Bundle;
import android.util.Log;
import android.view.MotionEvent;
import android.view.View;
import android.view.View.OnClickListener;
import android.view.View.OnTouchListener;
import android.widget.Button;
```

Our activity will implement the OnCompletionListener, as did the previous example, but will also implement the OnTouchListener, so that it can respond to touch events, and the OnClickListener, so that it can respond when a user clicks a button.

```
public class CustomAudioPlayer extends Activity implements OnCompletionListener,
OnTouchListener, OnClickListener {
```

Of course, we'll need a reference to the MediaPlayer object. We need access to a View so that we can register that we want touch events, and we'll need access to any buttons that we define in the Layout XML file—in this case, a button for stopping playback and a button for starting playback.

```
MediaPlayer mediaPlayer;
View theView;
Button stopButton, startButton;
```

We'll declare a variable that will contain a saved position in the audio file. We'll use this position later to determine where to start playing the audio file.

```
int position = 0;

@Override
public void onCreate(Bundle savedInstanceState) {
    super.onCreate(savedInstanceState);
    setContentView(R.layout.main);
```

Using our normal findViewById function, we'll get access to the Buttons and the View that are defined in the Layout XML.

```
stopButton = (Button) this.findViewById(R.id.StopButton);
startButton = (Button) this.findViewById(R.id.StartButton);
```

Since our activity can respond to Click events, we'll make it so that it is registered as the listener on both Buttons.

```
startButton.setOnClickListener(this);
stopButton.setOnClickListener(this);

theView = this.findViewById(R.id.theview);
```

Then we'll make our activity (this) respond to the touch events.

```
theView.setOnTouchListener(this);
```

In this application, our audio file is called goodmorningandroid.mp3, and it has been placed in the res/raw folder of our project. We'll create our MediaPlayer object using this file. Also, as in the previous example, we are setting our activity to be the OnCompletionListener for our MediaPlayer.

```
mediaPlayer = MediaPlayer.create(this, R.raw.goodmorningandroid);
mediaPlayer.setOnCompletionListener(this);
mediaPlayer.start();
}
```

Here our onCompletion method is defined. It gets called whenever the MediaPlayer has finished playing our audio file. In this case, we'll call start first to make the audio play and then call seek to the saved position. The audio needs to be playing before we can seek.

```
public void onCompletion(MediaPlayer mp) {
    mediaPlayer.start();
    mediaPlayer.seekTo(position);
}
```

When the user triggers a touch event, the onTouch method is called. In this method, we are paying attention only to the ACTION_MOVE touch event, which is triggered when the user drags a finger across the surface of the View. In this case, we'll make sure the MediaPlayer is playing and then calculate where we should seek to based upon where on the screen the touch event occurs. If it occurs toward the right boundary of the screen, we'll seek toward the end of the file. If it occurs toward the left boundary of the screen, we'll seek to near the beginning of the file. We save this value in the position variable, so that when the audio file finishes, it will seek back to that point when it starts playing again (in the onCompletion method).

```
public boolean onTouch(View v, MotionEvent me) {

    if (me.getAction() == MotionEvent.ACTION_MOVE)
    {
        if (mediaPlayer.isPlaying()) {
            position = (int) (me.getX() *
                mediaPlayer.getDuration()/theView.getWidth());
            Log.v("SEEK",""+position);
            mediaPlayer.seekTo(position);
        }
    }

    return true;
}
```

Last we have an onClick method that responds to the Button clicks. These clicks pause and start the audio playback.

```
public void onClick(View v) {
    if (v == stopButton) {
        mediaPlayer.pause();
    } else if (v == startButton) {
        mediaPlayer.start();
    }

}
}
```

Here is the Layout XML file that is being referred to in the foregoing code example:

```
<?xml version="1.0" encoding="utf-8"?>
<LinearLayout xmlns:android="http://schemas.android.com/apk/res/android"
    android:orientation="vertical"
    android:layout_width="fill_parent"
    android:layout_height="fill_parent"
    >
    <Button android:text="Start" android:id="@+id/StartButton"↵
    android:layout_width="wrap_content" android:layout_height="wrap_content"></Button>
```

```
        <Button android:text="Stop" android:id="@+id/StopButton"↵
         android:layout_width="wrap_content" android:layout_height="wrap_content"></Button>
        <View android:layout_width="fill_parent" android:layout_height="fill_parent"↵
         android:id="@+id/theview" />
</LinearLayout>
```

As you can see, building a custom audio player on Android opens up some interesting possibilities. Applications can be built that do more than just play audio straight through. Turning this into a full-fledged DJ application for the phone could be fun.

MediaStore for Audio

We explored using the MediaStore for images early on in this book. Much of what we learned can be leveraged for the storage and retrieval of other types of media, including audio. In order to provide a robust mechanism for browsing and searching for audio, Android includes a MediaStore.Audio package, which defines the standard content provider.

Accessing Audio from the MediaStore

Accessing audio files that are stored using the MediaStore provider is consistent with our previous uses of the MediaStore. In this case, we'll be using the android.provider.MediaStore.Audio package.

One of the easiest ways to illustrate the use of the MediaStore for audio is to go through a sample application. The following code creates an activity that queries the MediaStore for any audio file and simply plays the first one returned.

```
package com.apress.proandroidmedia.ch5.audioplayer;

import java.io.File;
import android.app.Activity;
import android.content.Intent;
import android.database.Cursor;
import android.net.Uri;
import android.os.Bundle;
import android.util.Log;
import android.provider.MediaStore;

public class AudioPlayer extends Activity {

    @Override
    public void onCreate(Bundle savedInstanceState) {
        super.onCreate(savedInstanceState);
        setContentView(R.layout.main);
```

To use the MediaStore, we need to specify which data we want returned. We do this by creating an array of strings using the constants located in the android.provider.MediaStore.Audio.Media class. Those constants are all of the standard fields that are saved in the MediaStore for use with audio.

In this case, we are asking for the DATA column, which contains the path to the actual audio file. We are also asking for the internal ID, the Title, Display Name, MIME-Type, Artist, Album, and which type of audio file it is, alarm, music, ring tone, or notification type.

Other columns such as date added (DATE_ADDED), date modified (DATE_MODIFIED), file size (SIZE), and so on are available as well.

```
String[] columns = {
    MediaStore.Audio.Media.DATA,
    MediaStore.Audio.Media._ID,
    MediaStore.Audio.Media.TITLE,
    MediaStore.Audio.Media.DISPLAY_NAME,
    MediaStore.Audio.Media.MIME_TYPE,
    MediaStore.Audio.Media.ARTIST,
    MediaStore.Audio.Media.ALBUM,
    MediaStore.Audio.Media.IS_RINGTONE,
    MediaStore.Audio.Media.IS_ALARM,
    MediaStore.Audio.Media.IS_MUSIC,
    MediaStore.Audio.Media.IS_NOTIFICATION
};
```

We query the MediaStore by calling the managedQuery method in Activity. The managedQuery method takes in the Uri for the content provider, in this case, the audio MediaStore, android.provider.MediaStore.Audio.Media.EXTERNAL_CONTENT_URI. This Uri specifies that we want audio stored on the SD card. If we wanted audio files that are stored in the internal memory, we would use android.provider.MediaStore.Audio.Media.INTERNAL_CONTENT_URI.

In addition to the Uri to the MediaStore, the managedQuery method takes in the array of columns that we want returned, an SQL WHERE clause, the values for the WHERE clause, and an SQL ORDER BY clause.

In this example, we aren't using the WHERE and ORDER BY clauses, so we'll pass in null for those arguments.

```
Cursor cursor = managedQuery(MediaStore.Audio.Media.EXTERNAL_CONTENT_URI,↵
columns, null, null, null);
```

The managedQuery method returns a Cursor object. The Cursor class allows interaction with a dataset returned from a database query.

The first thing we'll do is create a couple of variables to hold the column numbers for some of the columns we want to access from the results. This isn't absolutely necessary, but it is nice to have the index around so we don't have to call the method on the Cursor object each time we need them. The way we get them is to pass in the constant value for the column we want to the getColumnIndex method on the Cursor.

```
int fileColumn = cursor.getColumnIndex (MediaStore.Audio.Media.DATA);
```

The first one is the index of the column containing the path to the actual audio file. We got the foregoing index by passing in the constant that represents that column, android.provider.MediaStore.Audio.Media.DATA.

Next we are getting a couple of other indexes, not all of which we are actually using, so the extras are here merely for illustration purposes.

```
int titleColumn = cursor.getColumnIndex (MediaStore.Audio.Media.TITLE);
int displayColumn = cursor.getColumnIndex (MediaStore.Audio.Media.DISPLAY_NAME);
int mimeTypeColumn = cursor.getColumnIndex (MediaStore.Audio.Media.MIME_TYPE);
```

The data returned by the MediaStore available in the Cursor is organized in rows as well as by columns. We can get the first result returned by calling the moveToFirst method and retrieving the results from there. The method will return a Boolean false if no rows are returned, so we can wrap it in an if statement to make sure there is data.

```
if (cursor.moveToFirst()) {
```

To get the actual data, we call one of the "get" methods on the Cursor and pass in the index for the column we want to retrieve. If the data is expected to be a String, we call getString. If it is expected to be an integer, we call getInt. There are corresponding "get" methods for all of the primitive data types.

```
String audioFilePath = cursor.getString(fileColumn);
String mimeType = cursor.getString(mimeTypeColumn);

Log.v("AUDIOPLAYER",audioFilePath);
Log.v("AUDIOPLAYER",mimeType);
```

Once we have the path to the file and the MIME type, we can use those to construct the intent to launch the built-in audio player application and play that file. (Alternatively we could use the MediaPlayer class as illustrated previously to play the audio file directly.) In order to turn the path to the audio file into a Uri that we can pass into the intent, we construct a File object and use the Uri.fromFile method to get the Uri. There are other ways to do the same, but this is probably the most straightforward.

```
Intent intent = new Intent(android.content.Intent.ACTION_VIEW);
File newFile = new File(audioFilePath);
intent.setDataAndType(Uri.fromFile(newFile), mimeType);
startActivity(intent);
            }
        }
}
```

That finishes off our basic illustration of using the MediaStore for audio.

Now, let's take it a step further and create an application that allows us to narrow down the results returned and browse them, allowing the user to select the audio file to play.

Browsing Audio in the MediaStore

Audio files, in particular music files, can be found by album, artist, and genre as well as directly in the MediaStore. Each of these has an Uri that can be used with a managedQuery to search with.

- *Album*:
  android.provider.MediaStore.Audio.Albums.EXTERNAL_CONTENT_URI

- *Artist*: android.provider.MediaStore.Artists.EXTERNAL_CONTENT_URI

- *Genre*: android.provider.MediaStore.Genres.EXTERNAL_CONTENT_URI

Here is how you would use the album Uri to query for all of the albums on the device:

```
String[] columns = { android.provider.MediaStore.Audio.Albums._ID,
        android.provider.MediaStore.Audio.Albums.ALBUM};
Cursor cursor = managedQuery(MediaStore.Audio.Albums.EXTERNAL_CONTENT_URI, columns,↵
null, null, null);
if (cursor != null) {
    while (cursor.moveToNext()) {
        Log.v("OUTPUT",
            cursor.getString(cursor.getColumnIndex(MediaStore.Audio.Albums.ALBUM)));
    }
}
```

In the foregoing code snippet, you see that we are asking the MediaStore to return the _ID and the ALBUM columns. The ALBUM constant indicates that we want the name of the album returned. Other columns available are listed in the android.provider.MediaStore.Audio.Albums class and are inherited from android.provider.BaseColumns and android.provider.MediaStore.Audio.AlbumColumns.

We are calling the managedQuery method giving just the Uri and the list of columns, leaving the other parameters as null. This will give us all of the albums available on the device.

Finally, we are outputting the list of albums. To iterate through the list returned inside the Cursor object, we first check that the Cursor contains results (cursor != null) and then use the moveToNext method.

Album Browsing App Example

What follows is an example that uses the foregoing as a starting point to allow the user to see the names of all of the albums. The user can indicate which album he or she would like to see the songs on. It will then present the list of songs, and if the user selects one of those, it will play that song.

```
package com.apress.proandroidmedia.ch5.audiobrowser;

import java.io.File;

import android.app.ListActivity;
import android.content.Intent;
import android.database.Cursor;
import android.net.Uri;
import android.os.Bundle;
import android.provider.MediaStore;
import android.util.Log;
import android.view.View;
import android.widget.ListView;
import android.widget.SimpleCursorAdapter;
```

Instead of extending a generic activity, let's extend ListActivity. This allows us to present and manage a basic ListView.

```
public class AudioBrowser extends ListActivity {

    Cursor cursor;
```

Let's create a couple of constants that will help us keep track of where the user is in the application and respond appropriately when the user performs an action. This will be kept track of in the `currentState` variable that is initially set to `STATE_SELECT_ALBUM`.

```
public static int STATE_SELECT_ALBUM = 0;
public static int STATE_SELECT_SONG = 1;

int currentState = STATE_SELECT_ALBUM;
```

Just like a normal activity, we have an `onCreate` method where we can perform the initial commands.

```
@Override
public void onCreate(Bundle savedInstanceState) {
    super.onCreate(savedInstanceState);
    setContentView(R.layout.main);
```

After setting the layout (via the `main.xml` layout XML file), we create an array of Strings that represents the columns we want returned from the `MediaStore` when we run our query. In this case, it is the same as the foregoing snippet of code—we want the `_ID` and the name of the album, `ALBUM`. Both are constants in the `MediaStore.Audio.Albums` class.

```
String[] columns = {
    android.provider.MediaStore.Audio.Albums._ID,
    android.provider.MediaStore.Audio.Albums.ALBUM
};
```

We call the `managedQuery` method with only the Uri representing the album search and the columns, leaving everything else null. This should give us a list of all of the albums available.

```
    cursor = managedQuery(MediaStore.Audio.Albums.EXTERNAL_CONTENT_URI, columns,
null, null, null);
```

Once we do this, we are returned a `Cursor` object that contains the results of our query.

Since we are using a `ListActivity`, we have the ability to have it automagically manage the list of data for us. We can use the `setListAdapter` method to bind our `Cursor` object to `ListView`.

First we create an array of Strings that is the name of the columns in the `Cursor` that we want displayed. In our case, we just want the name of the album— `MediaStore.Audio.Albums.ALBUM` is our constant for that.

Next we list the View objects that will display the data from those columns. Since we just have one column, we need only one View object. It is `android.R.id.text1`. This View is available to us, as it is part of the `android.R.layout.simple_list_item_1` layout that we'll be using in the next step.

Last we call the `setListAdapter` method, passing in a `SimpleCursorAdapter`, which we are creating inline. The `SimpleCursorAdapter` is a simple adapter from a `Cursor` object containing data to a `ListActivity`. In creating the `SimpleCursoryAdapter`, we pass in our activity (`this`) as the Context, a standard `ListView` layout that is already defined for us (`android.R.layout.simple_list_item_1`), the `Cursor` object containing the data, and the two arrays we just defined.

```
        String[] displayFields = new String[] {MediaStore.Audio.Albums.ALBUM};
        int[] displayViews = new int[] {android.R.id.text1};
        setListAdapter(new SimpleCursorAdapter(this,↵
                android.R.layout.simple_list_item_1, cursor, displayFields,↵
displayViews));

    }
```

If we were to run this as is, we would get a simple list of the albums available on our device as shown in Figure 5–3. We are going to take it a step further, though, and allow the user to select an album.

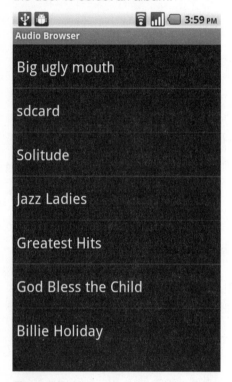

Figure 5–3. Albums listed in basic `ListView`

To allow the user to actually select one of the albums, we need to override the default `onListItemClick` method that is provided by our `ListActivity` parent class.

```
    protected void onListItemClick(ListView l, View v, int position, long id) {
        if (currentState == STATE_SELECT_ALBUM) {
```

When an album in the list is selected, this method will be called. Since our `currentState` variable starts off as `STATE_SELECT_ALBUM` the first time this method is called it should be true.

The position of the selected album in the list will be passed in and can be used with the `Cursor` object to get at the data about which album it was by calling the `moveToPosition` method.

```
        if (cursor.moveToPosition(position)) {
```

Assuming the moveToPosition was successful, we are going to start all over again querying the MediaStore. This time, though, we are going to run our managedQuery on MediaStore.Audio.Media.EXTERNAL_CONTENT_URI as we want access to the individual media files.

First we choose the columns that we want returned.

```
        String[] columns = {
                MediaStore.Audio.Media.DATA,
                MediaStore.Audio.Media._ID,
                MediaStore.Audio.Media.TITLE,
                MediaStore.Audio.Media.DISPLAY_NAME,
                MediaStore.Audio.Media.MIME_TYPE,
        };
```

Next we need to construct an SQL WHERE clause for our query. Since we want only media files that belong to a specific album, our WHERE clause should indicate that.

In normal SQL, the WHERE clause would look like this:

```
WHERE album = 'album name'
```

Since we are working with a managedQuery, we don't need the word WHERE and we don't need to pass in what it should be equal to. Instead we substitute in a '?'. Therefore for the foregoing version, the String would be as follows:

```
album = ?
```

Since we don't know the actual name of the column as we are working with a constant. We'll use that to construct the WHERE clause.

```
        String where = android.provider.MediaStore.Audio.Media.ALBUM + "=?";
```

Finishing off the WHERE clause, we need the data that will be substituted in for the ?s in the WHERE. This will be an array of Strings, one for each of the ?s used. In our case, we want to use the name of the album that was selected. Since we have the Cursor in the right position, we simply need to call the Cursor's getString method on the right column, which we get by calling the Cursor's getColumnIndex method on the column name.

```
        String whereVal[] = ↵
{cursor.getString(cursor.getColumnIndex(MediaStore.Audio.Albums.ALBUM))};
```

Last we can specify that we want the results to be ordered by a specific column's value. For this let's create a String variable that will contain the name of the column that we want the results ordered by.

```
        String orderBy = android.provider.MediaStore.Audio.Media.TITLE;
```

Finally, we can run our managedQuery method, passing in the Uri, the columns, the WHERE clause variable, the WHERE clause data, and the ORDER BY variable.

```
        cursor = managedQuery(MediaStore.Audio.Media.EXTERNAL_CONTENT_URI,↵
columns, where, whereVal, orderBy);
```

Again, we'll use the `ListActivity` methods to manage the `Cursor` object and present the results in a list.

```
                    String[] displayFields = new String[]↵
{MediaStore.Audio.Media.DISPLAY_NAME};
                    int[] displayViews = new int[] {android.R.id.text1};
                    setListAdapter(new SimpleCursorAdapter(this,↵
                        android.R.layout.simple_list_item_1, cursor, displayFields,↵
displayViews));
```

The last thing we'll do is change the `currentState` variable to be `STATE_SELECT_SONG` so that the next time through this method, we skip all of this as the user will be selecting a song and not an album.

```
                    currentState = STATE_SELECT_SONG;
                }
            } else if (currentState == STATE_SELECT_SONG) {
```

When the user selects a song from the list after selecting an album, he or she will enter this part of the method as `currentState` will equal `STATE_SELECT_SONG`.

```
                if (cursor.moveToPosition(position)) {
```

Using the same `moveToPosition` call on the `Cursor` object as we did previously, we can get at the song that was actually selected. In this case, we are getting at the column that contains the path to the file and the MIME-type of that file. We are converting it to a `File` and creating an intent to start the built-in music player application.

```
                    int fileColumn = cursor.getColumnIndex (MediaStore.Audio.Media.DATA);
                    int mimeTypeColumn = cursor.getColumnIndex↵
(MediaStore.Audio.Media.MIME_TYPE);

                    String audioFilePath = cursor.getString(fileColumn);
                    String mimeType = cursor.getString(mimeTypeColumn);

                    Intent intent = new Intent(android.content.Intent.ACTION_VIEW);

                    File newFile = new File(audioFilePath);
                    intent.setDataAndType(Uri.fromFile(newFile), mimeType);

                    startActivity(intent);
                }
            }
        }
    }
}
```

Here is the layout XML file that is being used by the foregoing code. You'll notice that it contains a ListView with the ID `list`. This is the default ID that needs to be used with the ListActivity that we are extending.

```
<?xml version="1.0" encoding="utf-8"?>
<LinearLayout xmlns:android="http://schemas.android.com/apk/res/android"
    android:orientation="vertical"
    android:layout_width="fill_parent"
    android:layout_height="fill_parent"
    >
```

```
<ListView android:id="@+android:id/list" android:layout_width="wrap_content"↵
    android:layout_height="wrap_content"></ListView>
</LinearLayout>
```

That wraps up our sample application, which allows us to browse and select songs to play by album using the MediaStore. Using very similar methods, we could build it out so that we could browse and select music based upon artist and genre as well.

Summary

As we have discovered throughout this chapter, Android provides a rich set of capabilities for working with audio files. The capabilities it offers are implemented in a manner similar to those we have used with the image capture capabilities; specifically, we can use the built-in applications through an intent or create our own custom playback application. Also, the MediaStore has special capabilities for audio beyond querying for individual audio files—we can use it to search and browse for audio based on artist, album, genre, and more.

In the next chapter, we'll take this a step further and look at the world opened up by harnessing audio not stored on the device, but rather available via the Internet.

Chapter 6

Background and Networked Audio

In the last chapter, we explored Android's basic audio playback capabilities. While those capabilities are fantastic, we need to push a bit further to make them generally useful. In this chapter, we'll look at how we can do things like play audio files in the background so that the application playing the audio doesn't need to be running. We'll take a look at how we can synthesize sound rather than just playing sound files, and we'll look at how to leverage streaming audio that is available on the Internet.

Background Audio Playback

So far we have concentrated on building applications that are centered around being in the foreground and have their user interface in front of the user. In the last chapter, we looked at how to add audio playback capabilities to those types of applications.

What happens, though, if we want to build an application that plays music or audio books, but we would like the user to be able to do other things with the phone while continuing to listen? We might have some trouble making that happen if we limit ourselves to just building *activities*. The Android operating system reserves the right to kill activities that aren't in the front and in use by the user. It does this in order to free up memory to make room for other applications to run. If the OS kills an activity that is playing audio, this would stop the audio from playing, making the user experience not so great.

Fortunately, there is a solution. Instead of playing our audio in an activity, we can use a Service.

Services

In order to ensure that the audio continues to play when the application is no longer in the front and its activity is not in use, we need to create a Service. A Service is a component of an Android application that is meant to run tasks in the background without requiring any interaction from the user.

Local vs. Remote Services

There are a couple of different classes of Services in use by Android. The first and what we'll be exploring is called a Local Service. Local Services exist as part of a specific application and are accessed and controlled only by that application. Remote Services are the other type. They can communicate with, be accessed, and be controlled by other applications. As mentioned, we'll be concentrating on using a Local Service to provide audio playback capabilities. Developing Remote Services is a very large topic and is unfortunately out of the scope of this book.

Simple Local Service

To demonstrate a Service, let's go through this very simple example.

First we'll need an activity with an interface that allows us to start and stop the Service.

```
package com.apress.proandroidmedia.ch06.simpleservice;

import android.app.Activity;
import android.content.Intent;
import android.os.Bundle;
import android.view.View;
import android.view.View.OnClickListener;
import android.widget.Button;

public class SimpleServiceActivity extends Activity implements OnClickListener {
```

Our activity will have two Buttons—one for starting the Service and one for stopping it.

```
    Button startServiceButton;
    Button stopServiceButton;
```

In order to start or stop the Service, we use a standard intent.

```
    Intent serviceIntent;

    @Override
    public void onCreate(Bundle savedInstanceState) {
        super.onCreate(savedInstanceState);
        setContentView(R.layout.main);
```

Our activity implements OnClickListener, so we set the OnClickListener for each of the Buttons to be "this".

```
        startServiceButton = (Button) this.findViewById(R.id.StartServiceButton);
        stopServiceButton = (Button) this.findViewById(R.id.StopServiceButton);

        startServiceButton.setOnClickListener(this);
        stopServiceButton.setOnClickListener(this);
```

When instantiating the intent that will be used to start and stop the Service, we pass in our activity as the Context followed by the Service's class.

```
            serviceIntent = new Intent(this, SimpleServiceService.class);
    }

    public void onClick(View v) {
        if (v == startServiceButton) {
```

When the `startServiceButton` is clicked, we call the `startService` method, passing in the intent just created to refer to our Service. The `startService` method is a part of the Context class of which activity is a child.

```
            startService(serviceIntent);
        }
        else if (v == stopServiceButton) {
```

When the `stopServiceButton` is clicked, we call the `stopService` method, passing in the same intent that refers to our Service. As with `startService`, `stopService` is part of the Context class.

```
            stopService(serviceIntent);
        }
    }
}
```

Here is our `main.xml` file that defines the layout for the foregoing activity. It contains the StartService and StopService Buttons as well as a TextView.

```
<?xml version="1.0" encoding="utf-8"?>
<LinearLayout xmlns:android="http://schemas.android.com/apk/res/android"
    android:orientation="vertical"
    android:layout_width="fill_parent"
    android:layout_height="fill_parent"
    >
    <TextView
        android:layout_width="fill_parent"
        android:layout_height="wrap_content"
        android:text="Simple Service"
    />
    <Button android:layout_width="wrap_content" android:layout_height="wrap_content"↵
android:id="@+id/StartServiceButton" android:text="Start Service"></Button>
    <Button android:layout_width="wrap_content" android:layout_height="wrap_content"↵
android:text="Stop Service" android:id="@+id/StopServiceButton"></Button>
</LinearLayout>
```

Now we can move on to the code for the Service itself. In this example, we aren't accomplishing anything in the Service, just using Toast to tell us when the Service has started and stopped.

```
package com.apress.proandroidmedia.ch06.simpleservice;

import android.app.Service;
import android.content.Intent;
import android.os.IBinder;
import android.util.Log;
```

Services extend the `android.app.Service` class. The `Service` class is abstract, so in order to extend it, we have to at the very least implement the onBind method. In this very simple example, we aren't going to be "binding" to the Service. Therefore we'll just return null in our onBind method.

```java
public class SimpleServiceService extends Service {

    @Override
    public IBinder onBind(Intent intent) {
        return null;
    }
```

The next three methods represent the Service's life cycle. The onCreate method, as in the *Activity,* is called when the Service is instantiated. It will be the first method called.

```java
    @Override
    public void onCreate() {
        Log.v("SIMPLESERVICE","onCreate");
    }
```

The onStartCommand method will be called whenever startService is called with an intent that matches this Service. Therefore it may be called more than once. The onStartCommand returns an integer value that represents what the OS should do if it kills the Service. START_STICKY, which we are using here, indicates that the Service will be restarted if killed.

```java
    @Override
    public int onStartCommand(Intent intent, int flags, int startId) {
        Log.v("SIMPLESERVICE","onStartCommand");
        return START_STICKY;
    }
```

onStartCommand vs. onStart

The onStartCommand method was introduced with Android 2.0 (API level 5). Previous to that, the method used was onStart. onStart's parameters are an intent and an int for startId. It does not include the int flags parameter and doesn't have a return. If you are targeting a phone that is running something earlier than 2.0, you can use the onStart method.

```java
    @Override
public void onStart(Intent intent, int startid) {
        Log.v("SIMPLESERVICE","onStart");
    }
```

The onDestroy method is called when the OS is destroying a Service. In this example, it is triggered when the stopService method is called by our activity. This method should be used to do any cleanup that needs to be done when a Service is being shut down.

```java
    public void onDestroy() {
        Log.v("SIMPLESERVICE","onDestroy");
    }
}
```

Finally, in order to make this example work, we need to add an entry to our manifest file (AndroidManifest.xml) that specifies our Service.

```xml
<?xml version="1.0" encoding="utf-8"?>
```

```
<manifest xmlns:android="http://schemas.android.com/apk/res/android"
    package="com.apress.proandroidmedia.ch06.simpleservice"
    android:versionCode="1"
    android:versionName="1.0">
  <application android:icon="@drawable/icon" android:label="@string/app_name">
    <activity android:name=".SimpleServiceActivity"
            android:label="@string/app_name">
        <intent-filter>
            <action android:name="android.intent.action.MAIN" />
            <category android:name="android.intent.category.LAUNCHER" />
        </intent-filter>
    </activity>
    <service android:name=".SimpleServiceService" />
  </application>
  <uses-sdk android:minSdkVersion="5" />
</manifest>
```

Of course, this example doesn't do anything other than output to the log indicating when the Service has been started and stopped. Let's move forward and have our Service actually do something.

Local Service plus MediaPlayer

Now that we have created an example Service, we can use it as a template to create an application to play audio files in the background. Here is a Service, and an activity to control the Service that does just that, allows us to play audio files in the background. It works in a similar manner to the custom audio player example from the last chapter, as it is using the same underlying MediaPlayer class that Android makes available to us.

```
package com.apress.proandroidmedia.ch06.backgroundaudio;
```

```
import android.app.Service;
import android.content.Intent;
import android.media.MediaPlayer;
import android.media.MediaPlayer.OnCompletionListener;
import android.os.IBinder;
import android.util.Log;
```

The Service implements OnCompletionListener so that it can be notified when the MediaPlayer has finished playing an audio file.

```
public class BackgroundAudioService extends Service implements OnCompletionListener
{
```

We declare an object of type MediaPlayer. This object will handle the playback of the audio as shown in the custom audio player example in the last chapter.

```
    MediaPlayer mediaPlayer;

    @Override
    public IBinder onBind(Intent intent) {
        return null;
    }

    @Override
```

```
public void onCreate() {
    Log.v("PLAYERSERVICE","onCreate");
```

In the onCreate method, we instantiate the MediaPlayer. We are passing it a specific reference to an audio file called goodmorningandroid.mp3, which should be placed in the raw resources (res/raw) directory of our project. If this directory doesn't exist, it should be created. Putting the audio file in that location allows us to refer to it by a constant in the generated R class, R.raw.goodmorningandroid. More detail about placing audio in the raw resources directory is available in Chapter 5 in the "Creating a Custom Audio-Playing Application" section.

```
mediaPlayer = MediaPlayer.create(this, R.raw.goodmorningandroid);
```

We also set our Service, this class, to be the OnCompletionListener for the MediaPlayer object.

```
mediaPlayer.setOnCompletionListener(this);
}
```

When the startService command is issued on this Service, the onStartCommand method will be triggered. In this method, we first check that the MediaPlayer object isn't already playing, as this method may be called multiple times, and if it isn't, we start it. Since we are using the onStartCommand method rather than the onStart method, this example runs only in Android 2.0 and above.

```
@Override
public int onStartCommand(Intent intent, int flags, int startId) {
    Log.v("PLAYERSERVICE","onStartCommand");

    if (!mediaPlayer.isPlaying()) {
        mediaPlayer.start();
    }
    return START_STICKY;
}
```

When the Service is destroyed, the onDestroy method is triggered. Since this doesn't guarantee that the MediaPlayer will stop playing, we invoke its stop method here if it is playing and also call its release method to get rid of any memory usage and or resource locks.

```
public void onDestroy() {
    if (mediaPlayer.isPlaying())
    {
        mediaPlayer.stop();
    }
    mediaPlayer.release();
    Log.v("SIMPLESERVICE","onDestroy");
}
```

Because we are implementing OnCompletionListener and the Service itself is set to be the MediaPlayer's OnCompletionListener, the following onCompletion method is called when the MediaPlayer has finished playing an audio file. Since this Service is only meant to play one song and that's it, we call stopSelf, which is analogous to calling stopService in our activity.

```
    public void onCompletion(MediaPlayer _mediaPlayer) {
        stopSelf();
    }
}
```

Here is the activity that corresponds to the foregoing Service. It has a very simple interface with two buttons to control the starting and stopping of the Service. In each case, it calls finish directly after to illustrate that the Service is not dependent on the activity and runs independently.

```
package com.apress.proandroidmedia.ch06.backgroundaudio;

import android.app.Activity;
import android.content.Intent;
import android.os.Bundle;
import android.view.View;
import android.view.View.OnClickListener;
import android.widget.Button;

public class BackgroundAudioActivity extends Activity implements OnClickListener {

    Button startPlaybackButton, stopPlaybackButton;
    Intent playbackServiceIntent;

    @Override
    public void onCreate(Bundle savedInstanceState) {
        super.onCreate(savedInstanceState);
        setContentView(R.layout.main);

        startPlaybackButton = (Button) this.findViewById(R.id.StartPlaybackButton);
        stopPlaybackButton = (Button) this.findViewById(R.id.StopPlaybackButton);

        startPlaybackButton.setOnClickListener(this);
        stopPlaybackButton.setOnClickListener(this);

        playbackServiceIntent = new Intent(this,BackgroundAudioService.class);
    }

    public void onClick(View v) {
        if (v == startPlaybackButton) {
            startService(playbackServiceIntent);
            finish();
        } else if (v == stopPlaybackButton) {
            stopService(playbackServiceIntent);
            finish();
        }
    }
}
```

Here is the main.xml layout XML file in use by the foregoing activity.

```
<?xml version="1.0" encoding="utf-8"?>
<LinearLayout xmlns:android="http://schemas.android.com/apk/res/android"
    android:orientation="vertical"
    android:layout_width="fill_parent"
    android:layout_height="fill_parent"
    >
    <TextView
```

```
                    android:layout_width="fill_parent"
                    android:layout_height="wrap_content"
                    android:text="Background Audio Player"
                    />
            <Button android:text="Start Playback" android:id="@+id/StartPlaybackButton"↩
              android:layout_width="wrap_content" android:layout_height="wrap_content"></Button>
            <Button android:text="Stop Playback" android:id="@+id/StopPlaybackButton"↩
              android:layout_width="wrap_content" android:layout_height="wrap_content"></Button>
        </LinearLayout>
```

Finally, here is the AndroidManifest.xml for this project.

```
<?xml version="1.0" encoding="utf-8"?>
<manifest xmlns:android="http://schemas.android.com/apk/res/android"
        package="com.apress.proandroidmedia.ch06.backgroundaudio"
        android:versionCode="1"
        android:versionName="1.0">
    <application android:icon="@drawable/icon" android:label="@string/app_name">
        <activity android:name=".BackgroundAudioActivity"
                    android:label="@string/app_name">
            <intent-filter>
                <action android:name="android.intent.action.MAIN" />
                <category android:name="android.intent.category.LAUNCHER" />
            </intent-filter>
        </activity>
        <service android:name=".BackgroundAudioService" />
    </application>
    <uses-sdk android:minSdkVersion="5" />
</manifest>
```

As shown, simply using the MediaPlayer to start and stop audio playback within a Service is very straightforward. Let's now look at how we can take that a step further.

Controlling a MediaPlayer in a Service

Unfortunately, when using a Service, issuing commands to the MediaPlayer from the user-facing activity becomes more complicated.

In order to allow the MediaPlayer to be controlled, we need to bind the activity and Service together. Once we do that, since the activity and Service are running in the same process, we can call methods in the Service directly. If we were creating a remote Service, we would have to take further steps.

Let's add a Button labeled "Have Fun" to the foregoing activity. When this Button is pressed, we'll have the MediaPlayer seek back a few seconds and continuing playing the audio file.

We'll start by adding the Button to the layout XML:

```
<?xml version="1.0" encoding="utf-8"?>
<LinearLayout xmlns:android="http://schemas.android.com/apk/res/android"
    android:orientation="vertical"
    android:layout_width="fill_parent"
    android:layout_height="fill_parent"
    >
    <TextView
```

```
            android:layout_width="fill_parent"
            android:layout_height="wrap_content"
            android:text="Background Audio Player"
            />
    <Button android:text="Start Playback" android:id="@+id/StartPlaybackButton"↵
     android:layout_width="wrap_content" android:layout_height="wrap_content"></Button>
    <Button android:text="Stop Playback" android:id="@+id/StopPlaybackButton"↵
     android:layout_width="wrap_content" android:layout_height="wrap_content"></Button>
    <Button android:text="Have Fun" android:id="@+id/HaveFunButton"↵
     android:layout_width="wrap_content" android:layout_height="wrap_content"></Button>
</LinearLayout>
```

Then in the activity, we'll get a reference to it and set its onClickListener to be the activity itself, just like the existing Buttons.

```
package com.apress.proandroidmedia.ch06.backgroundaudiobind;

import android.app.Activity;
import android.content.ComponentName;
import android.content.Context;
import android.content.Intent;
import android.content.ServiceConnection;
import android.os.Bundle;
import android.os.IBinder;
import android.view.View;
import android.view.View.OnClickListener;
import android.widget.Button;

public class BackgroundAudioActivity extends Activity implements OnClickListener {

    Button startPlaybackButton, stopPlaybackButton;
    Button haveFunButton;
    Intent playbackServiceIntent;

    @Override
    public void onCreate(Bundle savedInstanceState) {
        super.onCreate(savedInstanceState);
        setContentView(R.layout.main);

        startPlaybackButton = (Button) this.findViewById(R.id.StartPlaybackButton);
        stopPlaybackButton = (Button) this.findViewById(R.id.StopPlaybackButton);
        haveFunButton = (Button) this.findViewById(R.id.HaveFunButton);

        startPlaybackButton.setOnClickListener(this);
        stopPlaybackButton.setOnClickListener(this);
        haveFunButton.setOnClickListener(this);

        playbackServiceIntent = new Intent(this,BackgroundAudioService.class);
    }
```

In order for us to have this Button interact with the MediaPlayer that is running in the Service, we have to bind to the Service. The means to do this is with the bindService method. This method takes in an intent; in fact, we can re-use the playbackServiceIntent that we are using to start the Service, a ServiceConnection object, and some flags for what to do when the Service isn't running.

In the following onClick method in our activity, we bind to the Service right after we start it, when the startPlaybackButton is pressed. We unbind from the Service when the stopPlaybackButton is called.

```
public void onClick(View v) {
    if (v == startPlaybackButton) {
        startService(playbackServiceIntent);
        bindService(playbackServiceIntent, serviceConnection,
                    Context.BIND_AUTO_CREATE);
    } else if (v == stopPlaybackButton) {
        unbindService(serviceConnection);
        stopService(playbackServiceIntent);
    }
```

You'll probably notice that we are using a new object that we haven't defined, serviceConnection. This we'll take care of in a moment.

We also need to finish off the onClick method. Since our new Button has its onClickListener set to be the activity, we should handle that case as well and close out the onClick method.

```
    else if (v == haveFunButton) {
        baService.haveFun();
    }
}
```

In the new section, we are using another new object, baService. baService is an object that is of type BackgroundAudioService. We'll declare it now and take care of creating when we create our ServiceConnection object.

```
private BackgroundAudioService baService;
```

As mentioned, we are still missing the declaration and instantiation of an object called serviceConnection. serviceConnection will be an object of type ServiceConnection, which is an Interface for monitoring the state of a bound Service.

Let's take care of creating our serviceConnection now:

```
private ServiceConnection serviceConnection = new ServiceConnection() {
```

The onServiceConnected method shown here will be called when a connection with the Service has been established through a bindService command that names this object as the ServiceConnection (such as we are doing in our bindService call).

One thing that is passed into this method is an IBinder object that is actually created and delivered from the Service itself. In our case, this IBinder object will be of type BackgroundAudioServiceBinder, which we'll create in our Service. It will have a method that returns our Service itself, called getService. The object returned by this can be operated directly on, as we are doing when the haveFunButton is clicked.

```
public void onServiceConnected(ComponentName className, IBinder baBinder) {
    baService =
((BackgroundAudioService.BackgroundAudioServiceBinder)baBinder).getService();
    }
```

We also need an onServiceDisconnected method to handle cases when the Service goes away.

```
        public void onServiceDisconnected(ComponentName className) {
            baService = null;
        }
    };
}
```

.

Now we can turn our attention to what we need to change in the Service itself.

```
package com.apress.proandroidmedia.ch06.backgroundaudiobind;

import android.app.Service;
import android.content.Intent;
import android.media.MediaPlayer;
import android.media.MediaPlayer.OnCompletionListener;
import android.os.Binder;
import android.os.IBinder;
import android.util.Log;

public class BackgroundAudioService extends Service implements OnCompletionListener
{
    MediaPlayer mediaPlayer;
```

The first change that we'll need to make in our Service is to create an inner class that extends Binder that can return our Service itself when asked.

```
    public class BackgroundAudioServiceBinder extends Binder {
        BackgroundAudioService getService() {
            return BackgroundAudioService.this;
        }
    }
```

Following that, we'll instantiate that as an object called basBinder.

```
    private final IBinder basBinder = new BackgroundAudioServiceBinder();
```

And override the implementation of onBind to return that.

```
    @Override
    public IBinder onBind(Intent intent) {
        // Return the BackgroundAudioServiceBinder object
        return basBinder;
    }
```

That's it for the binding. Now we just need to deal with "Having Fun."

As mentioned, when the haveFunButton is clicked, we want the MediaPlayer to seek back a few seconds. In this implementation, it will seek back 2,500 milliseconds or 2.5 seconds.

```
        public void haveFun() {
        if (mediaPlayer.isPlaying()) {
            mediaPlayer.seekTo(mediaPlayer.getCurrentPosition() - 2500);
        }
    }
```

That's it for updates on the Service. Here is the rest of the code for good measure.

```java
@Override
public void onCreate() {
    Log.v("PLAYERSERVICE","onCreate");

    mediaPlayer = MediaPlayer.create(this, R.raw.goodmorningandroid);
    mediaPlayer.setOnCompletionListener(this);
}

@Override
public int onStartCommand(Intent intent, int flags, int startId) {
    Log.v("PLAYERSERVICE","onStartCommand");

    if (!mediaPlayer.isPlaying()) {
        mediaPlayer.start();
    }
    return START_STICKY;
}

public void onDestroy() {
    if (mediaPlayer.isPlaying())
    {
        mediaPlayer.stop();
    }
    mediaPlayer.release();
    Log.v("SIMPLESERVICE","onDestroy");
}

public void onCompletion(MediaPlayer _mediaPlayer) {
    stopSelf();
}

}
```

Finally, here is the `AndroidManifest.xml` file that is required by the foregoing example.

```xml
<?xml version="1.0" encoding="utf-8"?>
<manifest xmlns:android="http://schemas.android.com/apk/res/android"
      android:versionCode="1"
      android:versionName="1.0" package="com.apress.proandroidmedia⏎
.ch06.backgroundaudiobind">
    <application android:icon="@drawable/icon" android:label="@string/app_name">
        <activity android:name=".BackgroundAudioActivity"
                android:label="@string/app_name">
            <intent-filter>
                <action android:name="android.intent.action.MAIN" />
                <category android:name="android.intent.category.LAUNCHER" />
            </intent-filter>
        </activity>
        <service android:name=".BackgroundAudioService" />
    </application>
    <uses-sdk android:minSdkVersion="5" />
</manifest>
```

Now that the foundation is in place, we can add whatever functionality we like into the Service and call the various methods such as haveFun directly from our activity by binding to it. Without binding to the Service, we would be unable to do anything more than start and stop the Service.

The foregoing examples should give a good starting point for building an application that plays audio files in the background, allowing users to continue doing other tasks while the audio continues playing. The second example can be extended to build a full-featured audio playback application.

Networked Audio

Moving our attention forward, let's look at how we can further leverage Android's audio playback capabilities to harness media that lives elsewhere, in particular audio that lives online. With posting MP3 files, podcasting, and streaming all becoming more and more popular, it only makes sense that we would want to build audio playback applications that can leverage those services.

Fortunately, Android has rich capabilities for dealing with various types of audio available on the network.

Let's start with examining how to leverage web-based audio or audio delivered via HTTP.

HTTP Audio Playback

The simplest case to explore would simply be to play an audio file that lives online and is accessible via HTTP.

One such file would be this, which is available on my server: http://www.mobvcasting.com/android/audio/goodmorningandroid.mp3

Here is an example activity that uses the MediaPlayer to illustrate how to play audio available via HTTP.

```
package com.apress.proandroidmedia.ch06.audiohttp;

import java.io.IOException;

import android.app.Activity;
import android.media.MediaPlayer;
import android.os.Bundle;
import android.util.Log;

public class AudioHTTPPlayer extends Activity {
    MediaPlayer mediaPlayer;

    @Override
    public void onCreate(Bundle savedInstanceState) {
        super.onCreate(savedInstanceState);
        setContentView(R.layout.main);
```

When our activity is created, we do a generic instantiation of a MediaPlayer object by calling the MediaPlayer constructor with no arguments. This is a different way of using the `MediaPlayer` than we have previously seen and requires us to take some additional steps before we can play the audio.

```
mediaPlayer = new MediaPlayer();
```

Specifically, we need to call the `setDataSource` method, passing in the HTTP location of the audio file we would like to play. This method can throw an `IOException`, so we have to catch and deal with that as well.

```
try {
    mediaPlayer.setDataSource(
        "http://www.mobvcasting.com/android/audio/goodmorningandroid.mp3");
```

Following that we call the prepare method and then the `start` method, after which the audio should start playing.

```
        mediaPlayer.prepare();
        mediaPlayer.start();
    } catch (IOException e) {
        Log.v("AUDIOHTTPPLAYER",e.getMessage());
    }
    }
}
```

Running this example, you will probably notice a significant lag time from when the application loads to when the audio plays. The length of the delay is due to the speed of the data network that the phone is using for its Internet connection (among other variables).

If we add Log or Toast messages throughout the code, we would see that this delay happens between the call to the prepare method and the start method. During the running of the `prepare` method, the `MediaPlayer` is filling up a buffer so that the audio playback can run smoothly even if the network is slow.

The `prepare` method actually blocks while it is doing this. This means that applications that use this method will likely become unresponsive until the `prepare` method is complete. Fortunately, there is a way around this, and that is to use the `prepareAsync` method. This method returns immediately and does the buffering and other work in the background, allowing the application to continue.

The issue then becomes one of paying attention to the state of the `MediaPlayer` object and implementing various callbacks that help us keep track of its state.

To get a handle on the various states that a `MediaPlayer` object may be in, it is helpful to look over the diagram from the `MediaPlayer` page on the Android API Reference, shown in Figure 6–1.

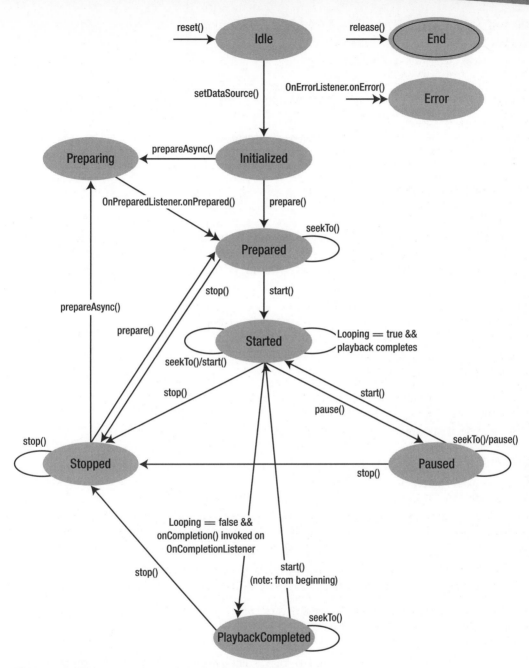

Figure 6–1. *MediaPlayer state diagram from Android API Reference*

Here is a full MediaPlayer example that uses prepareAsync and implements several listeners to keep track of its state.

```
package com.apress.proandroidmedia.ch06.audiohttpasync;

import java.io.IOException;
import android.app.Activity;
import android.media.MediaPlayer;
import android.media.MediaPlayer.OnBufferingUpdateListener;
import android.media.MediaPlayer.OnCompletionListener;
import android.media.MediaPlayer.OnErrorListener;
import android.media.MediaPlayer.OnInfoListener;
import android.media.MediaPlayer.OnPreparedListener;
import android.os.Bundle;
import android.util.Log;
import android.view.View;
import android.view.View.OnClickListener;
import android.widget.Button;
import android.widget.TextView;
```

In this version of our HTTP audio player, we are implementing several interfaces. Two of them, OnPreparedListener and OnCompletionListener, will help us keep track of the state of the MediaPlayer so that we don't attempt to play or stop audio when we shouldn't.

```
public class AudioHTTPPlayer extends Activity
    implements OnClickListener, OnErrorListener, OnCompletionListener,
    OnBufferingUpdateListener, OnPreparedListener {

    MediaPlayer mediaPlayer;
```

The interface for this activity has start and stop Buttons, a TextView for displaying the status, and a TextView for displaying the percentage of the buffer that has been filled.

```
    Button stopButton, startButton;
    TextView statusTextView, bufferValueTextView;

    @Override
    public void onCreate(Bundle savedInstanceState) {
        super.onCreate(savedInstanceState);
        setContentView(R.layout.main);
```

In the onCreate method, we set the stopButton and startButton to be disabled. They'll be enabled or disabled throughout the running of the application. This is to illustrate when the methods they trigger are and aren't available.

```
        stopButton = (Button) this.findViewById(R.id.EndButton);
        startButton = (Button) this.findViewById(R.id.StartButton);
        stopButton.setOnClickListener(this);
        startButton.setOnClickListener(this);
        stopButton.setEnabled(false);
        startButton.setEnabled(false);

        bufferValueTextView = (TextView) this.findViewById(R.id.BufferValueTextView);
        statusTextView = (TextView) this.findViewById(R.id.StatusDisplayTextView);
        statusTextView.setText("onCreate");
```

After we instantiate the MediaPlayer object, we register the activity to be the OnCompletionListener, the OnErrorListener, the OnBufferingUpdateListener, and the OnPreparedListener.

```
        mediaPlayer = new MediaPlayer();

        mediaPlayer.setOnCompletionListener(this);
        mediaPlayer.setOnErrorListener(this);
        mediaPlayer.setOnBufferingUpdateListener(this);
        mediaPlayer.setOnPreparedListener(this);

        statusTextView.setText("MediaPlayer created");
```

Next we call setDataSource with the URL to the audio file.

```
        try {
            mediaPlayer.setDataSource(
                "http://www.mobvcasting.com/android/audio/goodmorningandroid.mp3");

            statusTextView.setText("setDataSource done");
            statusTextView.setText("calling prepareAsync");
```

Last, we'll call prepareAsync, which will start the buffering of the audio file in the background and return. When the preparation is complete, our activity's onCompletion method will be called due to our activity being registered as the OnCompletionListener for the MediaPlayer.

```
            mediaPlayer.prepareAsync();

        } catch (IOException e) {
            Log.v("AUDIOHTTPPLAYER",e.getMessage());
        }
    }
```

What follows is the implementation of the onClick method for the two Buttons. When the stopButton is pressed, the MediaPlayer's pause method will be called. When the startButton is pressed, the MediaPlayer's start method is called.

```
    public void onClick(View v) {
        if (v == stopButton) {
            mediaPlayer.pause();
            statusTextView.setText("pause called");
            startButton.setEnabled(true);
        } else if (v == startButton) {
            mediaPlayer.start();
            statusTextView.setText("start called");
            startButton.setEnabled(false);
            stopButton.setEnabled(true);
        }
    }
```

If the MediaPlayer enters into an error state, the onError method will be called on the object that is registered as the MediaPlayer's OnErrorListener. The following onError method shows the various constants that are specified in the MediaPlayer class.

```
    public boolean onError(MediaPlayer mp, int what, int extra) {
        statusTextView.setText("onError called");

        switch (what) {
            case MediaPlayer.MEDIA_ERROR_NOT_VALID_FOR_PROGRESSIVE_PLAYBACK:
                statusTextView.setText(
                    "MEDIA ERROR NOT VALID FOR PROGRESSIVE PLAYBACK " + extra);
```

```
            Log.v(
                "ERROR","MEDIA ERROR NOT VALID FOR PROGRESSIVE PLAYBACK " + extra);
            break;
        case MediaPlayer.MEDIA_ERROR_SERVER_DIED:
            statusTextView.setText("MEDIA ERROR SERVER DIED " + extra);
            Log.v("ERROR","MEDIA ERROR SERVER DIED " + extra);
            break;
        case MediaPlayer.MEDIA_ERROR_UNKNOWN:
            statusTextView.setText("MEDIA ERROR UNKNOWN " + extra);
            Log.v("ERROR","MEDIA ERROR UNKNOWN " + extra);
            break;
    }

    return false;
}
```

When the MediaPlayer completes playback of an audio file, the onCompletion method of the object registered as the OnCompletionListener will be called. This indicates that we could start playback again.

```
public void onCompletion(MediaPlayer mp) {
    statusTextView.setText("onCompletion called");
    stopButton.setEnabled(false);
    startButton.setEnabled(true);
}
```

While the MediaPlayer is buffering, the onBufferingUpdate method of the object registered as the MediaPlayer's onBufferingUpdateListener is called. The percentage of the buffer that is filled is passed in.

```
public void onBufferingUpdate(MediaPlayer mp, int percent) {
    bufferValueTextView.setText("" + percent + "%");
}
```

When the prepareAsync method finishes, the onPrepared method of the object registered as the OnPreparedListener will be called. This indicates that the audio is ready for playback, and therefore, in the following method, we are setting the startButton to be enabled.

```
public void onPrepared(MediaPlayer mp) {
    statusTextView.setText("onPrepared called");
    startButton.setEnabled(true);
}
}
```

Here is the Layout XML associated with the foregoing activity:

```
<?xml version="1.0" encoding="utf-8"?>
<LinearLayout xmlns:android="http://schemas.android.com/apk/res/android"
    android:orientation="vertical"
    android:layout_width="fill_parent"
    android:layout_height="fill_parent"
    >
    <TextView android:text="Status" android:id="@+id/TextView01"↵
 android:layout_width="wrap_content" android:layout_height="wrap_content"></TextView>
    <TextView android:text="Unknown" android:id="@+id/StatusDisplayTextView"↵
 android:layout_width="wrap_content" android:layout_height="wrap_content"></TextView>
    <TextView android:text="0%" android:id="@+id/BufferValueTextView"↵
```

```
android:layout_width="wrap_content" android:layout_height="wrap_content"></TextView>
    <Button android:layout_width="wrap_content" android:layout_height="wrap_content"↵
android:text="Start" android:id="@+id/StartButton"></Button>
    <Button android:layout_width="wrap_content" android:layout_height="wrap_content"↵
android:id="@+id/EndButton" android:text="Stop"></Button>
</LinearLayout>
```

As just shown, the MediaPlayer has a nice set of capabilities for handling audio files that are available online via HTTP.

Streaming Audio via HTTP

One way that live audio is commonly delivered online is via HTTP streaming. There are a variety of streaming methods that fall under the umbrella of HTTP streaming from server push, which has historically been used for displaying continually refreshing webcam images in browsers to a series of new methods being put forth by Apple, Adobe, and Microsoft for use by their respective media playback applications.

The main method for streaming live audio over HTTP is one developed in 1999 by a company called Nullsoft, which was subsequently purchased by AOL. Nullsoft was the creator of WinAMP, a popular MP3 player, and they developed a live audio streaming server that used HTTP, called SHOUTcast. SHOUTcast uses the ICY protocol, which extends HTTP. Currently, a large number of servers and playback software products support this protocol, so many, in fact, that it may be considered the de facto standard for online radio.

Fortunately, the MediaPlayer class on Android is capable of playing ICY streams without requiring us developers to jump through hoops.

Unfortunately for us, Internet radio stations don't typically advertise the direct URL to their streams. This is for good reason; unfortunately, browsers don't support ICY streams directly and require a helper application or plug-in to play the stream. In order to know to open a helper application, an intermediary file with a specific MIME-type is delivered by the Internet radio station, which contains a pointer to the actual live stream. In the case of ICY streams, this is typically either a PLS file or an M3U file.

- A PLS file is a multimedia playlist file and has the MIME-type "audio/x-scpls".

- An M3U file is also a file that stores multimedia playlists but in a more basic format. Its MIME-type is "audio/x-mpegurl".

The following illustrates the contents of an M3U file that points to a fake live stream.

```
#EXTM3U
#EXTINF:0,Live Stream Name
http://www.nostreamhere.org:8000/
```

The first line, #EXTM3U, is required and specifies that what follows is an Extended M3U file that can contain extra information. Extra information about a playlist entry is specified on the line above the entry and starts with #EXTINF:, followed by the duration in seconds, a comma, and then the name of the media.

An M3U file can have multiple entries as well, specifying one file or stream after another.

```
#EXTM3U
#EXTINF:0,Live Stream Name
http://www.nostreamhere.org:8000/
#EXTINF:0,Other Live Stream Name
http://www.nostreamthere.org/
```

Unfortunately, the MediaPlayer on Android doesn't handle the parsing of M3U files for us. Therefore, to create an HTTP streaming audio player on Android, we have to handle the parsing ourselves and use the MediaPlayer for the actual media playback.

Here is an example activity that parses and plays an M3U file delivered from an online radio station or any M3U file as entered in the URL field.

```
package  com.apress.proandroidmedia.ch06.httpaudioplaylistplayer;

import java.io.BufferedReader;
import java.io.IOException;
import java.io.InputStream;
import java.io.InputStreamReader;
import java.util.Vector;

import org.apache.http.HttpResponse;
import org.apache.http.HttpStatus;
import org.apache.http.client.ClientProtocolException;
import org.apache.http.client.HttpClient;
import org.apache.http.client.methods.HttpGet;
import org.apache.http.impl.client.DefaultHttpClient;

import android.app.Activity;
import android.media.MediaPlayer;
import android.media.MediaPlayer.OnCompletionListener;
import android.media.MediaPlayer.OnPreparedListener;
import android.os.Bundle;
import android.util.Log;
import android.view.View;
import android.view.View.OnClickListener;
import android.widget.Button;
import android.widget.EditText;
```

As in our previous example, this activity will extend OnCompletionListener and OnPreparedListener to track the state of the MediaPlayer.

```
public class HTTPAudioPlaylistPlayer extends Activity
   implements OnClickListener, OnCompletionListener, OnPreparedListener {
```

We'll use a Vector to hold the list of items in the playlist. Each item will be a PlaylistFile object that is defined in an inner class at the end of this class.

```
    Vector playlistItems;
```

We'll have a few Buttons on the interface as well as an EditText object, which will contain the URL to the M3U file.

```
    Button parseButton;
    Button playButton;
    Button stopButton;
```

```
EditText editTextUrl;
String baseURL = "";
MediaPlayer mediaPlayer;
```

The following integer is used keep track of which item from the `playlistItems` Vector we are currently on.

```
int currentPlaylistItemNumber = 0;

@Override
public void onCreate(Bundle savedInstanceState) {
    super.onCreate(savedInstanceState);
    setContentView(R.layout.main);

    parseButton = (Button) this.findViewById(R.id.ButtonParse);
    playButton = (Button) this.findViewById(R.id.PlayButton);
    stopButton = (Button) this.findViewById(R.id.StopButton);
```

We are setting the text of the `editTextUrl` object to be the URL of an M3U file from an online radio station. The first one, which is commented out, is the URL for KBOO, a community radio station in Portland, Oregon (`www.kboo.fm/`). The second, which is not commented out, is for KMFA, a classical station in Austin, Texas (`www.kmfa.org/`).

The user can edit this to be the URL to any M3U file available on the Internet.

```
    editTextUrl = (EditText) this.findViewById(R.id.EditTextURL);
    //editTextUrl.setText("http://live.kboo.fm:8000/high.m3u");
    editTextUrl.setText("http://pubint.ic.llnwd.net/stream/pubint_kmfa.m3u");

    parseButton.setOnClickListener(this);
    playButton.setOnClickListener(this);
    stopButton.setOnClickListener(this);
```

Initially the `playButton` and `stopButton` will not be enabled; the user will not be able to press them. The `parseButton`, on the other hand, will be enabled. After the M3U file is retrieved and parsed, the `playButton` will be enabled, and after the audio is playing, the `stopButton` will be enabled. This is how we'll guide the user through the flow of the application.

```
    playButton.setEnabled(false);
    stopButton.setEnabled(false);

    mediaPlayer = new MediaPlayer();
    mediaPlayer.setOnCompletionListener(this);
    mediaPlayer.setOnPreparedListener(this);
}
```

Each of the Buttons has their `OnClickListener` set to be this activity. Therefore the following `onClick` method will be called when any of these are clicked. This drives most of the application's flow.

When the `parseButton` is pressed, the `parsePlaylistFile` method is called. When the `playButton` is pressed, the `playPlaylistItems` method is called.

```
public void onClick(View view) {
    if (view == parseButton) {
        parsePlaylistFile();
    } else if (view == playButton) {
        playPlaylistItems();
    } else if (view == stopButton) {
        stop();
    }
}
```

The first method that will be triggered is parsePlaylistFile. This method downloads the M3U file that is specified by the URL in the editTextUrl object and parses it. The act of parsing it picks out any lines that represent files to play and creates a PlaylistItem object, which is added to the playlistItems Vector.

```
private void parsePlaylistFile() {
```

We'll start out with an empty Vector. If a new M3U file is parsed, anything previously in here will be thrown away.

```
playlistItems = new Vector();
```

To retrieve the M3U file off of the Web, we can use the Apache Software Foundation's HttpClient library, which is included with Android.

First we create an HttpClient object, which represents something along the lines of a web browser, and then an HttpGet object, which represents the specific request for a file. The HttpClient will execute the HttpGet and return an HttpResponse.

```
HttpClient httpClient = new DefaultHttpClient();
HttpGet getRequest = new HttpGet(editTextUrl.getText().toString());

Log.v("URI",getRequest.getURI().toString());

try {
    HttpResponse httpResponse = httpClient.execute(getRequest);
    if (httpResponse.getStatusLine().getStatusCode() != HttpStatus.SC_OK) {
        // ERROR MESSAGE
        Log.v("HTTP ERROR",httpResponse.getStatusLine().getReasonPhrase());
    } else {
```

After we make the request, we can retrieve an InputStream from the HttpResponse. This InputStream contains the contents of the file requested.

```
InputStream inputStream = httpResponse.getEntity().getContent();
BufferedReader bufferedReader =
    new BufferedReader(new InputStreamReader(inputStream));
```

With the aid of a BufferedReader, we can go through the file line by line.

```
String line;
while ((line = bufferedReader.readLine()) != null) {
    Log.v("PLAYLISTLINE","ORIG: " + line);
```

If the line starts with a "#", we'll ignore it for now. As described earlier, these lines are metadata.

```
if (line.startsWith("#")) {
    // Metadata
    // Could do more with this but not fo now
```

Otherwise, if it isn't a blank line, it has a length greater than 0, and we'll assume that it is a playlist item.

```
} else if (line.length() > 0) {
```

If the line starts with "http://", we treat it as a full URL to the stream, otherwise we treat it as a relative URL and tack on the URL of the original request for the M3U file.

```
String filePath = "";

if (line.startsWith("http://")) {
    // Assume it's a full URL
    filePath = line;
} else {
    // Assume it's relative
    filePath = getRequest.getURI().resolve(line).toString();
}
```

We then add it to our Vector of playlist items.

```
PlaylistFile playlistFile = new PlaylistFile(filePath);
playlistItems.add(playlistFile);
        }
    }
    inputStream.close();
}
} catch (ClientProtocolException e) {
    e.printStackTrace();
} catch (IOException e) {
    e.printStackTrace();
}
```

Last, now that we are done parsing the file, we enable the playButton.

```
playButton.setEnabled(true);
}
```

When the user clicks the playButton, the playPlaylistItems method is called. This method takes the first item from the playlistItems Vector and hands it to the MediaPlayer object for preparation.

```
private void playPlaylistItems() {
    playButton.setEnabled(false);

    currentPlaylistItemNumber = 0;
    if (playlistItems.size() > 0)
    {
        String path =
        ((PlaylistFile)playlistItems.get(currentPlaylistItemNumber)).getFilePath();
        try {
```

After extracting the path to the file or stream, we use that in a setDataSource method call on the MediaPlayer.

```
mediaPlayer.setDataSource(path);
```

Then we call prepareAsync, which allows the MediaPlayer to buffer and prepare to play the audio in the background. When the buffering and other preparation is done, the activity's onPrepared method will be called since the activity is registered as the OnPreparedListener.

```
            mediaPlayer.prepareAsync();

        } catch (IllegalArgumentException e) {
            e.printStackTrace();
        } catch (IllegalStateException e) {
            e.printStackTrace();
        } catch (IOException e) {
            e.printStackTrace();
        }
    }
}
```

Once the onPrepared method has been called, the stopButton is enabled and the MediaPlayer object is triggered to start playing the audio.

```
public void onPrepared(MediaPlayer _mediaPlayer) {
    stopButton.setEnabled(true);
    Log.v("HTTPAUDIOPLAYLIST","Playing");
    mediaPlayer.start();
}
```

When the audio playback is complete, the onCompletion method is triggered in this activity since the activity extends and is registered as the MediaPlayer's OnCompletionListener.

The onCompletion method cues up the next item in the playlistItems Vector.

```
public void onCompletion(MediaPlayer mediaPlayer) {
    Log.v("ONCOMPLETE","called");
    mediaPlayer.stop();
    mediaPlayer.reset();
    if (playlistItems.size() > currentPlaylistItemNumber + 1) {
        currentPlaylistItemNumber++;
        String path =
        ((PlaylistFile)playlistItems.get(currentPlaylistItemNumber)).getFilePath();
        try {
            mediaPlayer.setDataSource(path);
            mediaPlayer.prepareAsync();
        } catch (IllegalArgumentException e) {
            e.printStackTrace();
        } catch (IllegalStateException e) {
            e.printStackTrace();
        } catch (IOException e) {
            e.printStackTrace();
        }
    }
}
```

The stop method is called when the user presses the stopButton. This method causes the MediaPlayer to pause rather than stop. The MediaPlayer has a stop method, but that puts the MediaPlayer in an unprepared state. The pause method just pauses playback.

```
    private void stop() {
        mediaPlayer.pause();
        playButton.setEnabled(true);
        stopButton.setEnabled(false);
    }
```

Last, we have an inner class called `PlaylistFile`. One `PlaylistFile` object is created for each file represented in the M3U file.

```
class PlaylistFile {
    String filePath;

    public PlaylistFile(String _filePath) {
        filePath = _filePath;
    }

    public void setFilePath(String _filePath) {
        filePath = _filePath;
    }

    public String getFilePath() {
        return filePath;
    }
}
}
```

Here is the layout XML file (`main.xml`) for the foregoing activity.

```
<?xml version="1.0" encoding="utf-8"?>
<LinearLayout xmlns:android="http://schemas.android.com/apk/res/android"
    android:orientation="vertical"
    android:layout_width="fill_parent"
    android:layout_height="fill_parent"
    >
    <TextView android:layout_width="wrap_content" android:layout_height="wrap_content"↵
     android:text="Enter URL" android:id="@+id/EnterURLTextView"></TextView>
    <EditText android:layout_width="wrap_content" android:layout_height="wrap_content"↵
     android:id="@+id/EditTextURL" android:text="http://www.mobvcasting.com/android/↵
    audio/test.m3u"></EditText>
    <Button android:layout_width="wrap_content" android:layout_height="wrap_content"↵
     android:id="@+id/ButtonParse" android:text="Parse"></Button>
    <TextView android:layout_width="wrap_content" android:layout_height="wrap_content"↵
     android:id="@+id/PlaylistTextView"></TextView>
    <Button android:layout_width="wrap_content" android:layout_height="wrap_content"↵
     android:id="@+id/PlayButton" android:text="Play"></Button>
    <Button android:layout_width="wrap_content" android:layout_height="wrap_content"↵
     android:id="@+id/StopButton" android:text="Stop"></Button>
</LinearLayout>
```

This example requires that the following permission be added to the `AndroidManifest.xml` file

```
<uses-permission android:name="android.permission.INTERNET" />
```

As you can see in the foregoing example, working with a live audio stream via HTTP is as straightforward as working with a file delivered via HTTP. Figure 6–2 shows the example in action.

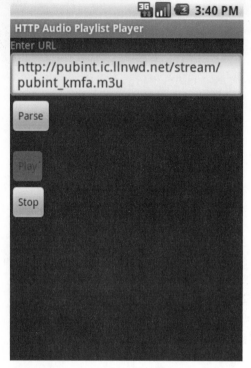

Figure 6–2. *HTTP Audio Playlist Player example shown after audio started playback*

RTSP Audio Streaming

Android supports one more protocol for streaming audio through the MediaPlayer. This is called the Real Time Streaming Protocol or RTSP. RTSP has been in use for quite some time and was made popular in the mid- to late 1990s by RealNetworks, as it is the protocol they used in their audio and video streaming software.

The same code in use for the preceding HTTP streaming example works with an RTSP audio stream. We'll get into more RTSP specifics in Chapter 10.

Summary

As we have seen throughout this chapter, Android's rich advanced audio capabilities help it to move beyond just being a playback device. Out of the box, it has capabilities that allow us as developers to take advantage of the wide variety of audio available online, from individual MP3 files to live radio streams.

In the next chapter, we'll look at using Android as an audio production device as well.

Chapter 7

Audio Capture

Developing audio playback applications isn't the only way to work with audio on Android. We can also write applications that involve capturing audio. In this chapter, we'll explore three different methods that can be used for audio capture. Each method has relative strengths and weaknesses. The first method, using an intent, is the easiest but least flexible, followed by a method using the `MediaRecorder` class, which is a bit harder to use but offers more flexibility. The final method uses the `AudioRecord` class, and offers the most flexibility but does the least amount of work for us.

Audio Capture with an Intent

The easiest way to simply allow audio recording capabilities in an application is to leverage an existing application through an intent that provides recording capabilities. In the case of audio, Android ships with a sound recorder application that can be triggered in this manner.

The action used to create the intent is available as a constant called `RECORD_SOUND_ACTION` within the `MediaStore.Audio.Media` class. Here is the basic code to trigger the built-in sound recorder.

```
Intent intent = new Intent(MediaStore.Audio.Media.RECORD_SOUND_ACTION);
startActivity(intent);
```

Figure 7–1 shows the built-in audio recording application as triggered by an intent.

Figure 7–1. *Android's built-in sound recorder triggered with an intent*

Of course, in order to retrieve the recording that the user creates, we'll want to use startActivityForResult rather than just startActivity.

Here is an example that triggers the built-in sound recorder via an intent. When the user finishes, the audio file is played back using the MediaPlayer.

```
package  com.apress.proandroidmedia.ch07.intentaudiorecord;

import android.app.Activity;
import android.content.Intent;
import android.media.MediaPlayer;
import android.media.MediaPlayer.OnCompletionListener;
import android.net.Uri;
import android.os.Bundle;
import android.provider.MediaStore;
import android.view.View;
import android.view.View.OnClickListener;
import android.widget.Button;
```

Our activity implements OnClickListener so that it can respond to Button presses, and OnCompletionListener so that it can be notified when audio is finished playing in the MediaPlayer.

```
public class IntentAudioRecorder extends Activity implements OnClickListener,↵
 OnCompletionListener {
```

We'll create a constant called RECORD_REQUEST that we can pass into the startActivityForResult function so that we can identify the source of any calls to onActivityResult, which is called when the sound recorder is complete.

The onActivityResult method would be called by any returning activity when triggered by a startActivityForResult function. Passing in a unique constant along with the intent allows us to differentiate between them within the onActivityResult method.

```
public static int RECORD_REQUEST = 0;

Button createRecording, playRecording;
```

We need a Uri object that we will use to contain the Uri to the audio file that is recorded by the sound recorder activity.

```
Uri audioFileUri;

@Override
public void onCreate(Bundle savedInstanceState) {
    super.onCreate(savedInstanceState);
    setContentView(R.layout.main);
```

After we set the content view, we can obtain references to the Button objects. Each one's click listener is set to this so that our activity's onClick method will be called. Also, we'll set the playRecording button to not be enabled until we have an audio file to play (get a result from the sound recorder activity).

```
        createRecording = (Button) this.findViewById(R.id.RecordButton);
        createRecording.setOnClickListener(this);

        playRecording = (Button) this.findViewById(R.id.PlayButton);
        playRecording.setOnClickListener(this);
        playRecording.setEnabled(false);
}
```

When we click either of the Buttons, our onClick method is triggered. If the createRecording Button was clicked, we trigger the sound recorder activity through the MediaStore.Audio.Media.RECORD_SOUND_ACTION action in an intent passed into startActivityForResult.

```
public void onClick(View v) {
    if (v == createRecording) {
        Intent intent =
        new Intent(MediaStore.Audio.Media.RECORD_SOUND_ACTION);
        startActivityForResult(intent, RECORD_REQUEST);
    } else if (v == playRecording) {
```

If the playRecording Button was pressed, we create a MediaPlayer and set it to play the audio file represented by the Uri that was returned from the sound recorder activity and saved in our audioFileUri object.

We also set the OnCompletionListener of the MediaPlayer to be ourselves so that our OnCompletion method is called when it is done playing, and we disable the playRecording Button so that the user cannot trigger the playback to happen again until we are ready.

```
        MediaPlayer mediaPlayer = MediaPlayer.create(this, audioFileUri);
        mediaPlayer.setOnCompletionListener(this);
        mediaPlayer.start();
        playRecording.setEnabled(false);
    }
}
```

Our onActivityResult method is triggered when the sound recorder activity is complete. The resultCode should equal the RESULT_OK constant, and the requestCode should equal the value we passed into the startActivityForResult method, RECORD_REQUEST. If both of those are true, then we can retrieve the Uri of the recorded audio file by getting it out of the intent that is passed back to us through its getData method. Once all of that is done, we enable the playRecording Button so that we can play the returned audio file.

```
protected void onActivityResult (int requestCode, int resultCode, Intent data) {
    if (resultCode == RESULT_OK && requestCode == RECORD_REQUEST) {
        audioFileUri = data.getData();
        playRecording.setEnabled(true);
    }
}
```

Finally, in our onCompletion method, which is called when the MediaPlayer is done playing a file, we re-enable the playRecording Button so the user may listen to the audio file again if he or she so chooses.

```
public void onCompletion(MediaPlayer mp) {
    playRecording.setEnabled(true);
}
}
```

Here is the layout XML that is in use by our activity.

```
<?xml version="1.0" encoding="utf-8"?>
<LinearLayout xmlns:android="http://schemas.android.com/apk/res/android"
    android:orientation="vertical"
    android:layout_width="fill_parent"
    android:layout_height="fill_parent"
    >
    <Button android:text="Record Audio" android:id="@+id/RecordButton"↵
     android:layout_width="wrap_content" android:layout_height="wrap_content"></Button>
    <Button android:text="Play Recording" android:id="@+id/PlayButton"↵
     android:layout_width="wrap_content" android:layout_height="wrap_content"></Button>
</LinearLayout>
```

As you can see, simply adding audio recording capabilities is straightforward. It doesn't allow much in the way of control over the user interface or other aspects of the recording, but it does give a no-frills usable interface to the user without much work on our part.

Custom Audio Capture

Of course, using an intent to trigger the sound recorder isn't the only way we can capture audio. The Android SDK includes a MediaRecorder class, which we can leverage to build our own audio recording functionality. Doing so enables a lot more flexibility, such as controlling the length of time audio is recorded for.

The MediaRecorder class is used for both audio and video capture. After constructing a MediaRecorder object, to capture audio, the setAudioEncoder and setAudioSource methods must be called. If these methods are not called, audio will not be recorded. (The same goes for video. If setVideoEncoder and setVideoSource methods are not called, video will not be recorded. We won't be dealing with video in this chapter; therefore we won't use either of these methods.)

Additionally, two other methods are generally called before having the MediaRecorder prepare to record. These are setOutputFormat and setOutputFile. setOutputFormat allows us to choose what file format should be used for the recording and setOutputFile allows us to specify the file that we will record to. It is important to note that the order of each of these calls matters quite a bit.

MediaRecorder Audio Sources

The first method that should be called after the MediaRecorder is instantiated is setAudioSource. setAudioSource takes in a constant that is defined in the AudioSource inner class. Generally we will want to use MediaRecorder.AudioSource.MIC, but it is interesting to note that MediaRecorder.AudioSource also contains constants for VOICE_CALL, VOICE_DOWNLINK, and VOICE_UPLINK. Unfortunately, it appears as though there aren't any handsets or versions of Android where recording audio from the call actually works. Also of note, as of Froyo, Android version 2.2, there are constants for CAMCORDER and VOICE_RECOGNITION. These may be used if the device has more than one microphone.

```
MediaRecorder recorder = new MediaRecorder();
recorder.setAudioSource(MediaRecorder.AudioSource.MIC);
```

MediaRecorder Output Formats

The next method to be called in sequence is setOutputFormat. The values this takes in are specified as constants in the MediaRecorder.OutputFormat inner class.

- *MediaRecorder.OutputFormat.MPEG_4*: This specifies that the file written will be an MPEG-4 file. It may contain both audio and video tracks.

- *MediaRecorder.OutputFormat.RAW_AMR*: This represents a raw file without any type of container. This should be used only when capturing audio without video and when the audio encoder is AMR_NB.

- *MediaRecorder.OutputFormat.THREE_GPP*: This specifies that the file written will be a 3GPP file (extension .3gp). It may contain both audio and video tracks.

```
recorder.setOutputFormat(MediaRecorder.OutputFormat.THREE_GPP);
```

MediaRecorder Audio Encoders

Following the setting of the output format, we can call setAudioEncoder to set the codec that should be used. The possible values are specified as constants in the MediaRecorder.AudioEncoder class and other than DEFAULT, only one other value exists: MediaRecorder.AudioEncoder.AMR_NB, which is the Adaptive Multi-Rate Narrow Band codec. This codec is tuned for speech and is therefore not a great choice for anything other than speech. By default it has a sample rate of 8 kHz and a bitrate between 4.75 and 12.2 kbps, both of which are very low for recoding anything but speech. Unfortunately, this is our only choice for use with the MediaRecorder at the moment.

```
recorder.setAudioEncoder(MediaRecorder.AudioEncoder.AMR_NB);
```

MediaRecorder Output and Recording

Last, we'll want to call setOutputFile with the location of the file we want to record to. The following snippet of code creates a file using File.createTempFile in the preferred file location for applications that need to store files on the SD card.

```
File path = new File(Environment.getExternalStorageDirectory().getAbsolutePath() +
  "/Android/data/com.apress.proandroidmedia.ch07.customrecorder/files/");
path.mkdirs();
audioFile = File.createTempFile("recording", ".3gp", path);
recorder.setOutputFile(audioFile.getAbsolutePath());
```

Now we can actually call prepare, which signals the end of the configuration stage and tells the MediaRecorder to get ready to start recording. We call the start method to actually start recording.

```
recorder.prepare();
recorder.start();
```

To stop recording, we call the stop method.

```
recorder.stop();
```

MediaRecorder State Machine

The MediaRecorder, similar to the MediaPlayer, operates as a state machine. Figure 7–2 shows a diagram from the Android API reference page for MediaRecorder, which describes the various states and the methods that may be called from each state.

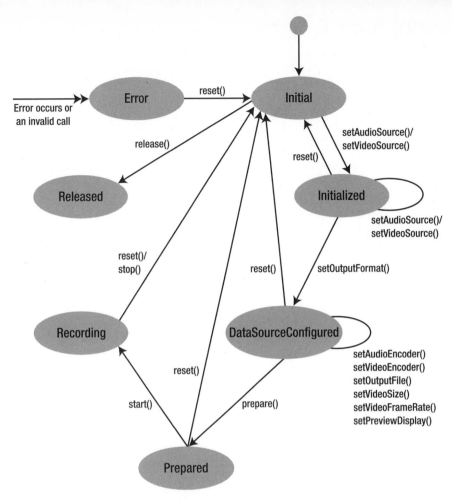

MediaRecorder state diagram

Figure 7–2. *MediaRecorder state diagram from Android API Reference*

MediaRecorder Example

Here is the code for a full custom audio capture and playback example using the
MediaRecorder class.

```
package com.apress.proandroidmedia.ch07.customrecorder;

import java.io.File;
import java.io.IOException;

import android.app.Activity;
import android.media.MediaPlayer;
import android.media.MediaRecorder;
import android.media.MediaPlayer.OnCompletionListener;
```

```
import android.os.Bundle;
import android.os.Environment;
import android.view.View;
import android.view.View.OnClickListener;
import android.widget.Button;
import android.widget.TextView;
```

Our `CustomRecorder` activity implements `OnClickListener` so that it may be notified when Buttons are pressed, and `OnCompletionListener` so that it can respond when `MediaPlayer` has completed playing audio.

```
public class CustomRecorder extends Activity implements OnClickListener,↵
  OnCompletionListener {
```

We'll have a series of user interface components. The first, a `TextView` called `statusTextView`, will report the status of the application to the user: "Recording," "Ready to Play," and so on.

```
    TextView statusTextView;
```

A series of buttons will be used for controlling various aspects. The names of the Buttons describe their use.

```
    Button startRecording, stopRecording, playRecording, finishButton;
```

We'll have a `MediaRecorder` for recording the audio and a `MediaPlayer` for playing it back.

```
    MediaRecorder recorder;
    MediaPlayer player;
```

Finally, we have a `File` object called `audioFile`, which will reference the file that is recorded to.

```
    File audioFile;

    @Override
    public void onCreate(Bundle savedInstanceState) {
        super.onCreate(savedInstanceState);
        setContentView(R.layout.main);
```

When the activity starts up, we'll set the text of the `statusTextView` to be "Ready."

```
        statusTextView = (TextView) this.findViewById(R.id.StatusTextView);
        statusTextView.setText("Ready");

        stopRecording = (Button) this.findViewById(R.id.StopRecording);
        startRecording = (Button) this.findViewById(R.id.StartRecording);
        playRecording = (Button) this.findViewById(R.id.PlayRecording);
        finishButton = (Button) this.findViewById(R.id.FinishButton);
```

We'll set all of the Buttons' `onClickListeners` to be this so that our `onClick` method is called when any of them are pressed.

```
        startRecording.setOnClickListener(this);
        stopRecording.setOnClickListener(this);
        playRecording.setOnClickListener(this);
        finishButton.setOnClickListener(this);
```

Finally, in the onCreate method, we'll disable the stopRecording and playRecording Buttons since they won't work until we either start recording or finish recording respectively.

```
        stopRecording.setEnabled(false);
        playRecording.setEnabled(false);
    }
```

In the following onClick method, we handle all of the Button presses.

```
    public void onClick(View v) {
        if (v == finishButton) {
```

If the finishButton is pressed, we finish the activity.

```
            finish();
        } else if (v == stopRecording) {
```

If the stopRecording Button is pressed, we call stop and release on the MediaRecorder object.

```
            recorder.stop();
            recorder.release();
```

We then construct a MediaPlayer object and have it prepare to play back the audio file that we just recorded.

```
            player = new MediaPlayer();
            player.setOnCompletionListener(this);
```

The following two methods that we are using on the MediaPlayer, setDataSource and prepare, may throw a variety of exceptions. In the following code, we are simply throwing them. In your application development, you will probably want to catch and deal with them more elegantly, such as alerting the user when a file doesn't exist.

```
            try {
                player.setDataSource(audioFile.getAbsolutePath());
            } catch (IllegalArgumentException e) {
                throw new RuntimeException(
                    "Illegal Argument to MediaPlayer.setDataSource", e);
            } catch (IllegalStateException e) {
                throw new RuntimeException(
                    "Illegal State in MediaPlayer.setDataSource", e);
            } catch (IOException e) {
                throw new RuntimeException(
                    "IOException in MediaPalyer.setDataSource", e);
            }

            try {
                player.prepare();
            } catch (IllegalStateException e) {
                throw new RuntimeException(
                    "IllegalStateException in MediaPlayer.prepare", e);
            } catch (IOException e) {
                throw new RuntimeException("IOException in MediaPlayer.prepare", e);
            }
```

We set the statusTextView to indicate to the user that we are ready to play the audio file.

```
statusTextView.setText("Ready to Play");
```

We then set the playRecording and startRecording Buttons to be enabled and disable the stopRecording Button, as we are not currently recording.

```
playRecording.setEnabled(true);
stopRecording.setEnabled(false);
startRecording.setEnabled(true);
} else if (v == startRecording) {
```

When the startRecording Button is pressed, we construct a new MediaRecorder and call setAudioSource, setOutputFormat, and setAudioEncoder.

```
recorder = new MediaRecorder();

recorder.setAudioSource(MediaRecorder.AudioSource.MIC);
recorder.setOutputFormat(MediaRecorder.OutputFormat.THREE_GPP);
recorder.setAudioEncoder(MediaRecorder.AudioEncoder.AMR_NB);
```

We then create a new File on the SD card and call setOutputFile on the MediaRecorder object.

```
File path = new File(Environment.getExternalStorageDirectory()↵
.getAbsolutePath() + "/Android/data/com.apress.proandroidmedia.ch07↵
.customrecorder/files/");
path.mkdirs();

try {
    audioFile = File.createTempFile("recording", ".3gp", path);
} catch (IOException e) {
    throw new RuntimeException("Couldn't create recording audio file",e);
}

recorder.setOutputFile(audioFile.getAbsolutePath());
```

We call prepare on the MediaRecorder and start to begin the recording.

```
try {
    recorder.prepare();
} catch (IllegalStateException e) {
    throw new RuntimeException(
        "IllegalStateException on MediaRecorder.prepare", e);
} catch (IOException e) {
    throw new RuntimeException("IOException on MediaRecorder.prepare",e);
}

recorder.start();
```

Last, we update the statusTextView and change which Buttons are enabled and disabled.

```
statusTextView.setText("Recording");

playRecording.setEnabled(false);
stopRecording.setEnabled(true);
startRecording.setEnabled(false);
} else if (v == playRecording) {
```

The last Button that we need to respond to is playRecording. When the stopRecording Button is pressed, the MediaPlayer object, player, is constructed and configured. All that we need to do when the playRecording Button is pushed is to start the playback, set the status message, and change which Buttons are enabled.

```
            player.start();
            statusTextView.setText("Playing");
            playRecording.setEnabled(false);
            stopRecording.setEnabled(false);
            startRecording.setEnabled(false);
        }
    }
```

The onCompletion method is called when the MediaPlayer object has completed playback of a recording. We use it to change the status message and set which Buttons are enabled.

```
    public void onCompletion(MediaPlayer mp) {
        playRecording.setEnabled(true);
        stopRecording.setEnabled(false);
        startRecording.setEnabled(true);
        statusTextView.setText("Ready");
    }
}
```

Here is the layout XML file, main.xml, for the foregoing activity.

```
<?xml version="1.0" encoding="utf-8"?>
<LinearLayout xmlns:android="http://schemas.android.com/apk/res/android"
    android:orientation="vertical"
    android:layout_width="fill_parent"
    android:layout_height="fill_parent"
    >
    <TextView android:layout_width="wrap_content" android:layout_height=
"wrap_content" android:id="@+id/StatusTextView" android:text="Status"
 android:textSize="35dip"></TextView>

    <Button android:text="Start Recording" android:id="@+id/StartRecording"
android:layout_width="wrap_content" android:layout_height="wrap_content"></Button>
    <Button android:text="Stop Recording" android:id="@+id/StopRecording"
android:layout_width="wrap_content" android:layout_height="wrap_content"></Button>
    <Button android:text="Play Recording" android:id="@+id/PlayRecording"
android:layout_width="wrap_content" android:layout_height="wrap_content"></Button>
    <Button android:layout_width="wrap_content" android:layout_height="wrap_content"
android:id="@+id/FinishButton" android:text="Finish"></Button>
</LinearLayout>
```

We'll also need to add the following permissions to the AndroidManifest.xml file.

```
<uses-permission android:name="android.permission.RECORD_AUDIO"></uses-permission>
<uses-permission android:name="android.permission.WRITE_EXTERNAL_STORAGE">
</uses-permission>
```

As we have seen, developing a custom audio capture application using MediaRecorder is not too cumbersome. Now let's look at how we can use the MediaRecorder's other methods to add other features.

Other MediaRecorder Methods

MediaRecorder has a variety of other methods available that we can use in relation to audio capture.

- *getMaxAmplitude*: Allows us to request the maximum amplitude of audio that has been recorded by the MediaPlayer. The value is reset each time the method is called, so each call will return the maximum amplitude from the last time it is called. An audio level meter may be implemented by calling this method periodically.

- *setMaxDuration*: Allows us to specify a maximum recording duration in milliseconds. This method must be called after the setOutputFormat method but before the prepare method.

- *setMaxFileSize*: Allows us to specify a maximum file size for the recording in bytes. As with setMaxDuration, this method must be called after the setOutputFormat method but before the prepare method.

Here is an update to the custom recorder application we went through previously that includes a display of the current amplitude.

```
package com.apress.proandroidmedia.ch07.customrecorder;

import java.io.File;
import java.io.IOException;

import android.app.Activity;
import android.media.MediaPlayer;
import android.media.MediaRecorder;
import android.media.MediaPlayer.OnCompletionListener;
import android.os.AsyncTask;
import android.os.Bundle;
import android.os.Environment;
import android.view.View;
import android.view.View.OnClickListener;
import android.widget.Button;
import android.widget.TextView;

public class CustomRecorder extends Activity implements OnClickListener,
        OnCompletionListener {
```

In this version, we have added a TextView called amplitudeTextView. This will display the numeric amplitude of the audio input.

```
    TextView statusTextView, amplitudeTextView;
    Button startRecording, stopRecording, playRecording, finishButton;
    MediaRecorder recorder;
    MediaPlayer player;
    File audioFile;
```

We'll need an instance of a new class called RecordAmplitude. This class is an inner class that is defined toward the end of this source code listing. It uses a Boolean called isRecording that will be set to true when we start the MediaRecorder.

```
RecordAmplitude recordAmplitude;
boolean isRecording = false;

@Override
public void onCreate(Bundle savedInstanceState) {
    super.onCreate(savedInstanceState);
    setContentView(R.layout.main);

    statusTextView = (TextView) this.findViewById(R.id.StatusTextView);
    statusTextView.setText("Ready");
```

We'll use a TextView to display the current amplitude of the audio as it is captured.

```
    amplitudeTextView = (TextView) this
            .findViewById(R.id.AmplitudeTextView);
    amplitudeTextView.setText("0");

    stopRecording = (Button) this.findViewById(R.id.StopRecording);
    startRecording = (Button) this.findViewById(R.id.StartRecording);
    playRecording = (Button) this.findViewById(R.id.PlayRecording);
    finishButton = (Button) this.findViewById(R.id.FinishButton);

    startRecording.setOnClickListener(this);
    stopRecording.setOnClickListener(this);
    playRecording.setOnClickListener(this);
    finishButton.setOnClickListener(this);

    stopRecording.setEnabled(false);
    playRecording.setEnabled(false);
}

public void onClick(View v) {
    if (v == finishButton) {
        finish();
    } else if (v == stopRecording) {
```

When we finish the recording, we set the isRecording Boolean to false and call cancel on our RecordAmplitude class. Since RecordAmplitude extends AsyncTask, calling cancel with true as the parameter will interrupt its thread if necessary.

```
        isRecording = false;
        recordAmplitude.cancel(true);

        recorder.stop();
        recorder.release();

        player = new MediaPlayer();
        player.setOnCompletionListener(this);
        try {
            player.setDataSource(audioFile.getAbsolutePath());
        } catch (IllegalArgumentException e) {
            throw new RuntimeException(
                    "Illegal Argument to MediaPlayer.setDataSource", e);
        } catch (IllegalStateException e) {
            throw new RuntimeException(
                    "Illegal State in MediaPlayer.setDataSource", e);
        } catch (IOException e) {
            throw new RuntimeException(
```

```
                        "IOException in MediaPalyer.setDataSource", e);
            }

            try {
                player.prepare();
            } catch (IllegalStateException e) {
                throw new RuntimeException(
                        "IllegalStateException in MediaPlayer.prepare", e);
            } catch (IOException e) {
                throw new RuntimeException(
                        "IOException in MediaPlayer.prepare", e);
            }

            statusTextView.setText("Ready to Play");

            playRecording.setEnabled(true);
            stopRecording.setEnabled(false);
            startRecording.setEnabled(true);

        } else if (v == startRecording) {
            recorder = new MediaRecorder();

            recorder.setAudioSource(MediaRecorder.AudioSource.MIC);
            recorder.setOutputFormat(MediaRecorder.OutputFormat.THREE_GPP);
            recorder.setAudioEncoder(MediaRecorder.AudioEncoder.AMR_NB);

            File path = new File(Environment.getExternalStorageDirectory()⏎
                    .getAbsolutePath() + "/Android/data/com.apress.proandroidmedia.ch07⏎
.customrecorder/files/");
            path.mkdirs();
            try {
                audioFile = File.createTempFile("recording", ".3gp", path);
            } catch (IOException e) {
                throw new RuntimeException(
                        "Couldn't create recording audio file", e);
            }
            recorder.setOutputFile(audioFile.getAbsolutePath());

            try {
                recorder.prepare();
            } catch (IllegalStateException e) {
                throw new RuntimeException(
                        "IllegalStateException on MediaRecorder.prepare", e);
            } catch (IOException e) {
                throw new RuntimeException(
                        "IOException on MediaRecorder.prepare", e);
            }
            recorder.start();
```

After we start the recording, we set the isRecording Boolean to true and create a new instance of RecordAmplitude. Since RecordAmplitude extends AsyncTask, we'll call the execute method to start the RecordAmplitude's task running.

```
            isRecording = true;
            recordAmplitude = new RecordAmplitude();
            recordAmplitude.execute();

            statusTextView.setText("Recording");

            playRecording.setEnabled(false);
            stopRecording.setEnabled(true);
            startRecording.setEnabled(false);
        } else if (v == playRecording) {
            player.start();
            statusTextView.setText("Playing");
            playRecording.setEnabled(false);
            stopRecording.setEnabled(false);
            startRecording.setEnabled(false);
        }
    }

    public void onCompletion(MediaPlayer mp) {
        playRecording.setEnabled(true);
        stopRecording.setEnabled(false);
        startRecording.setEnabled(true);
        statusTextView.setText("Ready");
    }
```

Here is the definition of RecordAmplitude. It extends AsyncTask, which is a nice utility class in Android that provides a thread to run long-running tasks without tying up the user interface or making an application unresponsive.

```
    private class RecordAmplitude extends AsyncTask<Void, Integer, Void> {
```

The doInBackground method runs on a separate thread and is run when the execute method is called on the object. This method loops as long as isRecording is true and calls Thread.sleep(500), which causes it to not do anything for half a second. Once that is complete, it calls publishProgress and passes in the result of getMaxAmplitude on the MediaRecorder object.

```
        @Override
        protected Void doInBackground(Void... params) {
            while (isRecording) {

                try {
                    Thread.sleep(500);
                } catch (InterruptedException e) {
                    e.printStackTrace();
                }

                publishProgress(recorder.getMaxAmplitude());
            }
            return null;
        }
```

The preceding call to publishProgress calls the onProgressUpdate method defined here, which runs on the main thread so it can interact with the user interface. In this case, it is updating the amplitudeTextView with the value that is passed in from the publishProgress method call.

```
        protected void onProgressUpdate(Integer... progress) {
            amplitudeTextView.setText(progress[0].toString());
        }
    }
}
```

Of course, we'll need to update the layout XML to include the TextView for displaying the amplitude.

```
<?xml version="1.0" encoding="utf-8"?>
<LinearLayout xmlns:android="http://schemas.android.com/apk/res/android"
    android:orientation="vertical"
    android:layout_width="fill_parent"
    android:layout_height="fill_parent"
    >
        <TextView android:layout_width="wrap_content" android:layout_height=
"wrap_content" android:id="@+id/StatusTextView" android:text="Status"
android:textSize="35dip"></TextView>
        <TextView android:layout_width="wrap_content" android:layout_height=
"wrap_content" android:id="@+id/AmplitudeTextView" android:textSize="35dip"
android:text="0"></TextView>
        <Button android:text="Start Recording" android:id="@+id/StartRecording"
android:layout_width="wrap_content" android:layout_height="wrap_content"></Button>
        <Button android:text="Stop Recording" android:id="@+id/StopRecording"
android:layout_width="wrap_content" android:layout_height="wrap_content"></Button>
        <Button android:text="Play Recording" android:id="@+id/PlayRecording"
android:layout_width="wrap_content" android:layout_height="wrap_content"></Button>
        <Button android:layout_width="wrap_content" android:layout_height=
"wrap_content" android:id="@+id/FinishButton" android:text="Finish"></Button>
</LinearLayout>
```

As we can see, using an AsyncTask to do something periodically is a nice way to provide automatically updating information to the user while something else is in progress. This provides a nicer user experience for our MediaRecorder example. Using the getMaxAmplitude method provides the user with some feedback about the recording that is currently happening.

In Android 2.2, Froyo, the following methods were made available:

- *setAudioChannels*: Allows us to specify the number of audio channels that will be recorded. Typically this will be either one channel (mono) or two channels (stereo). This method must be called prior to the prepare method.

- *setAudioEncodingBitRate*: Allows us to specify the number of bits per second that will be used by the encoder when compressing the audio. This method must be called prior to the prepare method.

- *setAudioSamplingRate*: Allows us to specify the sampling rate of the audio as it is captured and encoded. The applicable rates are determined by the hardware and codec being used. This method must be called prior to the prepare method.

Inserting Audio into the MediaStore

Audio recordings may be put into the MediaStore content provider so they are available to other applications. The process is very similar to the process we used earlier to add images to the MediaStore. In this case though, we'll add them after they are created.

We create a ContentValues object to hold the data that we'll insert into the MediaStore. A ContentValues object is made up of a series of key/value pairs. The keys that may be used are defined as constants in the MediaStore.Audio.Media class (and those classes it inherits from).

The MediaStore.Audio.Media.DATA constant is the key for the path to the recorded file. It is the only required pair in order to insert the file into the MediaStore.

To do the actual insert into the MediaStore, we use the insert method on a ContentResolver object with the Uri to the table for audio files on the SD card and the ContentValues object containing the data. The Uri is defined as a constant in MediaStore.Audio.Media named EXTERNAL_CONTENT_URI.

Here is a snippet that may be plugged into the CustomRecorder example just after the release method is called on the MediaRecorder (recorder.release()). It will cause the recording to be inserted into the MediaStore and made available to other applications that use the MediaStore for finding audio to play back.

```
ContentValues contentValues = new ContentValues();
contentValues.put(MediaStore.MediaColumns.TITLE, "This Isn't Music");
contentValues.put(MediaStore.MediaColumns.DATE_ADDED, System.currentTimeMillis());
contentValues.put(MediaStore.Audio.Media.DATA, audioFile.getAbsolutePath());
Uri newUri =
  getContentResolver().insert(
    MediaStore.Audio.Media.EXTERNAL_CONTENT_URI, contentValues);
```

Of course, in order to use the foregoing snippet, we'll need to add these imports:

```
import android.content.ContentValues;
import android.net.Uri;
import android.provider.MediaStore;
```

Raw Audio Recording with AudioRecord

Aside from using an intent to launch the sound recorder and using the MediaRecorder, Android offers a third method to capture audio, using a class called AudioRecord. AudioRecord is the most flexible of the three methods in that it allows us access to the raw audio stream but has the least number of built-in capabilities, such as not automatically compressing the audio.

The basics for using AudioRecord are straightforward. We simply need to construct an object of type AudioRecord, passing in various configuration parameters.

The first value we'll need to specify is the audio source. The values for use here are the same as we used for the MediaRecorder and are defined in MediaRecorder.AudioSource. Essentially this means that we have MediaRecorder.AudioSource.MIC available to us.

```
int audioSource = MediaRecorder.AudioSource.MIC;
```

The next value that we'll need to specify is the sample rate of the recording. This should be specified in Hz. As we know, the MediaRecorder samples audio at 8 kHz or 8,000 Hz. CD quality audio is typically 44.1 kHz or 44,100 Hz. Hz or hertz is the number of samples per second. Different Android handset hardware will be able to sample at different sample rates. For our example application, we'll sample at 11,025 Hz, which is another commonly used sample rate.

```
int sampleRateInHz = 11025;
```

Next, we need to specify the number of channels of audio to capture. The constants for this parameter are specified in the AudioFormat class and are self-explanatory.

- `AudioFormat.CHANNEL_CONFIGURATION_MONO`
- `AudioFormat.CHANNEL_CONFIGURATION_STEREO`
- `AudioFormat.CHANNEL_CONFIGURATION_INVALID`
- `AudioFormat.CHANNEL_CONFIGURATION_DEFAULT`

We'll use a mono configuration for now.

```
int channelConfig = AudioFormat.CHANNEL_CONFIGURATION_MONO;
```

Following that, we need to specify the audio format. The possibilities here are also specified in the AudioFormat class.

- `AudioFormat.ENCODING_DEFAULT`
- `AudioFormat.ENCODING_INVALID`
- `AudioFormat.ENCODING_PCM_16BIT`
- `AudioFormat.ENCODING_PCM_8BIT`

Among these four, our choices boil down to PCM 16-bit and PCM 8-bit. PCM stands for Pulse Code Modulation, which is essentially the raw audio samples. We can therefore set the resolution of each sample to be 16 bits or 8 bits. Sixteen bits will take up more space and processing power, while the representation of the audio will be closer to reality.

For our example, we'll use the 16-bit version.

```
int audioFormat = AudioFormat.ENCODING_PCM_16BIT;
```

Last, we'll need to specify the buffer size. We can actually ask the AudioRecord class what the minimum buffer size should be with a static method call, getMinBufferSize, passing in the sample rate, channel configuration, and audio format.

```
int bufferSizeInBytes = AudioRecord.getMinBufferSize(sampleRateInHz, channelConfig, ↵
  audioFormat);
```

Now we can construct the actual AudioRecord object.

```
AudioRecord audioRecord = new AudioRecord(audioSource, sampleRateInHz, channelConfig, ↵
  audioFormat, bufferSizeInBytes);
```

The AudioRecord class doesn't actually save the captured audio anywhere. We need to do that manually as the audio comes in. The first thing we'll probably want to do is record it to a file.

To do that, we'll need to create a file.

```
File recordingFile;
File path = new File(Environment.getExternalStorageDirectory()↵
                .getAbsolutePath() + "/Android/data/com.apress.proandroidmedia.ch07↵
.altaudiorecorder /files/");
path.mkdirs();
try {
    recordingFile = File.createTempFile("recording", ".pcm", path);
} catch (IOException e1) {
    throw new RuntimeException("Couldn't create file on SD card", e);
}
```

Next we create an OutputStream to that file, specifically one wrapped in a BufferedOutputStream and a DataOutputStream for performance and convenience reasons.

```
DataOutputStream dos = new DataOutputStream(new BufferedOutputStream(new↵
 FileOutputStream(recordingFile)));
```

Now we can start the capture and write the audio samples to the file. We'll use an array of shorts to hold the audio we read from the AudioRecord object. We'll make the array smaller than the buffer that the AudioRecord object has so that buffer won't fill up before we read it out.

To make sure this array is smaller than the buffer size, we divide by 4. The size of the buffer is in bytes and each short takes up 2 bytes, so dividing by 2 won't be enough. Dividing by 4 will make it so that this array is half the size of the AudioRecord object's internal buffer.

```
short[] buffer = new short[bufferSize/4];
```

We simply call the startRecording method on the AudioRecord object to kick things off.

```
audioRecord.startRecording();
```

After recording has started, we can construct a loop to continuously read from the AudioRecord object into our array of shorts and write that to the DataOutputStream for the file.

```
while (true) {
    int bufferReadResult = audioRecord.read(buffer, 0, bufferSize/4);
    for (int i = 0; i < bufferReadResult; i++) {
        dos.writeShort(buffer[i]);
    }
}
audioRecord.stop();
dos.close();
```

When we are done, we call stop on the AudioRecord object and close on the DataOutputStream.

Of course, in the real world, we wouldn't put this in a while (true) loop as it will never complete. We also probably want to run this in some kind of thread so that it doesn't tie up the user interface and anything else we might want the application to do while recording.

Before going through a full example, let's look at how we can play back audio as it is captured using the AudioRecord class.

Raw Audio Playback with AudioTrack

AudioTrack is a class in Android that allows us to play raw audio samples. This allows for the playback of audio captured with AudioRecord that otherwise wouldn't be playable using a MediaPlayer object.

To construct an AudioTrack object, we need to pass in a series of configuration variables describing the audio to be played.

- The first argument is the stream type. The possible values are defined as constants in the AudioManager class. We'll be using AudioManager.STREAM_MUSIC, which is the audio stream used for normal music playback.

- The second argument is the sample rate in hertz of the audio data that will be played back. In our example, we'll be capturing audio at 11,025 Hz, and therefore, to play it back, we need to specify the same value.

- The third argument is the channel configuration. The possible values, the same as those used when constructing an AudioRecord object, are defined as constants in the AudioFormat class. Their names are self-explanatory.

    - AudioFormat.CHANNEL_CONFIGURATION_MONO

    - AudioFormat.CHANNEL_CONFIGURATION_STEREO

    - AudioFormat.CHANNEL_CONFIGURATION_INVALID

    - AudioFormat.CHANNEL_CONFIGURATION_DEFAULT

- The fourth argument is the format of the audio. The possible values are the same as those used when constructing an AudioRecord object, and they are defined in AudioFormat as constants. The value used should match the value of the audio that will be passed in.

    - AudioFormat.ENCODING_DEFAULT

    - AudioFormat.ENCODING_INVALID

    - AudioFormat.ENCODING_PCM_16BIT

    - AudioFormat.ENCODING_PCM_8BIT

- The fifth argument is the size of the buffer that will be used in the object to store the audio. To determine the smallest buffer size to use, we can call getMinBufferSize, passing in the sample rate, the channel configuration, and audio format.

```
int frequency = 11025;
int channelConfiguration = AudioFormat.CHANNEL_CONFIGURATION_MONO;
int audioEncoding = AudioFormat.ENCODING_PCM_16BIT;

int bufferSize = AudioTrack.getMinBufferSize(frequency, channelConfiguration, ↵
 audioEncoding);
```

- The last argument is the mode. The possible values are defined as constants in the AudioTrack class.

  - *AudioTrack.MODE_STATIC*: The audio data will all be transferred to the AudioTrack object before playback occurs.

  - *AudioTrack.MODE_STREAM*: The audio data will continue to be transferred to the AudioTrack object while playback is in progress.

Here is our AudioTrack configuration:

```
AudioTrack audioTrack = new AudioTrack(AudioManager.STREAM_MUSIC, frequency,
            channelConfiguration, audioEncoding, bufferSize,
            AudioTrack.MODE_STREAM);
```

Once the AudioTrack is constructed, we need to open an audio source, read the audio data into a buffer, and pass it to the AudioTrack object.

We'll construct a DataInputStream from a file containing raw PCM data in the right format (11,025 Hz, 16 bit, mono).

```
DataInputStream dis = new DataInputStream(
            new BufferedInputStream(new FileInputStream(recordingFile)));
```

We can then call play on the AudioTrack and start writing audio in from the DataInputStream.

```
audioTrack.play();

while (isPlaying && dis.available() > 0) {
    int i = 0;
    while (dis.available() > 0 && i < audiodata.length) {
        audiodata[i] = dis.readShort();
        i++;
    }
    audioTrack.write(audiodata, 0, audiodata.length);
}

dis.close();
```

That covers the basics of using AudioTrack to play back audio from a file as it is recorded from an AudioRecorder.

Raw Audio Capture and Playback Example

Here is a full example that records using AudioRecord and plays back using AudioTrack. Each of these operations lives in their own thread through the use of AsyncTask, so that they don't make the application become unresponsive by running in the main thread.

```
package com.apress.proandroidmedia.ch07.altaudiorecorder;
```

```
import java.io.BufferedInputStream;
import java.io.BufferedOutputStream;
import java.io.DataInputStream;
import java.io.DataOutputStream;
import java.io.File;
import java.io.FileInputStream;
import java.io.FileOutputStream;
import java.io.IOException;

import android.app.Activity;
import android.media.AudioFormat;
import android.media.AudioManager;
import android.media.AudioRecord;
import android.media.AudioTrack;
import android.media.MediaRecorder;
import android.os.AsyncTask;
import android.os.Bundle;
import android.os.Environment;
import android.util.Log;
import android.view.View;
import android.view.View.OnClickListener;
import android.widget.Button;
import android.widget.TextView;
```

```
public class AltAudioRecorder extends Activity implements OnClickListener {
```

We have two inner classes defined—one for the recording and one for the playback. Each one extends AsyncTask.

```
    RecordAudio recordTask;
    PlayAudio playTask;

    Button startRecordingButton, stopRecordingButton, startPlaybackButton,
            stopPlaybackButton;
    TextView statusText;

    File recordingFile;
```

We'll use Booleans to keep track of whether we should be recording and playing. These will be used in the loops in recording and playback tasks.

```
    boolean isRecording = false;
    boolean isPlaying = false;
```

Here are the variables that we'll use to define the configuration of both the AudioRecord and AudioTrack objects.

```
    // These should really be constants themselves
    int frequency = 11025;
```

```
int channelConfiguration = AudioFormat.CHANNEL_CONFIGURATION_MONO;
int audioEncoding = AudioFormat.ENCODING_PCM_16BIT;

@Override
public void onCreate(Bundle savedInstanceState) {
    super.onCreate(savedInstanceState);
    setContentView(R.layout.main);

    statusText = (TextView) this.findViewById(R.id.StatusTextView);

    startRecordingButton = (Button) this .findViewById(R.id.StartRecordingButton);
    stopRecordingButton = (Button) this .findViewById(R.id.StopRecordingButton);
    startPlaybackButton = (Button) this .findViewById(R.id.StartPlaybackButton);
    stopPlaybackButton = (Button) this.findViewById(R.id.StopPlaybackButton);

    startRecordingButton.setOnClickListener(this);
    stopRecordingButton.setOnClickListener(this);
    startPlaybackButton.setOnClickListener(this);
    stopPlaybackButton.setOnClickListener(this);

    stopRecordingButton.setEnabled(false);
    startPlaybackButton.setEnabled(false);
    stopPlaybackButton.setEnabled(false);
```

The last thing we'll do in the constructor is create the file that we'll record to and play back from. In this case, we are creating the file in the preferred location for files associated with an application on the SD card.

```
    File path = new File(Environment.getExternalStorageDirectory()↩
            .getAbsolutePath() + "/Android/data/com.apress.proandroidmedia.ch07↩
.altaudiorecorder/files/");
    path.mkdirs();
    try {
        recordingFile = File.createTempFile("recording", ".pcm", path);
    } catch (IOException e) {
        throw new RuntimeException("Couldn't create file on SD card", e);
    }
}
```

The onClick method handles the Button presses generated by the user. Each one corresponds to a specific method.

```
public void onClick(View v) {
    if (v == startRecordingButton) {
        record();
    } else if (v == stopRecordingButton) {
        stopRecording();
    } else if (v == startPlaybackButton) {
        play();
    } else if (v == stopPlaybackButton) {
        stopPlaying();
    }
}
```

To start playback, we construct a new PlayAudio object and call its execute method, which is inherited from AsyncTask.

```
    public void play() {
```

```
            startPlaybackButton.setEnabled(true);

            playTask = new PlayAudio();
            playTask.execute();

            stopPlaybackButton.setEnabled(true);
        }
```

To stop playback, we set the isPlaying Boolean to false and that's it. This will cause the PlayAudio object's loop to finish.

```
        public void stopPlaying() {
            isPlaying = false;
            stopPlaybackButton.setEnabled(false);
            startPlaybackButton.setEnabled(true);
        }
```

To start recording, we construct a RecordAudio object and call its execute method.

```
        public void record() {
            startRecordingButton.setEnabled(false);
            stopRecordingButton.setEnabled(true);

            // For Fun
            startPlaybackButton.setEnabled(true);

            recordTask = new RecordAudio();
            recordTask.execute();
        }
```

To stop recording, we simply set the isRecording Boolean to false. This allows the RecordAudio object to stop looping and perform any cleanup.

```
        public void stopRecording() {
        '   isRecording = false;
        }
```

Here is our PlayAudio inner class. This class extends AsyncTask and uses an AudioTrack object to play back the audio.

```
        private class PlayAudio extends AsyncTask<Void, Integer, Void> {
            @Override
            protected Void doInBackground(Void... params) {
                isPlaying = true;

                int bufferSize = AudioTrack.getMinBufferSize(frequency,
                        channelConfiguration, audioEncoding);
                short[] audiodata = new short[bufferSize/4];

                try {
                    DataInputStream dis = new DataInputStream(
                            new BufferedInputStream(new FileInputStream(
                                    recordingFile)));

                    AudioTrack audioTrack = new AudioTrack(
                            AudioManager.STREAM_MUSIC, frequency,
                            channelConfiguration, audioEncoding, bufferSize,
                            AudioTrack.MODE_STREAM);
```

```
            audioTrack.play();

            while (isPlaying && dis.available() > 0) {
                int i = 0;
                while (dis.available() > 0 && i < audiodata.length) {
                    audiodata[i] = dis.readShort();
                    i++;
                }
                audioTrack.write(audiodata, 0, audiodata.length);
            }

            dis.close();

            startPlaybackButton.setEnabled(false);
            stopPlaybackButton.setEnabled(true);

        } catch (Throwable t) {
            Log.e("AudioTrack", "Playback Failed");
        }

        return null;
    }
}
```

Last is our RecordAudio class, which extends AsyncTask. This class runs an AudioRecord object in the background and calls publishProgress to update the UI with an indication of recording progress.

```
private class RecordAudio extends AsyncTask<Void, Integer, Void> {
    @Override
    protected Void doInBackground(Void... params) {
        isRecording = true;

        try {
            DataOutputStream dos = new DataOutputStream(
                    new BufferedOutputStream(new FileOutputStream(
                        recordingFile)));

            int bufferSize = AudioRecord.getMinBufferSize(frequency,
                    channelConfiguration, audioEncoding);

            AudioRecord audioRecord = new AudioRecord(
                    MediaRecorder.AudioSource.MIC, frequency,
                    channelConfiguration, audioEncoding, bufferSize);

            short[] buffer = new short[bufferSize];
            audioRecord.startRecording();

            int r = 0;
            while (isRecording) {
                int bufferReadResult = audioRecord.read(buffer, 0,
                        bufferSize);
                for (int i = 0; i < bufferReadResult; i++) {
                    dos.writeShort(buffer[i]);
                }

                publishProgress(new Integer(r));
```

```
            r++;
        }

        audioRecord.stop();
        dos.close();
    } catch (Throwable t) {
        Log.e("AudioRecord", "Recording Failed");
    }

    return null;
}
```

When publishProgress is called, onProgressUpdate is the method called.

```
protected void onProgressUpdate(Integer... progress) {
    statusText.setText(progress[0].toString());
}
```

When the doInBackground method completes, the following onPostExecute method is called.

```
protected void onPostExecute(Void result) {
    startRecordingButton.setEnabled(true);
    stopRecordingButton.setEnabled(false);
    startPlaybackButton.setEnabled(true);
    }
  }
}
```

Here is the layout XML for the foregoing example:

```
<?xml version="1.0" encoding="utf-8"?>
<LinearLayout xmlns:android="http://schemas.android.com/apk/res/android"
    android:orientation="vertical"
    android:layout_width="fill_parent"
    android:layout_height="fill_parent"
    >
    <TextView
        android:layout_width="fill_parent"
        android:layout_height="wrap_content" android:text="Status" android:id=↵
    "@+id/StatusTextView"/>

    <Button android:layout_width="wrap_content" android:layout_height="wrap_content"↵
     android:text="Start Recording" android:id="@+id/StartRecordingButton"></Button>
    <Button android:layout_width="wrap_content" android:layout_height="wrap_content"↵
     android:text="Stop Recording" android:id="@+id/StopRecordingButton"></Button>
    <Button android:layout_width="wrap_content" android:layout_height="wrap_content"↵
     android:text="Start Playback" android:id="@+id/StartPlaybackButton"></Button>
    <Button android:layout_width="wrap_content" android:layout_height="wrap_content"↵
     android:text="Stop Playback" android:id="@+id/StopPlaybakButton" ></Button>
</LinearLayout>
```

And, we'll need to add these permissions to AndroidManifest.xml.

```
<uses-permission android:name="android.permission.RECORD_AUDIO"></uses-permission>
    <uses-permission android:name="android.permission.WRITE_EXTERNAL_STORAGE">↵
</uses-permission>
```

As we have seen, using the AudioRecord and AudioTrack classes to create a capture and playback application is much more cumbersome than working with the MediaRecorder and MediaPlayer classes. But as we'll see in the next chapter, it is worth the effort when we need to do any type of audio processing or want to synthesize audio.

Summary

In this chapter, we looked at three different methods for recording audio on Android. Each of them comes with their own plusses and minuses. Using the built-in sound recorder is great for no-fuss audio recordings, where little or no programmatic control is needed. Using the MediaRecorder allows us to take it a step further, allowing control over the length of time media is recorded and other aspects but leaving the interface up to us. Last we investigated the ability to record raw samples with AudioRecord. Using this we have the most control and flexibility but have to do the most work in order to capture and work with the audio.

In the next chapter, we'll look more at audio possibilities, investigating audio processing and synthesis.

Chapter 8

Audio Synthesis and Analysis

At the end of the last chapter, we looked at a way to capture raw PCM audio and play it back using the `AudioRecord` and `AudioTrack` classes. In this chapter, we'll continue using those classes to both algorithmically synthesize audio and analyze recorded audio.

Digital Audio Synthesis

Digital audio synthesis is a very broad topic with a great deal of theory, mathematics, engineering, and history behind it. Unfortunately, most of the topic overall is out of the scope of what can be covered in this book. What we will do is look at some basic examples on how we can harness a few built-in classes on Android to create audio from scratch.

As you probably know, sound is formed by a repetitive change in pressure in air (or other substance) in the form of a wave. Certain frequencies of these oscillations, otherwise known as sound waves, are audible, meaning our ears are sensitive to that number of repetitions in a period of time. This range is somewhere between 12 Hz (12 cycles per second), which is a very low sound such as a rumble, and 20 kHz (20,000 cycles per second), which is a very high-pitched sound.

To create audio, we need to cause the air to vibrate at the frequency desired for the sound we want. In the digital realm, this is generally done with a speaker that is driven by an analog electric signal. Digital audio systems contain a chip or board that performs a digital-to-analog conversion (DAC). A DAC will take in data in the form of a series of numbers that represent audio samples and convert that into an electrical voltage, which is translated into sound by the speaker.

In order to synthesize audio, we simply need to synthesize the audio samples and feed them to the appropriate mechanism. In the case of Android, that mechanism is the `AudioTrack` class.

As we learned in the last chapter, the AudioTrack class allows us to play raw audio samples (such as those captured by the AudioRecord class).

Playing a Synthesized Sound

Here is a quick example showing how to construct an AudioTrack class and pass in data to play. For a full discussion of the parameters used to construct the AudioTrack object, please see the "Raw Audio Playback with AudioTrack" section of Chapter 7.

This example uses an inner class that extends AsyncTask, AudioSynthesisTask. AsyncTask defines a method called doInBackground, which runs any code that is placed inside it in a thread that is separate from the main thread of the activity. This allows the activity and its UI to be responsive, as the loop that feeds the write method of our AudioTrack object would otherwise tie it up.

```
package com.apress.proandroidmedia.ch08.audiosynthesis;

import android.app.Activity;
import android.media.AudioFormat;
import android.media.AudioManager;
import android.media.AudioTrack;
import android.os.AsyncTask;
import android.os.Bundle;
import android.view.View;
import android.view.View.OnClickListener;
import android.widget.Button;

public class AudioSynthesis extends Activity implements OnClickListener {

    Button startSound;
    Button endSound;

    AudioSynthesisTask audioSynth;

    boolean keepGoing = false;

    @Override
    public void onCreate(Bundle savedInstanceState) {
        super.onCreate(savedInstanceState);
        setContentView(R.layout.main);

        startSound = (Button) this.findViewById(R.id.StartSound);
        startSound.setOnClickListener(this);

        endSound = (Button) this.findViewById(R.id.EndSound);
        endSound.setOnClickListener(this);

        endSound.setEnabled(false);
    }

    @Override
    public void onPause() {
        super.onPause();
        keepGoing = false;
```

```java
            endSound.setEnabled(false);
            startSound.setEnabled(true);
    }

    public void onClick(View v) {
        if (v == startSound) {
            keepGoing = true;

            audioSynth = new AudioSynthesisTask();
            audioSynth.execute();

            endSound.setEnabled(true);
            startSound.setEnabled(false);
        } else if (v == endSound) {
            keepGoing = false;

            endSound.setEnabled(false);
            startSound.setEnabled(true);
        }
    }

    private class AudioSynthesisTask extends AsyncTask<Void, Void, Void>
    {
        @Override
        protected Void doInBackground(Void... params) {
            final int SAMPLE_RATE = 11025;

            int minSize = AudioTrack.getMinBufferSize(SAMPLE_RATE,
                    AudioFormat.CHANNEL_CONFIGURATION_MONO,
                    AudioFormat.ENCODING_PCM_16BIT);

            AudioTrack audioTrack = new AudioTrack(
                    AudioManager.STREAM_MUSIC, SAMPLE_RATE,
                    AudioFormat.CHANNEL_CONFIGURATION_MONO,
                    AudioFormat.ENCODING_PCM_16BIT,
                    minSize,
                    AudioTrack.MODE_STREAM);

            audioTrack.play();

            short[] buffer = {
                    8130,15752,22389,27625,31134,32695,32210,29711,25354,19410,12253,
                    4329,-3865,-11818,-19032,-25055,-29511,-32121,-32722,-31276,-27874,
                    -22728,-16160,-8582,-466
            };

            while (keepGoing) {
                    audioTrack.write(buffer, 0, buffer.length);
            }

            return null;
        }
    }
}
```

Here is the layout XML in use by the preceding activity.

```xml
<?xml version="1.0" encoding="utf-8"?>
<LinearLayout xmlns:android="http://schemas.android.com/apk/res/android"
    android:orientation="vertical"
    android:layout_width="fill_parent"
    android:layout_height="fill_parent"
    >
    <Button android:layout_width="wrap_content" android:layout_height="wrap_content"
     android:id="@+id/StartSound" android:text="Start Sound"></Button>
    <Button android:layout_width="wrap_content" android:layout_height="wrap_content"
     android:id="@+id/EndSound" android:text="End Sound"></Button>
</LinearLayout>
```

The key to the foregoing code is the array of shorts. These are the audio samples that are continuously being passed into the AudioTrack object through the write method. In this case, the samples oscillate from 8,130 to 32,695, down to -32,121 and back up to -466. If we plotted these values on a graph, these samples taken together will construct a waveform. Since sound is created with oscillating pressure, and each of the samples represents a pressure value, having these samples represent a waveform is required to create sound. Varying this waveform allows us to create different kinds of audio. The following set of samples describes a short waveform, only ten samples, and therefore represents a high-frequency sound, one that has many oscillations per second. Low-frequency sounds would have a waveform that spans many more samples at a fixed sample rate.

```java
short[] buffer = {
    8130,15752,32695,12253,4329,
    -3865,-19032,-32722,-16160,-466
};
```

Generating Samples

Using a little bit of math, we can algorithmically create these samples. The classic sine wave can be reproduced. This example produces a sine wave at 440 Hz.

```java
package com.apress.proandroidmedia.ch08.audiosynthesis;

import android.app.Activity;
import android.media.AudioFormat;
import android.media.AudioManager;
import android.media.AudioTrack;
import android.os.AsyncTask;
import android.os.Bundle;
import android.util.Log;
import android.view.View;
import android.view.View.OnClickListener;
import android.widget.Button;

public class AudioSynthesis extends Activity implements OnClickListener {

    Button startSound;
    Button endSound;
```

```
    AudioSynthesisTask audioSynth;

    boolean keepGoing = false;

    float synth_frequency = 440; // 440 Hz, Middle A

    @Override
    public void onCreate(Bundle savedInstanceState) {
        super.onCreate(savedInstanceState);
        setContentView(R.layout.main);

        startSound = (Button) this.findViewById(R.id.StartSound);
        startSound.setOnClickListener(this);

        endSound = (Button) this.findViewById(R.id.EndSound);
        endSound.setOnClickListener(this);

        endSound.setEnabled(false);
    }

    @Override
    public void onPause() {
        super.onPause();
        keepGoing = false;

        endSound.setEnabled(false);
        startSound.setEnabled(true);
    }

    public void onClick(View v) {
        if (v == startSound) {
            keepGoing = true;

            audioSynth = new AudioSynthesisTask();
            audioSynth.execute();

            endSound.setEnabled(true);
            startSound.setEnabled(false);
        } else if (v == endSound) {
            keepGoing = false;

            endSound.setEnabled(false);
            startSound.setEnabled(true);
        }
    }

    private class AudioSynthesisTask extends AsyncTask<Void, Void, Void>
    {
        @Override
        protected Void doInBackground(Void... params) {
            final int SAMPLE_RATE= 11025;

            int minSize = AudioTrack.getMinBufferSize(SAMPLE_RATE,
                    AudioFormat.CHANNEL_CONFIGURATION_MONO,
                    AudioFormat.ENCODING_PCM_16BIT);

            AudioTrack audioTrack = new AudioTrack(AudioManager.STREAM_MUSIC,
```

```
                        SAMPLE_RATE,
                        AudioFormat.CHANNEL_CONFIGURATION_MONO,
                        AudioFormat.ENCODING_PCM_16BIT,
                        minSize,
                        AudioTrack.MODE_STREAM);

            audioTrack.play();

            short[] buffer = new short[minSize];


            float angular_frequency =
                (float)(2*Math.PI) * synth_frequency / SAMPLE_RATE;
            float angle = 0;

            while (keepGoing) {
                for (int i = 0; i < buffer.length; i++)
                {

                    buffer[i] = (short)(Short.MAX_VALUE * ((float) Math.sin(angle)));
                    angle += angular_frequency;
                }
                audioTrack.write(buffer, 0, buffer.length);
            }

            return null;
        }
    }
}
```

Here is the layout XML file for the foregoing activity:

```
<?xml version="1.0" encoding="utf-8"?>
<LinearLayout xmlns:android="http://schemas.android.com/apk/res/android"
    android:orientation="vertical"
    android:layout_width="fill_parent"
    android:layout_height="fill_parent"
    >

    <Button android:layout_width="wrap_content" android:layout_height="wrap_content"↵
        android:id="@+id/StartSound" android:text="Start Sound"></Button>
    <Button android:layout_width="wrap_content" android:layout_height="wrap_content"↵
        android:id="@+id/EndSound" android:text="End Sound"></Button>
</LinearLayout>
```

Changing the synth_frequency would allow us to reproduce any other frequency we would like. Of course, changing the function used to generate the values would change the sound as well. You may want to try clamping the samples to Short.MAX_VALUE or Short.MIN_VALUE to do a quick and dirty square wave example.

Of course, this just scratches the surface of what can be done with audio synthesis on Android. Given AudioTrack allows us to play raw PCM samples, almost any technique that can be used to generate digital audio can be utilized on Android, taking into account processor speed and memory limitations.

What follows is an example application that takes some techniques from Chapter 4 for tracking finger position on the touchscreen and the foregoing example code for generating audio. In this application, we'll generate audio and choose the frequency based upon the location of the user's finger on the x axis of the touchscreen.

```
package com.apress.proandroidmedia.ch08.fingersynthesis;
```

```
import android.app.Activity;
import android.media.AudioFormat;
import android.media.AudioManager;
import android.media.AudioTrack;
import android.os.AsyncTask;
import android.os.Bundle;
import android.util.Log;
import android.view.MotionEvent;
import android.view.View;
import android.view.View.OnTouchListener;
```

Our activity will implement OnTouchListener so that we can track the touch locations.

```
public class FingerSynthesis extends Activity implements OnTouchListener {
```

Just like the previous example, we'll use an AsyncTask to provide a thread for generating and playing the audio samples.

```
    AudioSynthesisTask audioSynth;
```

We need a base audio frequency that will be played when the finger is at the 0 position on the x axis. This will be lowest frequency played.

```
    static final float BASE_FREQUENCY = 440;
```

We'll be varying the synth_frequency float as the finger moves. When we start the app, we'll set it to the BASE_FREQUENCY.

```
    float synth_frequency = BASE_FREQUENCY;
```

We'll use the play Boolean to determine when we should actually being playing audio or not. It will be controlled by the touch events.

```
    boolean play = false;

    @Override
    public void onCreate(Bundle savedInstanceState) {
        super.onCreate(savedInstanceState);

        setContentView(R.layout.main);
```

In our layout, we have only one item, a LinearLayout with the ID of MainView. We'll get a reference to this and register the OnTouchListener to be our activity. This way our activity's onTouch method will be called when the user touches the screen.

```
        View mainView = this.findViewById(R.id.MainView);
        mainView.setOnTouchListener(this);

        audioSynth = new AudioSynthesisTask();
        audioSynth.execute();
    }

    @Override
    public void onPause() {
```

```
        super.onPause();
        play = false;

        finish();
    }
```

Our onTouch method, called when the user touches, stops touching, or drags a finger on the screen, will set the play Boolean to true or false depending on the action of the user. This will control whether audio samples are generated. It will also track the location of the user's finger on the x axis of the touchscreen and adjust the synth_frequency variable accordingly.

```
public boolean onTouch(View v, MotionEvent event) {
    int action = event.getAction();
    switch (action)
    {
        case MotionEvent.ACTION_DOWN:
            play = true;
            synth_frequency = event.getX() + BASE_FREQUENCY;
            Log.v("FREQUENCY",""+synth_frequency);
            break;
        case MotionEvent.ACTION_MOVE:
            play = true;
            synth_frequency = event.getX() + BASE_FREQUENCY;
            Log.v("FREQUENCY",""+synth_frequency);
            break;
        case MotionEvent.ACTION_UP:
            play = false;
            break;
        case MotionEvent.ACTION_CANCEL:
            break;
        default:
            break;
    }
    return true;
}

private class AudioSynthesisTask extends AsyncTask<Void, Void, Void>
{
    @Override
    protected Void doInBackground(Void... params) {
        final int SAMPLE_RATE= 11025;

        int minSize = AudioTrack.getMinBufferSize(SAMPLE_RATE,
                AudioFormat.CHANNEL_CONFIGURATION_MONO,
                AudioFormat.ENCODING_PCM_16BIT);

        AudioTrack audioTrack = new AudioTrack(AudioManager.STREAM_MUSIC,
                SAMPLE_RATE,
                AudioFormat.CHANNEL_CONFIGURATION_MONO,
                AudioFormat.ENCODING_PCM_16BIT,
                minSize,
                AudioTrack.MODE_STREAM);

        audioTrack.play();

        short[] buffer = new short[minSize];
```

```
            float angle = 0;
```

Finally, in the AudioSynthesisTask, in the loop that generates the audio, we'll check the play Boolean and do the calculations to generate the audio samples based on the synth_frequency variable, which we are changing based upon the user's finger position.

```
        while (true) {

            if (play)
            {
                for (int i = 0; i < buffer.length; i++)
                {
                    float angular_frequency =
                        (float)(2*Math.PI) * synth_frequency / SAMPLE_RATE;

                    buffer[i] =
                        (short)(Short.MAX_VALUE * ((float) Math.sin(angle)));
                    angle += angular_frequency;
                }
                audioTrack.write(buffer, 0, buffer.length);
            } else {
                try {
                    Thread.sleep(50);
                } catch (InterruptedException e) {
                    e.printStackTrace();
                }
            }
        }
    }
}
```

Here is the layout XML:

```
<?xml version="1.0" encoding="utf-8"?>
<LinearLayout xmlns:android="http://schemas.android.com/apk/res/android"
    android:orientation="vertical"
    android:layout_width="fill_parent"
    android:layout_height="fill_parent"
    android:id="@+id/MainView"
    >
</LinearLayout>
```

This example shows some of the power and flexibility of the AudioTrack class. Since we can algorithmically generate audio, we can use just about any method we would like to determine its features (its pitch or frequency in this example).

Audio Analysis

Now that we have gone over more advanced ways that AudioTrack may be used, how about looking at what else we might do with audio as it comes in through an AudioRecord object?

Capturing Sound for Analysis

As previously described, sound is vibration traveling through a substance. These vibrations can be captured by a microphone. Microphones convert the vibrations that travel through air into a constantly varying electrical current. When a microphone is used to capture sound by a computer, that sound is digitized. Specifically, amplitude samples of a specific size (sample size) are taken many times a second (sample rate). This stream of data is called a PCM (pulse code modulation) stream, which forms the foundation for digital audio. Taken all together, the samples represented in the PCM stream digitally represent the audio waveform that is captured. The higher the sample rate, the more accurate the representation and the higher the frequency of audio that can be captured.

As we learned in the previous chapter, when we started working with the AudioRecord class, these parameters may be passed into the constructor of the AudioRecord class when creating an object. To revisit what each of the parameters means, please see the "Raw Audio Recording with AudioRecord" section in Chapter 7.

> **NOTE:** The Nyquist sampling theorem, named after Harry Nyquist, who was an engineer for Bell Labs in the early to mid-twentieth century, explains that the highest frequency that may be captured by a digitizing system is one half of the sample rate used. Therefore, in order to capture audio at 440 Hz (middle A), our system needs to capture samples at 880 Hz or higher.

Here is a quick recap of the steps required to capture audio using an object of type AudioRecord.

```
int frequency = 8000;
int channelConfiguration = AudioFormat.CHANNEL_CONFIGURATION_MONO;
int audioEncoding = AudioFormat.ENCODING_PCM_16BIT;

int bufferSize = AudioRecord.getMinBufferSize(frequency,
            channelConfiguration, audioEncoding);

AudioRecord audioRecord = new AudioRecord(
            MediaRecorder.AudioSource.MIC, frequency,
            channelConfiguration, audioEncoding, bufferSize);

short[] buffer = new short[blockSize];
audioRecord.startRecording();

while (started) {
    int bufferReadResult = audioRecord.read(buffer, 0, blockSize);
}

audioRecord.stop();
```

The foregoing code doesn't actually do anything with the audio that is captured. Normally we would want to write it to a file or to analyze it in some other manner.

Visualizing Frequencies

One common way that people typically use to analyze audio is to visualize the frequencies that exist within it. Commonly these types of visuals are employed with equalizers that allow the adjustment of the levels of various frequency ranges.

The technique used to break an audio signal down into component frequencies employs a mathematic transformation called a discrete Fourier transform (DFT). A DFT is commonly used to translate data from a time base to a frequency base. One algorithm used to perform DFT is a fast Fourier transform (FFT), which is very efficient but unfortunately complex.

Fortunately, many implementations of FFT algorithms exist that are in the public domain or are open source and that we may employ. One such version is a Java port of the FFTPACK library, originally developed by Paul Swarztrauber of the National Center for Atmospheric Research. The Java port was performed by Baoshe Zhang of the University of Lethbridge in Alberta, Canada. Various implementations are available online at www.netlib.org/fftpack/. The one we'll be using is archived in a file called jfftpack.tgz linked off of that page. It is directly downloadable via www.netlib.org/fftpack/jfftpack.tgz.

To use this or any other package containing Java source code in an Eclipse Android project, we need to import the source into our project. This archive contains the correct directory structure for the package, so we just drag the top-level folder in the javasource directory (ca) into the src directory of our project.

Here is an example that draws the graphic portion of a graphic equalizer.

```
package com.apress.proandroidmedia.ch08.audioprocessing;

import android.app.Activity;
import android.graphics.Bitmap;
import android.graphics.Canvas;
import android.graphics.Color;
import android.graphics.Paint;
import android.media.AudioFormat;
import android.media.AudioRecord;
import android.media.MediaRecorder;
import android.os.AsyncTask;
import android.os.Bundle;
import android.util.Log;
import android.view.View;
import android.view.View.OnClickListener;
import android.widget.Button;
import android.widget.ImageView;
```

We'll import the RealDoubleFFT class in the fftpack package.

```
import ca.uol.aig.fftpack.RealDoubleFFT;

public class AudioProcessing extends Activity implements OnClickListener {
```

We'll use a frequency of 8 kHz, one audio channel, and 16 bit samples in the AudioRecord object.

```
int frequency = 8000;
int channelConfiguration = AudioFormat.CHANNEL_CONFIGURATION_MONO;
int audioEncoding = AudioFormat.ENCODING_PCM_16BIT;
```

transformer will be our FFT object, and we'll be dealing with 256 samples at a time from the AudioRecord object through the FFT object. The number of samples we use will correspond to the number of component frequencies we will get after we run them through the FFT object. We are free to choose a different size, but we do need concern ourselves with memory and performance issues as the math required to the calculation is processor-intensive.

```
private RealDoubleFFT transformer;
int blockSize = 256;

Button startStopButton;
boolean started = false;
```

RecordAudio is an inner class defined here that extends AsyncTask.

```
RecordAudio recordTask;
```

We'll be using an ImageView to display a Bitmap image. This image will represent the levels of the various frequencies that are in the current audio stream. To draw these levels, we'll use Canvas and Paint objects constructed from the Bitmap.

```
ImageView imageView;
Bitmap bitmap;
Canvas canvas;
Paint paint;

@Override
public void onCreate(Bundle savedInstanceState) {
    super.onCreate(savedInstanceState);
    setContentView(R.layout.main);

    startStopButton = (Button) this.findViewById(R.id.StartStopButton);
    startStopButton.setOnClickListener(this);
```

The RealDoubleFFT class constructor takes in the number of samples that we'll deal with at a time. This also represents the number of distinct ranges of frequencies that will be output.

```
    transformer = new RealDoubleFFT(blockSize);
```

Here is the setup of the ImageView and related object for drawing.

```
    imageView = (ImageView) this.findViewById(R.id.ImageView01);
    bitmap = Bitmap.createBitmap((int)256,(int)100,Bitmap.Config.ARGB_8888);
    canvas = new Canvas(bitmap);
    paint = new Paint();
    paint.setColor(Color.GREEN);
    imageView.setImageBitmap(bitmap);
}
```

Most of the work in this activity is done in the following class, called RecordAudio, which extends AsyncTask. Using AsyncTask, we run the methods that will tie up the user interface on a separate thread. Anything that is placed in the doInBackground method will be run in this manner.

```
private class RecordAudio extends AsyncTask<Void, double[], Void> {
    @Override
    protected Void doInBackground(Void... params) {
        try {
```

We'll set up and use AudioRecord in the normal manner.

```
            int bufferSize = AudioRecord.getMinBufferSize(frequency,
                    channelConfiguration, audioEncoding);

            AudioRecord audioRecord = new AudioRecord(
                    MediaRecorder.AudioSource.MIC, frequency,
                    channelConfiguration, audioEncoding, bufferSize);
```

The short array, buffer, will take in the raw PCM samples from the AudioRecord object. The double array, toTransform, will hold the same data but in the form of doubles, as that is what the FFT class requires.

```
            short[] buffer = new short[blockSize];
            double[] toTransform = new double[blockSize];

            audioRecord.startRecording();

            while (started) {
                int bufferReadResult = audioRecord.read(buffer, 0, blockSize);
```

After we read the data from the AudioRecord object, we loop through and translate it from short values to double values. We can't do this directly by casting, as the values expected should be between -1.0 and 1.0 rather than the full range. Dividing the short by 32,768.0 will do that, as that value is the maximum value of short.

NOTE: There is a constant Short.MAX_VALUE that could be used instead.

```
                for (int i = 0; i < blockSize && i < bufferReadResult; i++) {
                    toTransform[i] = (double) buffer[i] / 32768.0; // signed 16 bit
                }
```

Next we'll pass the array of double values to the FFT object. The FFT object re-uses the same array to hold the output values. The data contained will be in the frequency domain rather than the time domain. This means that the first element in the array will not represent the first sample in time—rather, it will represent the levels of the first set of frequencies.

Since we are using 256 values (or ranges) and our sample rate is 8,000, we can determine that each element in the array will cover approximately 15.625 Hz. We come up with this figure by dividing the sample rate in half (as the highest frequency we can capture is half the sample rate) and then dividing by 256. Therefore the data represented in the first element of the array will represent the level of audio that is between 0 and 15.625 Hz.

```
            transformer.ft(toTransform);
```

Calling publishProgress calls onProgressUpdate.

```
            publishProgress(toTransform);
        }

        audioRecord.stop();
    } catch (Throwable t) {
        Log.e("AudioRecord", "Recording Failed");
    }

    return null;
}
```

onProgressUpdate runs on the main thread in our activity and can therefore interact with the user interface without problems. In this implementation, we are passing in the data after it has been run through the FFT object. This method takes care of drawing the data on the screen as a series of lines at most 100 pixels tall. Each line represents one of the elements in the array and therefore a range of 15.625 Hz. The first line represents frequencies ranging from 0 to 15.625 Hz, and the last line represents frequencies ranging from 3,984.375 to 4,000 Hz. Figure 8–1 shows what this looks like in action.

```
protected void onProgressUpdate(double[]... toTransform) {
    canvas.drawColor(Color.BLACK);

    for (int i = 0; i < toTransform[0].length; i++) {
        int x = i;
        int downy = (int) (100 - (toTransform[0][i] * 10));
        int upy = 100;

        canvas.drawLine(x, downy, x, upy, paint);
    }
    imageView.invalidate();
}
}

public void onClick(View v) {
    if (started) {
        started = false;
        startStopButton.setText("Start");
        recordTask.cancel(true);
    } else {
        started = true;
        startStopButton.setText("Stop");
        recordTask = new RecordAudio();
        recordTask.execute();
    }
}
}
```

Here is the layout XML file used by the AudioProcessing activity just defined.

```
<?xml version="1.0" encoding="utf-8"?>
<LinearLayout xmlns:android="http://schemas.android.com/apk/res/android"
    android:orientation="vertical"
    android:layout_width="fill_parent"
    android:layout_height="fill_parent"
    >
```

```
<TextView
    android:layout_width="fill_parent"
    android:layout_height="wrap_content"
    android:text="@string/hello"
/>
    <ImageView android:id="@+id/ImageView01" android:layout_width="wrap_content"↵
android:layout_height="wrap_content"></ImageView><Button android:text="Start"↵
android:id="@+id/StartStopButton" android:layout_width="wrap_content"↵
android:layout_height="wrap_content"></Button>
</LinearLayout>
```

Figure 8–1. *AudioProcessing activity running*

Summary

With this chapter, we have concluded our coverage of audio on Android and have done so by showing how flexible it can be. Although we only scratched the surface of both audio synthesis and analysis, doing so shows the potential of what can be done and how flexible the `AudioTrack` and `AudioRecord` classes in Android are.

Next we'll turn our attention to video.

Chapter 9

Introduction to Video

Continuing on our journey through Android's media capabilities, we'll now turn our attention to video. In this chapter, we'll explore the various means we can use for video playback on Android as well as what formats are supported.

Video Playback

Technically, some mobile phones have had video capabilities previous to 2004. In reality, though, video on mobile phones didn't really take off in the US until the introduction of the iPhone in 2007. Since then, every smartphone worth its name has supported video playback, if not video capture. As we'll explore throughout this chapter, Android is no exception.

Supported Formats

Before we get into the specific mechanics of how to play video, we should look at the types of video that we can play. Although Android supports playing back a variety of video formats and the types it can play back is slowly increasing, it certainly doesn't cover the wide range of video formats available.

In general Android's support is consistent with other mobile phones. It supports the 3GP (.3gp) and MPEG-4 (.mp4) file formats. 3GP is a video standard derived from MPEG-4 specifically for use by mobile devices.

As far as codecs go, Android supports H.263, a codec designed for low-latency and low-bitrate videoconferencing applications. H.263 video is supported in either MPEG-4 (.mp4) or 3GP (.3gp) files. Android also supports MPEG-4 Simple Profile in 3GP files (.3gp) as well as H.264.

H.264 is also referred to as MPEG-4 part 10 or AVC (Advanced Video Coding). It is one of the contenders for the video codec crown and probably offers the widest amount of support across software and hardware. H.264 is supported by Silverlight, Flash, iPhone/iPod, Blu-ray devices, and so on. Android supports H.264 encoded video in the MPEG-4 container format (.mp4).

Depending on when you are reading this book, Android probably also supports WebM (Android 3.0 and later), the open and royalty-free media container that holds VP8-encoded video and Vorbis-encoded audio. WebM was introduced shortly after Google acquired On2 Technologies and released the VP8 codec into the public domain.

A large number of desktop video conversion tools work to aid the conversion of video for use with Android devices. The hard part is getting the settings correct. In general, if the tool has a preset for Android devices, you are just fine. If not, it is more than likely any presets that a tool might have for the iPhone will also work with Android devices since the range of supported formats is very close between the two.

Playback Using an Intent

As with most of Android's capabilities that we have explored in this book, simply playing back a video can be done easily, using an intent to trigger the built-in Media Player application's playback activity.

For this example, I captured a video using QuickTime X on a Mac laptop with a built-in iSight. I exported this video using QuickTime X's Save As command and selected "iPhone" as the format. This created a video that I named Test_Movie.m4v. (The .m4v extension was given by QuickTime. Unfortunately, it isn't standard, which may indicate that the file may not be a fully standards-compliant MPEG-4 file. Nevertheless, it doesn't seem to present any issues on Android devices.) This video is available online at www.mobvcasting.com/android/video/Test_Movie.m4v for you to download if you would like to test with it.

The following code requires that this video be on root of the SD card on your Android device. To do this, you should be able to connect the device to your computer via a USB cable and select the menu item in the status bar pull-down that states "USB connected. Select to copy files to/from your computer." This should bring up a screen that allows you to "Turn on USB storage." Doing so should cause your phone to be mounted as a removable drive to your computer, and the video file can then be copied over. Don't forget to unmount the drive and "Turn off USB storage" before attempting to run the following code. If you don't, you'll get an error as the program running on the phone cannot access the SD card to read the video file while your computer has access to it.

To create the intent that will trigger the built-in Media Player application's playback activity, we'll construct an activity using the Intent.ACTION_VIEW constant and pass in the URI and the MIME-type of the file via the setDataAndType method. This allows Android to choose the preferred activity for playback. Figure 9–1 shows the built-in Media Player from Android 2.2 playing video specified in this manner.

```
package com.apress.proandroidmedia.ch09.videointent;

import android.app.Activity;
import android.content.Intent;
import android.net.Uri;
import android.os.Bundle;
import android.os.Environment;
```

```
import android.view.View;
import android.view.View.OnClickListener;
import android.widget.Button;

public class VideoPlayerIntent extends Activity implements OnClickListener {
    Button playButton;

    @Override
    public void onCreate(Bundle savedInstanceState) {
        super.onCreate(savedInstanceState);
        setContentView(R.layout.main);
        playButton = (Button) this.findViewById(R.id.PlayButton);
        playButton.setOnClickListener(this);
    }

    public void onClick(View v) {
        Intent intent = new Intent(android.content.Intent.ACTION_VIEW);
        Uri data = Uri.parse(Environment.getExternalStorageDirectory().getPath() +↵
"/Test_Movie.m4v");
        intent.setDataAndType(data, "video/mp4");
        startActivity(intent);
    }
}
```

Figure 9–1. *Built-in Media Player application playing video specified via an intent*

Playback Using VideoView

VideoView is a View that has video playback capabilities and can be used directly in a layout. It is very straightforward to use.

The following layout XML file, main.xml, specifies a VideoView inside a LinearLayout.

```
<?xml version="1.0" encoding="utf-8"?>
<LinearLayout xmlns:android="http://schemas.android.com/apk/res/android"
    android:orientation="vertical"
    android:layout_width="fill_parent"
    android:layout_height="fill_parent"
    >
```

```
    <VideoView android:layout_width="wrap_content" android:layout_height="wrap_content"↵
        android:id="@+id/VideoView"></VideoView>
</LinearLayout>
```

To utilize this VideoView, we simply have to gain a reference to it in the normal way, using findViewById, passing in the ID (R.id.VideoView). Once we have the object, we can set the Uri to the video file with setVideoURI and then call the start method to play.

```
package com.apress.proandroidmedia.ch09.videoview;

import android.app.Activity;
import android.net.Uri;
import android.os.Bundle;
import android.os.Environment;
import android.widget.VideoView;

public class ViewTheVideo extends Activity {
    VideoView vv;

    @Override
    public void onCreate(Bundle savedInstanceState) {
        super.onCreate(savedInstanceState);
        setContentView(R.layout.main);

        vv = (VideoView) this.findViewById(R.id.VideoView);
        Uri videoUri = Uri.parse(Environment.getExternalStorageDirectory().getPath() +↵
    "/Test_Movie.m4v");
        vv.setVideoURI(videoUri);
        vv.start();
    }
}
```

Figure 9–2 shows the foregoing example in action.

Figure 9–2. *VideoView example*

Adding Controls with MediaController

The VideoView has relatively few capabilities for controlling the playback of video. Specifically it has a start and a pause method. In order to provide more controls, we can instantiate a MediaController and set it via setMediaController to be the controller of the VideoView.

The default MediaController has rewind, pause, play, and fast-forward buttons along with a scrubber and progress bar combination that can be used to seek to any point in the video.

Here is an update to our VideoView example to include a MediaController within the onCreate method after the content view is set by the setContentView method.

```
vv = (VideoView) this.findViewById(R.id.VideoView);
vv.setMediaController(new MediaController(this));
Uri videoUri = Uri.parse(Environment.getExternalStorageDirectory().getPath() +↵
"/Test_Movie.m4v");
vv.setVideoURI(videoUri);
vv.start();
```

Figure 9–3. *VideoView with a default* `MediaController`

Playback Using a MediaPlayer

In Chapters 6 and 7, those dealing with audio and networked audio, we introduced the `MediaPlayer` class. The very same `MediaPlayer` class can also be used for video playback, in much the same manner.

Using a `MediaPlayer` object for video playback gives us the greatest amount of flexibility in the control of the playback itself, as compared with playing video using `VideoView` or via an intent. In fact, the mechanism used to handle the actual playback within the `VideoView` and the activity triggered via the intent is a `MediaPlayer`.

> **NOTE:** Unfortunately, none of the video playback classes are as flexible as the most flexible audio playback class, `AudioTrack`, which allows us to generate on the fly the data that will be played.

MediaPlayer States

MediaPlayer objects operate as a state machine. This means that operations need to be performed in a specific order and various methods should be called only when the object is in the correct state to handle them.

The MediaPlayer class defines several listeners that allow applications that use it to be notified of various state changes and act accordingly.

Let's go through a full MediaPlayer example to explore further. Figure 9–4 shows the diagram again for reference.

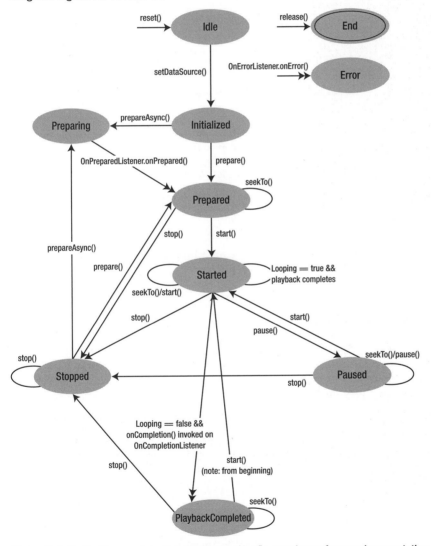

Figure 9–4. *MediaPlayer state diagram from* MediaPlayer *class reference documentation*

MediaPlayer Example

The following is a full example using the MediaPlayer to create a custom video playback application. Figure 9–5 shows the application running.

```
package com.apress.proandroidmedia.ch09.videoplayercustom;
```

```
import java.io.IOException;
```

```
import android.app.Activity;
import android.os.Bundle;
import android.os.Environment;
import android.util.Log;
import android.view.Display;
import android.widget.LinearLayout;
```

We are importing the MediaPlayer and several of its inner classes that are interfaces we'll be implementing.

```
import android.media.MediaPlayer;
import android.media.MediaPlayer.OnCompletionListener;
import android.media.MediaPlayer.OnErrorListener;
import android.media.MediaPlayer.OnInfoListener;
import android.media.MediaPlayer.OnPreparedListener;
import android.media.MediaPlayer.OnSeekCompleteListener;
import android.media.MediaPlayer.OnVideoSizeChangedListener;
```

SurfaceHolder and SurfaceView will be used to draw the video.

```
import android.view.SurfaceHolder;
import android.view.SurfaceView;
```

Our activity will implement all of the MediaPlayer state change listeners as well as the SurfaceHolder.Callback interface, which will enable us to get notified of changes to a SurfaceView.

```
public class CustomVideoPlayer extends Activity
    implements OnCompletionListener, OnErrorListener, OnInfoListener,
    OnPreparedListener, OnSeekCompleteListener, OnVideoSizeChangedListener,
    SurfaceHolder.Callback
{
    Display currentDisplay;

    SurfaceView surfaceView;
    SurfaceHolder surfaceHolder;
```

The workhorse of our application will be this MediaPlayer object.

```
    MediaPlayer mediaPlayer;

    int videoWidth = 0;
    int videoHeight = 0;

    boolean readyToPlay = false;

    public final static String LOGTAG = "CUSTOM_VIDEO_PLAYER";

    @Override
```

```
public void onCreate(Bundle savedInstanceState) {
    super.onCreate(savedInstanceState);
    setContentView(R.layout.main);
```

After we set the content view, we can get a reference to the `SurfaceView` defined in the layout XML and get a reference to the `SurfaceHolder`, which allows us to monitor what happens to the underlying `Surface`.

```
surfaceView = (SurfaceView) this.findViewById(R.id.SurfaceView);
surfaceHolder = surfaceView.getHolder();
```

Since our activity implements `SurfaceHolder.Callback`, we'll assign it to be the callback listener.

```
surfaceHolder.addCallback(this);
```

We need to make sure the underlying surface is a push buffer surface, which is currently required for video playback and camera previews.

```
surfaceHolder.setType(SurfaceHolder.SURFACE_TYPE_PUSH_BUFFERS);
```

Now we start constructing the actual `MediaPlayer` object. We aren't passing in any parameters, getting back a generic `MediaPlayer` in the "idle" state.

```
mediaPlayer = new MediaPlayer();
```

We'll also specify that our activity should be the listener for the various events.

```
mediaPlayer.setOnCompletionListener(this);
mediaPlayer.setOnErrorListener(this);
mediaPlayer.setOnInfoListener(this);
mediaPlayer.setOnPreparedListener(this);
mediaPlayer.setOnSeekCompleteListener(this);
mediaPlayer.setOnVideoSizeChangedListener(this);
```

Before we finish the onCreate method, we'll tell the `MediaPlayer` object what to play. In this example, we are using the same video file that we used in previous examples. You can download it from www.mobvcasting.com/android/video/Test_Movie.m4v or create your own file.

```
String filePath = Environment.getExternalStorageDirectory().getPath() + "/Test↵
_Movie iPhone.m4v";
```

The `setDataSource` method on the `MediaPlayer` can throw multiple exceptions, which we should handle gracefully. In this case, we are just quitting. In your application, you probably want to present the user with an opportunity to select a different file or explain what went wrong.

```
try {
    mediaPlayer.setDataSource(filePath);
} catch (IllegalArgumentException e) {
    Log.v(LOGTAG,e.getMessage());
    finish();
} catch (IllegalStateException e) {
    Log.v(LOGTAG,e.getMessage());
    finish();
} catch (IOException e) {
    Log.v(LOGTAG,e.getMessage());
```

```
        finish();
    }

    currentDisplay = getWindowManager().getDefaultDisplay();
}
```

Since our activity implements SurfaceHolder.Callback and is assigned to be the callback listener, the following three methods will get triggered.

surfaceCreated will be called when the underlying Surface in SurfaceView is created.

```
public void surfaceCreated(SurfaceHolder holder) {
    Log.v(LOGTAG,"surfaceCreated Called");
```

When the Surface is created, we can specify that the MediaPlayer use the Surface for playback by calling its setDisplay method, passing in the SurfaceHolder object.

```
    mediaPlayer.setDisplay(holder);
```

Finally, after we specify the Surface, we can call prepare. The prepare method blocks rather than doing the work in the background. To have it do the work in the background, so as to not tie up the application, we could use prepareAsync instead. Either way, since we have implemented the OnPreparedListener and our activity is set to be the listener, our onPrepared method will be called when it is done.

The prepare method can throw a couple of extensions that we need to take care of. For brevity we'll just log the error and quit. In your application, you'll probably want to intelligently handle these exceptions.

```
        try {
            mediaPlayer.prepare();
        } catch (IllegalStateException e) {
            Log.v(LOGTAG,e.getMessage());
            finish();
        } catch (IOException e) {
            Log.v(LOGTAG,e.getMessage());
            finish();
        }
    }
```

surfaceChanged will be called when the width, height, or other parameter of the Surface underlying the SurfaceView changes. In this example, we don't need to do anything in this case.

```
public void surfaceChanged(SurfaceHolder holder, int format, int width, int height){
    Log.v(LOGTAG,"surfaceChanged Called");
}
```

surfaceDestroyed will be called when the underlying Surface of our SurfaceView is destroyed. In this example, we won't be doing anything when this occurs.

```
public void surfaceDestroyed(SurfaceHolder holder) {
    Log.v(LOGTAG,"surfaceDestroyed Called");
}
```

Since we implement the MediaPlayer.OnCompletionListener and register ourselves as the listener, our onCompletion method will be called when the MediaPlayer finishes playing a file. We could use this to load another video or perform some other action such as loading another screen. In this example, we'll just quit.

```
public void onCompletion(MediaPlayer mp) {
    Log.v(LOGTAG,"onCompletion Called");
    finish();
}
```

Our activity implements the MediaPlayer.OnErrorListener, and it is registered as the error listener for our MediaPlayer object, so the following onError method will be called when one occurs. Unfortunately, not much error information is available, just two constants as shown here.

```
public boolean onError(MediaPlayer mp, int whatError, int extra) {
    Log.v(LOGTAG,"onError Called");

    if (whatError == MediaPlayer.MEDIA_ERROR_SERVER_DIED) {
        Log.v(LOGTAG,"Media Error, Server Died " + extra);
    } else if (whatError == MediaPlayer.MEDIA_ERROR_UNKNOWN) {
        Log.v(LOGTAG,"Media Error, Error Unknown " + extra);
    }
```

Returning false from the method indicates that the error wasn't handled. If an OnCompletionListener is registered, its onCompletion method will be called. The MediaPlayer object will be put into the "error" state. It can be put back to the "idle" state by calling the reset method.

```
    return false;
}
```

The onInfo method, specified in the OnInfoListener, is called when specific information about the playback of the media is available or if warnings need to be issued.

```
public boolean onInfo(MediaPlayer mp, int whatInfo, int extra) {
    if (whatInfo == MediaPlayer.MEDIA_INFO_BAD_INTERLEAVING) {
```

This will be triggered if the audio and video data in the file are not properly interleaved. A properly interleaved media file has audio and video samples arranged in an order that makes playback efficient and smooth.

```
        Log.v(LOGTAG,"Media Info, Media Info Bad Interleaving " + extra);
    } else if (whatInfo == MediaPlayer.MEDIA_INFO_NOT_SEEKABLE) {
```

This will be triggered if the media cannot be seeked (meaning it is probably a live stream).

```
        Log.v(LOGTAG,"Media Info, Media Info Not Seekable " + extra);
    } else if (whatInfo == MediaPlayer.MEDIA_INFO_UNKNOWN) {
```

This is self-explanatory, in that the information isn't specified or is otherwise unknown.

```
        Log.v(LOGTAG,"Media Info, Media Info Unknown " + extra);
    } else if (whatInfo == MediaPlayer.MEDIA_INFO_VIDEO_TRACK_LAGGING) {
```

This will be triggered if the device is having trouble playing the video. It is possible that the audio will play but the video is either too complex or the bitrate is too high.

```
        Log.v(LOGTAG,"MediaInfo, Media Info Video Track Lagging " + extra);
```

```
        } else if (whatInfo == MediaPlayer.MEDIA_INFO_METADATA_UPDATE) {
```

MEDIA_INFO_METADATA_UPDATE is available in Android 2.0 and higher. It is triggered when new metadata is available.

```
            Log.v(LOGTAG,"MediaInfo, Media Info Metadata Update " + extra);
        }
        return false;
    }
```

Following a successful preparation by the MediaPlayer to start playback, the onPrepared method will be called. This is specified as part of the OnPreparedListener interface that we are implementing. Once this method is called, the MediaPlayer has entered the "prepared" state and is ready to play.

```
    public void onPrepared(MediaPlayer mp) {
        Log.v(LOGTAG,"onPrepared Called");
```

Before we can play the video, we should set the size of the Surface to match the video or the display size, depending on which is smaller.

First we get the dimensions of the video using the getVideoWidth and getVideoHeight methods available on the MediaPlayer object.

```
        videoWidth = mp.getVideoWidth();
        videoHeight = mp.getVideoHeight();
```

If the width or height of the video is greater than the display, then we'll figure out the ratio we should use.

```
        if (videoWidth > currentDisplay.getWidth() ||
            videoHeight > currentDisplay.getHeight())
        {
            float heightRatio = (float)videoHeight/(float)currentDisplay.getHeight();
            float widthRatio = (float)videoWidth/(float)currentDisplay.getWidth();

            if (heightRatio > 1 || widthRatio > 1)
            {
```

We'll use whichever ratio is bigger and set the videoHeight and videoWidth by dividing the video size by the larger ratio.

```
                if (heightRatio > widthRatio) {
                    videoHeight = (int)Math.ceil((float)videoHeight/(float)heightRatio);
                    videoWidth = (int)Math.ceil((float)videoWidth/(float)heightRatio);
                } else {
                    videoHeight = (int)Math.ceil((float)videoHeight/(float)widthRatio);
                    videoWidth = (int)Math.ceil((float)videoWidth/(float)widthRatio);
                }
            }
        }
```

We can now set the size of the SurfaceView we are displaying the video in to be either the actual dimensions of the video or the resized dimensions if the video was bigger than the display.

```
        surfaceView.setLayoutParams(
            new LinearLayout.LayoutParams(videoWidth,videoHeight));
```

Finally, we can start the playback of the video by calling the start method on the MediaPlayer object.

```
mp.start();
    }
```

onSeekComplete is specified as part of the OnSeekListener that we are implementing, and our activity is the registered listener for our MediaPlayer. It is called when a seek command has completed.

```
public void onSeekComplete(MediaPlayer mp) {
    Log.v(LOGTAG,"onSeekComplete Called");
}
```

onVideoSizeChanged is specified as part of the OnVideoSizeChangedListener that we are implementing, and our activity is the registered listener for our MediaPlayer. It is called when a size change occurs. It will be called at least once after the data source is specified and the video metadata is read.

```
public void onVideoSizeChanged(MediaPlayer mp, int width, int height) {
    Log.v(LOGTAG,"onVideoSizeChanged Called");
    }
}
```

Here is the layout XML file, main.xml, for use with the foregoing activity.

```
<?xml version="1.0" encoding="utf-8"?>
<LinearLayout xmlns:android="http://schemas.android.com/apk/res/android"
    android:orientation="vertical"
    android:layout_width="fill_parent"
    android:layout_height="fill_parent"
    android:id="@+id/MainView"
    >
    <SurfaceView android:id="@+id/SurfaceView" android:layout_height="wrap_content"↵
    android:layout_width="wrap_content"></SurfaceView>
</LinearLayout>
```

Figure 9–5. *Video playing in* `CustomVideoPlayer` *activity*

MediaPlayer with MediaController

The `MediaController` view that we used in our `VideoView` example can also be used with a `MediaPlayer` as shown in Figure 9-6. Unfortunately, it takes significantly more work in order to have it work correctly.

First our class needs to implement `MediaController.MediaPlayerControl` in addition to other classes it already implements.

```
import android.widget.MediaController;
public class CustomVideoPlayer extends Activity
    implements OnCompletionListener, OnErrorListener, OnInfoListener,
    OnPreparedListener, OnSeekCompleteListener, OnVideoSizeChangedListener,
    SurfaceHolder.Callback, MediaController.MediaPlayerControl
{
```

This interface defines a series of functions that the `MediaController` uses to control the playback, and we need to implement them in our activity.

Here are the functions and their implementation in our `CustomVideoPlayer` example. For several of the functions, we just return `true`, meaning the capability is there. For the rest, we call the corresponding function on our `MediaPlayer` object.

```
    public boolean canPause() {
        return true;
    }
```

```
public boolean canSeekBackward() {
    return true;
}

public boolean canSeekForward() {
    return true;
}

public int getBufferPercentage() {
    return 0;
}

public int getCurrentPosition() {
    return mediaPlayer.getCurrentPosition();
}

public int getDuration() {
    return mediaPlayer.getDuration();
}

public boolean isPlaying() {
    return mediaPlayer.isPlaying();
}

public void pause() {
    if (mediaPlayer.isPlaying()) {
        mediaPlayer.pause();
    }
}

public void seekTo(int pos) {
    mediaPlayer.seekTo(pos);
}

public void start() {
    mediaPlayer.start();
}
```

Now we are free to add the actual MediaController object. We'll declare it with the rest of the instance variables.

```
MediaController controller;
```

In the onCreate method, we'll instantiate it.

```
controller = new MediaController(this);
```

We won't actually set it up and use it until after the MediaPlayer is prepared. At the end of the onPrepared method, we can add the following. First we specify the object that implements MediaController.MediaPlayerControl by calling the setMediaPlayer method. In this case, it is our activity, so we pass in this.

Then we set the root view of our activity so the MediaController can determine how to display itself. In the foregoing layout XML, we gave the root LinearLayout object an ID of MainView so we can reference it here.

Finally we enable it and show it.

```
controller.setMediaPlayer(this);
controller.setAnchorView(this.findViewById(R.id.MainView));
controller.setEnabled(true);
controller.show();
```

In order to bring the controller back up after it disappears (the default behavior of the MediaController is to auto-hide after a timeout), we can override onTouchEvent in our activity to show or hide it.

```
@Override
public boolean onTouchEvent(MotionEvent ev) {
    if (controller.isShowing()) {
        controller.hide();
    } else {
        controller.show();
    }
    return false;
}
```

Figure 9–6. *CustomVideoPlayer* **activity with** *MediaController*

Summary

As with many things in Android, there are many different ways that a task can be accomplished. In this chapter, we looked at three different ways that we can play video files. Simply using the built-in application via an intent is the easiest but least flexible. Using a VideoView allows us to play video within our own activity but doesn't offer much more in the way of control capabilities. The MediaPlayer allows for the greatest range of control but requires the most work.

Chapter 10

Advanced Video

In Chapter 9, we looked at how Android can play back a specific video file that is placed on the device's SD card. In this chapter, we'll take that a step further and look at accessing video that is made available by the MediaStore and video that is available on the Internet.

MediaStore for Retrieving Video

As discussed in Chapter 1, Android provides a standard means for sharing data across applications. The ContentProvider class is the base class that enables this. Also as discussed, the classes that extend the concept of a ContentProvider for media are the various MediaStore classes. We previously looked at using the MediaStore for images and audio and their related metadata. The MediaStore for use with video behaves in much the same way.

MediaStore.Video is the nested class within the MediaStore class for use with video files in particular. Within MediaStore.Video is MediaStore.Video.Media, which contains the constants that specify the columns available in the MediaStore related to the video media itself, many of which are inherited from other classes, such as MediaStore.MediaColumns. There is also a MediaStore.Video.Thumbnails, which contains the constants that specify the columns available in the MediaStore for thumbnail image storage that is related to video files.

To query the MediaStore for video content, we utilize the Uri specified in the constant MediaStore.Video.Media.EXTERNAL_CONTENT_URI as the data source for a query.

Using the managedQuery method available in the Activity class, we also need to pass in an array of columns that we would like returned. The array specified here indicates that we want the unique ID for the video in the MediaStore, MediaStore.Video.Media._ID. This is followed by MediaStore.Video.Media.DATA, which is the path to the video file itself. The next two specify that we want the title and the MIME-type of the file.

```
String[] mediaColumns = {
    MediaStore.Video.Media._ID,
    MediaStore.Video.Media.DATA,
    MediaStore.Video.Media.TITLE,
```

```
        MediaStore.Video.Media.MIME_TYPE
};
```

To query the MediaStore for video content, we utilize the Uri specified in the constant MediaStore.Video.Media.EXTERNAL_CONTENT_URI as the data source for a query.

```
Cursor cursor = managedQuery(MediaStore.Video.Media.EXTERNAL_CONTENT_URI,↵
 mediaColumns, null, null, null);
```

In return we get a cursor that we can loop through and extract the data.

```
if (cursor.moveToFirst()) {
    do {
        Log.v("VideoGallery",
            cursor.getString(cursor.getColumnIndex(MediaStore.Video.Media.DATA)));
        Log.v("VideoGallery",
            cursor.getString(cursor.getColumnIndex(MediaStore.Video.Media.TITLE)));
        Log.v("VideoGallery",
            cursor.getString(cursor.getColumnIndex(MediaStore.Video.Media.MIME_TYPE)));
    } while (cursor.moveToNext());
}
```

Video Thumbnails from the MediaStore

We could, starting with Android 2.0 (API Level 5), pull out the thumbnails associated with each video file from within the loop. We need the ID of the video file that is in our list of columns to select (MediaStore.Video.Media._ID), which we can then use in the "where" clause of the managedQuery.

```
int id = cursor.getInt(cursor.getColumnIndex(MediaStore.Video.Media._ID));
String[] thumbColumns = { MediaStore.Video.Thumbnails.DATA,
                        MediaStore.Video.Thumbnails.VIDEO_ID};
Cursor thumbCursor = managedQuery(MediaStore.Video.Thumbnails.EXTERNAL_CONTENT_URI,↵
 thumbColumns, MediaStore.Video.Thumbnails.VIDEO_ID + "=" + id, null, null);
if (thumbCursor.moveToFirst()) {
    Log.v("VideoGallery",thumbCursor.getColumnIndex(MediaStore.Video.Thumbnails.DATA));
}
```

Full MediaStore Video Example

Here is a full example that retrieves all of the available video files from the MediaStore and displays each of their thumbnail images and titles. Figure 10–1 shows the following example running. This example uses the MediaStore.Video.Thumbnails class which is available in Android 2.0 (API Level 5) and above.

```
package com.apress.proandroidmedia.ch10.videogallery;

import java.io.File;
import java.util.ArrayList;
import java.util.List;

import android.app.Activity;
import android.content.Context;
import android.content.Intent;
```

```
import android.database.Cursor;
import android.net.Uri;
import android.os.Bundle;
import android.provider.MediaStore;
import android.util.Log;
import android.view.LayoutInflater;
import android.view.View;
import android.view.ViewGroup;
import android.widget.AdapterView;
import android.widget.BaseAdapter;
import android.widget.ImageView;
import android.widget.ListView;
import android.widget.TextView;
import android.widget.AdapterView.OnItemClickListener;

public class VideoGallery extends Activity implements OnItemClickListener {
    Cursor cursor;
    @Override
    public void onCreate(Bundle savedInstanceState) {
        super.onCreate(savedInstanceState);
        setContentView(R.layout.main);
```

We'll use a `ListView` to display the list of videos.

```
        ListView listView = (ListView) this.findViewById(R.id.ListView);
```

Next is the list of columns we want from the `MediaStore.Video.Thumbnails` queries.

```
        String[] thumbColumns = {
            MediaStore.Video.Thumbnails.DATA,
            MediaStore.Video.Thumbnails.VIDEO_ID
        };
```

Then comes the list of columns we want from the `MediaStore.Video.Media` query.

```
        String[] mediaColumns = {
            MediaStore.Video.Media._ID,
            MediaStore.Video.Media.DATA,
            MediaStore.Video.Media.TITLE,
            MediaStore.Video.Media.MIME_TYPE
        };
```

In the main query, we'll select all of the videos that are represented in the `MediaStore`.

```
        cursor = managedQuery(MediaStore.Video.Media.EXTERNAL_CONTENT_URI,
                              mediaColumns, null, null, null);
```

Each row returned by the query will create an item in the following `ArrayList`. Each item will be a `VideoViewInfo` object, which is a class defined here specifically to hold information about a video for use in this activity.

```
        ArrayList<VideoViewInfo> videoRows = new ArrayList<VideoViewInfo>();
```

Here we loop through the data contained in the `Cursor` object, creating a `VideoViewInfo` object for each row and adding it to our `ArrayList`.

```
        if (cursor.moveToFirst())
        {
```

We are using a do while loop as we want it to run through the first row of data before moving to the next row. The do portion happens before the while clause is tested/executed. In our loop, we'll create a new VideoViewInfo object for each row of data returned.

```
do {

    VideoViewInfo newVVI = new VideoViewInfo();
```

We can then pull out all of the relevant data from the Cursor. As just described, we'll also make another query to pull out a thumbnail image for each video. Each of these pieces of data will be stored in the VideoViewInfo object.

```
int id =
  cursor.getInt(cursor.getColumnIndex(MediaStore.Video.Media._ID));
Cursor thumbCursor =
  managedQuery(MediaStore.Video.Thumbnails.EXTERNAL_CONTENT_URI,
               thumbColumns,
               MediaStore.Video.Thumbnails.VIDEO_ID + "=" + id,
               null, null);
if (thumbCursor.moveToFirst())
{
    newVVI.thumbPath = thumbCursor.getString(
        thumbCursor.getColumnIndex(MediaStore.Video.Thumbnails.DATA));
    Log.v("VideoGallery","Thumb " + newVVI.thumbPath);
}

newVVI.filePath = cursor.getString(
            cursor.getColumnIndexOrThrow(MediaStore.Video.Media.DATA));
newVVI.title = cursor.getString(
            cursor.getColumnIndexOrThrow(MediaStore.Video.Media.TITLE));
Log.v("VideoGallery","Title " + newVVI.title);
newVVI.mimeType = cursor.getString(
            cursor.getColumnIndexOrThrow(MediaStore.Video.Media.MIME_TYPE));
Log.v("VideoGallery","Mime " + newVVI.mimeType);
```

Finally, we add the VideoViewInfo to the videoRows ArrayList.

```
    videoRows.add(newVVI);
} while (cursor.moveToNext());
}
```

Once we are done getting all of the videos, we can continue on. We'll set the adapter of the ListView object to be a new instance of VideoGalleryAdapter, which is an inner class defined here. We'll also set this activity to be the OnItemClickListener for the ListView.

```
listView.setAdapter(new VideoGalleryAdapter(this,videoRows));
listView.setOnItemClickListener(this);
}
```

When an item in the ListView is clicked, the onItemClick method will be called. In this method, we extract the data we need from the Cursor and create an intent to launch the default media player application on the device to play back the video. We could have created our own MediaPlayer or used the VideoView class here instead.

```
public void onItemClick(AdapterView<?> l, View v, int position, long id) {
```

```
        if (cursor.moveToPosition(position)) {
            int fileColumn = cursor.getColumnIndexOrThrow(MediaStore.Video.Media.DATA);
            int mimeColumn =
              cursor.getColumnIndexOrThrow(MediaStore.Video.Media.MIME_TYPE);

            String videoFilePath = cursor.getString(fileColumn);
            String mimeType = cursor.getString(mimeColumn);

            Intent intent = new Intent(android.content.Intent.ACTION_VIEW);

            File newFile = new File(videoFilePath);
            intent.setDataAndType(Uri.fromFile(newFile), mimeType);

            startActivity(intent);
        }
    }
```

What follows is the very basic VideoViewInfo class, which is used to hold information about each video returned.

```
    class VideoViewInfo
    {
        String filePath;
        String mimeType;
        String thumbPath;
        String title;
    }
```

Since we are using a ListView in our activity to display each of the videos returned from the MediaStore query, we'll be using the ListView to display both the title of the video and a thumbnail. In order to hand the data to the ListView, we need to construct an Adapter. Next, we create an Adapter, VideoGalleryAdapter, which extends BaseAdapter. When this class is constructed, it gets passed the ArrayList that holds all of the videos returned from the MediaStore query.

BaseAdapter is an abstract class, so in order to extend it, we need to implement several methods. Most of them are straightforward and just operate on the ArrayList we passed in, such as getCount and getItem. The method that requires the most attention is the getView method.

```
    class VideoGalleryAdapter extends BaseAdapter
    {
        private Context context;
        private List<VideoViewInfo> videoItems;

        LayoutInflater inflater;

        public VideoGalleryAdapter(Context _context, ArrayList<VideoViewInfo> _items) {
            context = _context;
            videoItems = _items;

            inflater =
              (LayoutInflater) context.getSystemService(Context.LAYOUT_INFLATER_SERVICE);
        }

        public int getCount() {
```

```
        return videoItems.size();
    }

    public Object getItem(int position) {
        return videoItems.get(position);
    }

    public long getItemId(int position) {
        return position;
    }
```

The getView method is used to return the view for each row represented in the ListView. It is passed in the position that is meant to be returned (along with a View object representing the current View and an object that represents the parent ViewGroup).

```
    public View getView(int position, View convertView, ViewGroup parent) {
```

To construct the View to be returned, we need to inflate the layout that we are using for each row. In this case, we are using a layout defined in list_item.xml (shown here).

```
        View videoRow = inflater.inflate(R.layout.list_item, null);
```

After the layout is inflated, we can get at the individual Views that are defined and use the data from the ArrayList of VideoViewInfo objects to define what to display. Here is how that is done for the ImageView that is used to display each video's thumbnail.

```
        ImageView videoThumb = (ImageView) videoRow.findViewById(R.id.ImageView);
        if (videoItems.get(position).thumbPath != null) {
            videoThumb.setImageURI(Uri.parse(videoItems.get(position).thumbPath));
        }
```

Here we obtain a reference to the TextView for the video title and set the text according to the data in the ArrayList of VideoViewInfo object.

```
        TextView videoTitle = (TextView) videoRow.findViewById(R.id.TextView);
        videoTitle.setText(videoItems.get(position).title);
```

Finally, we return the newly constructed View.

```
        return videoRow;
    }
  }
}
```

Here is the main.xml file defining the layout for the activity.

```
<?xml version="1.0" encoding="utf-8"?>
<LinearLayout xmlns:android="http://schemas.android.com/apk/res/android"
    android:orientation="vertical"
    android:layout_width="fill_parent"
    android:layout_height="fill_parent"
    >
  <ListView android:layout_width="wrap_content" android:layout_height="wrap_content"
android:id="@+id/ListView"></ListView>
</LinearLayout>
```

Here is the list_item.xml file that is used to define the layout for each row of the ListView.

```
<?xml version="1.0" encoding="utf-8"?>
<LinearLayout
```

```
    xmlns:android="http://schemas.android.com/apk/res/android"
    android:layout_width="wrap_content"
    android:layout_height="wrap_content">
        <ImageView android:id="@+id/ImageView" android:layout_width="wrap_content"↵
    android:layout_height="wrap_content"></ImageView>
        <TextView android:text="@+id/TextView01" android:layout_width="wrap_content"↵
    android:layout_height="wrap_content" android:id="@+id/TextView"></TextView>
    </LinearLayout>
```

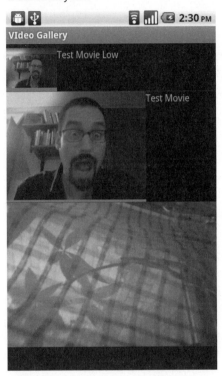

Figure 10–1. *VideoGallery activity*

You'll notice that the thumbnails displayed in Figure 10–1 from our example are different sizes. They are created by the MediaScanner service to be the same size as the video itself. To display the thumbnails at the same size, we can adjust the parameters in the ImageView item listed in list_item.xml.

```
<ImageView android:id="@+id/ImageView" android:layout_width="50dip"↵
    android:layout_height="50dip"></ImageView>
```

Now each of the video thumbnails will be displayed at 50 dip × 50 dip, as shown in Figure 10–2. (The term *dip* stands for "density independent pixel." 160 dips equal 1 inch on the display no matter what the resolution or density of the pixels on the display is.)

Figure 10–2. *VideoGallery activity with thumbnails the same size*

Networked Video

As more and more media moves onto the Internet, it makes sense for Android to have good support for playing it back, which it does. For the remainder of this chapter, we'll explore the details of what is supported in terms of protocols and video formats, and how to harness network video.

Supported Network Video Types

Android currently supports two different protocols for network delivered video.

HTTP

The first is media delivered via standard HTTP. As HTTP is broadly supported across networks and doesn't typically have problems with firewalls as other streaming protocols have had, a large amount of media is available in this manner. Media delivered via HTTP is commonly referred to as progressive download.

Android supports on-demand media within MPEG-4 and 3GP files delivered from a standard web server via HTTP. At this time, it does not support the delivery of live video via HTTP using any of the new techniques now being used by Apple, Microsoft, or Adobe.

There are several things to keep in mind when preparing video for delivery via progressive download. First, the media has to be encoded with a codec and in a format that Android supports (see Chapter 9 for details about the formats and codecs that Android supports).

There are many free and commercial tools available to prepare media for delivery via HTTP progressive download. A few of them, in no particular order, are QuickTime X, Adobe Media Encoder, HandBrake, and VLC. QuickTime X has presets for iPhone encoding that work well with Android. Adobe Media Encoder has presets for iPod that seem to work as well. In general, if a piece of software has presets for the iPhone, they will likely work for Android devices.

Second, the bitrate of the video should be in the range of what can be delivered over the network that will carry the video. For instance, GPRS bandwidth could be as low as 20 kbps, and therefore the audio and video should be encoded with that in mind. In general, when delivered via HTTP, the media will be buffered on the device, and playback will start when enough has been downloaded that the playback should be able to go straight through to the end of the file without having to pause while waiting for more media to download. If the delivery of the media is only 20 kbps and the media is encoded at 400 kbps, that means that for each second of video the user will have to be downloading for 20 seconds. This probably isn't ideal.

If, though, the user is on WiFi, 400 kbps is probably good and will provide nice-looking video as compared to video that is encoded at 20 kbps. In general, the speed of the network that will be used has to be weighed against the quality of the video. The nice thing about using HTTP progressive download is that this can be done: the media doesn't have to be delivered in real time as it does with RTSP, which we'll discuss next.

Finally, in order for the video to be played back while it is downloading, it has to be encoded in a manner that allows this. Specifically this means that the resulting file should have what is called the "moov atom" at the front of the file. The "moov atom" contains an index of what is in the file and how it is organized. In order for the video playback software to be able to start playing back the video, it needs to know this information. If the "moov atom" is at the end of the file, the playback software can't start playback until the entire file is downloaded so it can get the "moov atom."

Unfortunately, some video capture and encoding tools do not automatically perform this step. In some cases, it is simply a configuration setting; in other cases, you may need to do this step manually. A command-line application called qt-faststart has been developed and ported to many different operating systems and forms the basis for several GUI applications as well. It can be read about and downloaded from http://multimedia.cx/eggs/improving-qt-faststart/.

RTSP

The second protocol that Android supports for network delivery of video is RTSP. RTSP stands for Real Time Streaming Protocol and is technically not a media delivery protocol; rather, it is a control protocol that is used in support of media delivery. The form of media delivery that is supported along with RTSP in Android is RTP (the Real-time Transport Protocol) but only when paired with RTSP. In other words, RTP on Android doesn't work independently of RTSP.

RTSP and RTP are specific to real-time streaming. This is quite different from HTTP progressive download, in that the media is played as it is received over the network.

It also means that a special server is required to deliver the media. There are several RTSP servers on the market: Apple's Open Source Darwin Streaming Server, RealNetwork's Helix Server, and the Wowza Media Server are a few. Unfortunately, setting up and working with a server is out of the scope of what can be covered in this book. Fortunately, a highly reliable service exists that serves media via RTSP that we can test with (YouTube's mobile site, available at `http://m.youtube.com`).

As with progressive download, a couple of things need to be kept in mind when preparing media for delivery via RTSP. First the media needs to be encoded with a codec and in a file format that Android supports and that is streamable by an RTSP server. In general, streaming media for mobile devices is encoded as MP4 video and AAC audio in a 3GP container, although other codecs (H.264) and containers (MP4) are also supported.

> **NOTE:** Android currently has two underlying media frameworks, PacketVideo's OpenCORE and one particular to Android called Stagefright. OpenCORE is the original framework that has been used in Android, and it has been exclusive until Android 2.2, when Stagefright was introduced.
>
> In Android 2.2 (and all previous versions), OpenCORE is the framework that is used for streaming video (RTSP), although down the road this may change. The choice of which framework is used will be in the hands of the handset manufacturer, and both frameworks should be compatible on the API level. As this is all happening behind the scenes, with luck, we as developers will not need to be concerned with which underlying framework is being used.
>
> More information about what protocols, codecs, container formats, and streaming protocols are supported by OpenCORE can be found on `www.opencore.net/`. Specifically the OpenCORE Multimedia Framework Capabilities document is available at `www.opencore.net/files/opencore_framework_capabilities.pdf`. (Unfortunately, at this time, no public documentation with regards to Stagefright's capabilities exists.)

Last, the bitrate of the media needs to be something that can be delivered in real time to the end user depending on his or her network connection. These speeds vary quite a bit depending on the network type. Second-generation networks (GPRS) offer data speeds that top out in the 50 to 100 kbps range. Encoding live video to be delivered in real time over this type of network requires that the video be encoded in the 30 kbps range to account for overhead and varying connection qualities. Moving up to EDGE networks should allow video in the 50 kbps range to be delivered reliably, and a conservative bitrate for today's current 3G networks would be in the 100 kbps range, with many networks capable of supporting significantly higher bitrates.

Unlike HTTP progressive download, RTSP can be used for live streaming media as well. This is one of its main advantages over traditional HTTP delivery. RTSP also supports seeking within on-demand media. This means that users can seek to specific points in the video without having to download all of the media up to and including that point. The server takes care of only serving the media for that point in the file to the player.

Network Video Playback

Android supports HTTP and RTSP video playback in all three video playback methods discussed in Chapter 9. Using either the built-in Media Player activity via an intent or the VideoView class to play either form of network video requires no source code changes. Simply use the HTTP or RTSP URL as the video Uri, and it will work as long as the format is supported.

VideoView Network Video Player

Here is the ViewTheVideo activity example from Chapter 9 that uses a VideoView with an RTSP URL to a video from YouTube's mobile site. The only change is the string passed in to construct the videoUri.

```
package com.apress.proandroidmedia.ch10.videoview;

import android.app.Activity;
import android.net.Uri;
import android.os.Bundle;
import android.widget.MediaController;
import android.widget.VideoView;

public class ViewTheVideo extends Activity {
    VideoView vv;
    @Override
    public void onCreate(Bundle savedInstanceState) {
        super.onCreate(savedInstanceState);
        setContentView(R.layout.main);

        vv = (VideoView) this.findViewById(R.id.VideoView);
        Uri videoUri =
Uri.parse("rtsp://v2.cache2.c.youtube.com/CjgLENy73wIaLwm3JbT_↩
9HqWohMYESARFEIJbXYtZ29vZ2xlSARSB3Jlc3VsdHNg
_vSmsbeSyd5JDA==/0/0/0/video.3gp");
        vv.setMediaController(new MediaController(this));
        vv.setVideoURI(videoUri);
        vv.start();
    }
}
```

MediaPlayer Network Video Player

Working with the MediaPlayer for network video playback is similar to the MediaPlayer and MediaController code we went over in Chapter 9. In the following example, we'll highlight the portions that are specifically related to network playback. Figure 10–3 shows the example in action. For a full explanation of the MediaPlayer and MediaController, please refer to the examples in Chapter 9.

```
package com.apress.proandroidmedia.ch10.streamingvideoplayer;
```

```
import java.io.IOException;
import android.app.Activity;
import android.os.Bundle;
import android.media.MediaPlayer;
import android.media.MediaPlayer.OnBufferingUpdateListener;
import android.media.MediaPlayer.OnCompletionListener;
import android.media.MediaPlayer.OnErrorListener;
import android.media.MediaPlayer.OnInfoListener;
import android.media.MediaPlayer.OnPreparedListener;
import android.media.MediaPlayer.OnSeekCompleteListener;
import android.media.MediaPlayer.OnVideoSizeChangedListener;
import android.util.Log;
import android.view.Display;
import android.view.MotionEvent;
import android.view.SurfaceHolder;
import android.view.SurfaceView;
import android.view.View;
import android.widget.LinearLayout;
import android.widget.TextView;
import android.widget.MediaController;
```

The StreamingVideoPlayer activity implements many of the available listener and callback abstract classes from MediaPlayer, SurfaceHolder, and MediaController. The OnBufferingUpdateListener is particularly useful when dealing with network delivered media. This class specifies an onBufferingUpdate method that is repeatedly called while the media is buffering, allowing us to keep track of how full the buffer is.

```
public class StreamingVideoPlayer extends Activity implements
        OnCompletionListener, OnErrorListener, OnInfoListener,
        OnBufferingUpdateListener, OnPreparedListener, OnSeekCompleteListener,
        OnVideoSizeChangedListener, SurfaceHolder.Callback,
        MediaController.MediaPlayerControl {

    MediaController controller;
    Display currentDisplay;
    SurfaceView surfaceView;
    SurfaceHolder surfaceHolder;
    MediaPlayer mediaPlayer;

    View mainView;
```

In this version, we'll use a TextView called statusView to display status messages to the user. The reason we'll do so is that loading a video for playback via the Internet can take quite a bit of time, and without some sort of status message, the user may think the application has hung.

```
    TextView statusView;

    int videoWidth = 0;
    int videoHeight = 0;

    boolean readyToPlay = false;
```

```
public final static String LOGTAG = "STREAMING_VIDEO_PLAYER";

@Override
public void onCreate(Bundle savedInstanceState) {
    super.onCreate(savedInstanceState);

    setContentView(R.layout.main);
    mainView = this.findViewById(R.id.MainView);

    statusView = (TextView) this.findViewById(R.id.StatusTextView);

    surfaceView = (SurfaceView) this.findViewById(R.id.SurfaceView);
    surfaceHolder = surfaceView.getHolder();

    surfaceHolder.addCallback(this);
    surfaceHolder.setType(SurfaceHolder.SURFACE_TYPE_PUSH_BUFFERS);

    mediaPlayer = new MediaPlayer();

    statusView.setText("MediaPlayer Created");

    mediaPlayer.setOnCompletionListener(this);
    mediaPlayer.setOnErrorListener(this);
    mediaPlayer.setOnInfoListener(this);
    mediaPlayer.setOnPreparedListener(this);
    mediaPlayer.setOnSeekCompleteListener(this);
    mediaPlayer.setOnVideoSizeChangedListener(this);
```

Among the list of MediaPlayer event listeners, our activity implements and is registered to be the OnBufferingUpdateListener.

```
mediaPlayer.setOnBufferingUpdateListener(this);
```

Instead of playing back a file from the SD card, we'll be playing a file served from an RTSP server. The URL to the file is specified in the following String, filePath. We'll then use the MediaPlayer's setDataSource method, passing in the filePath String. The MediaPlayer knows how to handle loading and playing data from an RTSP server, so we don't have to do anything else different to handle it.

```
    String filePath = "rtsp://v2.cache2.c.youtube.com/CjgLENy73wIaLwm3JbT↵
_9HqWohMYESARFEIJbXYtZ29vZ2xlSARSB3Jlc3VsdHNg96LUzsKO781MDA==/0/0/0/video.3gp";
    try {
        mediaPlayer.setDataSource(filePath);
    } catch (IllegalArgumentException e) {
        Log.v(LOGTAG, e.getMessage());
        finish();
    } catch (IllegalStateException e) {
        Log.v(LOGTAG, e.getMessage());
        finish();
    } catch (IOException e) {
        Log.v(LOGTAG, e.getMessage());
        finish();
    }

    statusView.setText("MediaPlayer DataSource Set");
    currentDisplay = getWindowManager().getDefaultDisplay();
    controller = new MediaController(this);
```

```
    }

    public void surfaceCreated(SurfaceHolder holder) {
        Log.v(LOGTAG, "surfaceCreated Called");

        mediaPlayer.setDisplay(holder);
        statusView.setText("MediaPlayer Display Surface Set");
```

We'll use the MediaPlayer's prepareAsync method instead of prepare. The prepareAsync method does the preparation in the background on a separate thread. This makes it so that the user interface doesn't hang. This would allow the user to perform other actions or allow us as the developer to display a loading animation or something similar.

```
        try {
            mediaPlayer.prepareAsync();
        } catch (IllegalStateException e) {
            Log.v(LOGTAG, "IllegalStateException " + e.getMessage());
            finish();
        }
```

So the user knows what's happening while the prepareAsync method is running, we'll update the status message displayed by our statusView TextView.

```
        statusView.setText("MediaPlayer Preparing");
    }

    public void surfaceChanged(SurfaceHolder holder, int format, int width,
            int height) {
        Log.v(LOGTAG, "surfaceChanged Called");
    }

public void surfaceDestroyed(SurfaceHolder holder) {
        Log.v(LOGTAG, "surfaceDestroyed Called");
    }

    public void onCompletion(MediaPlayer mp) {
        Log.v(LOGTAG, "onCompletion Called");
        statusView.setText("MediaPlayer Playback Completed");
    }

    public boolean onError(MediaPlayer mp, int whatError, int extra) {
        Log.v(LOGTAG, "onError Called");
        statusView.setText("MediaPlayer Error");
        if (whatError == MediaPlayer.MEDIA_ERROR_SERVER_DIED) {
            Log.v(LOGTAG, "Media Error, Server Died " + extra);
        } else if (whatError == MediaPlayer.MEDIA_ERROR_UNKNOWN) {
            Log.v(LOGTAG, "Media Error, Error Unknown " + extra);
        }
        return false;
    }

    public boolean onInfo(MediaPlayer mp, int whatInfo, int extra) {
        statusView.setText("MediaPlayer onInfo Called");
        if (whatInfo == MediaPlayer.MEDIA_INFO_BAD_INTERLEAVING) {
            Log.v(LOGTAG, "Media Info, Media Info Bad Interleaving " + extra);
        } else if (whatInfo == MediaPlayer.MEDIA_INFO_NOT_SEEKABLE) {
            Log.v(LOGTAG, "Media Info, Media Info Not Seekable " + extra);
```

```
        } else if (whatInfo == MediaPlayer.MEDIA_INFO_UNKNOWN) {
            Log.v(LOGTAG, "Media Info, Media Info Unknown " + extra);
        } else if (whatInfo == MediaPlayer.MEDIA_INFO_VIDEO_TRACK_LAGGING) {
            Log.v(LOGTAG, "MediaInfo, Media Info Video Track Lagging " + extra);
        } else if (whatInfo == MediaPlayer.MEDIA_INFO_METADATA_UPDATE) {
            Log.v(LOGTAG, "MediaInfo, Media Info Metadata Update " + extra);
        }
        return false;
}

public void onPrepared(MediaPlayer mp) {
    Log.v(LOGTAG, "onPrepared Called");
    statusView.setText("MediaPlayer Prepared");

    videoWidth = mp.getVideoWidth();
    videoHeight = mp.getVideoHeight();

    Log.v(LOGTAG, "Width: " + videoWidth);
    Log.v(LOGTAG, "Height: " + videoHeight);

    if (videoWidth > currentDisplay.getWidth()
            || videoHeight > currentDisplay.getHeight()) {
        float heightRatio = (float) videoHeight
                / (float) currentDisplay.getHeight();
        float widthRatio = (float) videoWidth
                / (float) currentDisplay.getWidth();

        if (heightRatio > 1 || widthRatio > 1) {
            if (heightRatio > widthRatio) {
                videoHeight = (int) Math.ceil((float) videoHeight
                        / (float) heightRatio);
                videoWidth = (int) Math.ceil((float) videoWidth
                        / (float) heightRatio);
            } else {
                videoHeight = (int) Math.ceil((float) videoHeight
                        / (float) widthRatio);
                videoWidth = (int) Math.ceil((float) videoWidth
                        / (float) widthRatio);
            }
        }
    }


    surfaceView.setLayoutParams(
        new LinearLayout.LayoutParams(videoWidth, videoHeight));
    controller.setMediaPlayer(this);
    controller.setAnchorView(this.findViewById(R.id.MainView));
    controller.setEnabled(true);
    controller.show();

    mp.start();
    statusView.setText("MediaPlayer Started");
}

public void onSeekComplete(MediaPlayer mp) {
    Log.v(LOGTAG, "onSeekComplete Called");
```

```
        }

        public void onVideoSizeChanged(MediaPlayer mp, int width, int height) {
            Log.v(LOGTAG, "onVideoSizeChanged Called");

            videoWidth = mp.getVideoWidth();
            videoHeight = mp.getVideoHeight();

            Log.v(LOGTAG, "Width: " + videoWidth);
            Log.v(LOGTAG, "Height: " + videoHeight);

            if (videoWidth > currentDisplay.getWidth()
                    || videoHeight > currentDisplay.getHeight()) {
                float heightRatio = (float) videoHeight
                        / (float) currentDisplay.getHeight();
                float widthRatio = (float) videoWidth
                        / (float) currentDisplay.getWidth();

                if (heightRatio > 1 || widthRatio > 1) {
                    if (heightRatio > widthRatio) {
                        videoHeight = (int) Math.ceil((float) videoHeight
                                / (float) heightRatio);
                        videoWidth = (int) Math.ceil((float) videoWidth
                                / (float) heightRatio);
                    } else {
                        videoHeight = (int) Math.ceil((float) videoHeight
                                / (float) widthRatio);
                        videoWidth = (int) Math.ceil((float) videoWidth
                                / (float) widthRatio);
                    }
                }
            }


            surfaceView.setLayoutParams(
                new LinearLayout.LayoutParams(videoWidth, videoHeight));
        }
```

Since our activity implements the OnBufferingUpdateListener and is registered to be the listener for the MediaPlayer, the following method will be called periodically as media is downloaded and buffered. The buffering will occur during the preparation stage (after onPrepareAsync or onPrepare is called).

```
public void onBufferingUpdate(MediaPlayer mp, int bufferedPercent) {
    statusView.setText("MediaPlayer Buffering: " + bufferedPercent + "%");
    Log.v(LOGTAG, "MediaPlayer Buffering: " + bufferedPercent + "%");
}

public boolean canPause() {
    return true;
}

public boolean canSeekBackward() {
    return true;
}

public boolean canSeekForward() {
```

```java
            return true;
        }

        public int getBufferPercentage() {
            return 0;
        }

        public int getCurrentPosition() {
            return mediaPlayer.getCurrentPosition();
        }

        public int getDuration() {
            return mediaPlayer.getDuration();
        }

        public boolean isPlaying() {
            return mediaPlayer.isPlaying();
        }

        public void pause() {
            if (mediaPlayer.isPlaying()) {
                mediaPlayer.pause();
            }
        }

        public void seekTo(int pos) {
            mediaPlayer.seekTo(pos);
        }

        public void start() {
            mediaPlayer.start();
        }

        @Override
        public boolean onTouchEvent(MotionEvent ev) {
            if (controller.isShowing()) {
                controller.hide();
            } else {
                controller.show();
            }
            return false;
        }
    }
}
```

Figure 10–3. *Streaming* `MediaPlayer` *activity during playback of video file from YouTube*

Summary

Throughout this chapter, we looked at some more advanced video playback and streaming capabilities available on Android. As we learned, the `MediaStore` can be used for video in much the same way we previously used it for images and audio. It provides us as developers a truly comprehensive means for media metadata storage and retrieval on Android. We also learned that the three methods for media video playback can also be leveraged to provide network video playback, both streaming and web-based.

Chapter 11

Video Capture

In previous chapters, we have covered image capture and audio capture. Now we'll turn our attention to video capture. In this chapter, we'll explore capturing video using Android's built-in Camera application via an intent. We'll look at the formats and codecs that Android supports for video capture, and finally we'll build a custom video capture application.

Recording Video Using an Intent

It is becoming cliché, but as previously discussed, often the quickest and easiest way to perform some function on Android is to leverage an existing application that can be triggered by an intent from our application. Using the built-in Camera application to record video, triggered by an intent, is no exception.

Within the `android.provider.MediaStore` class is a constant named `ACTION_VIDEO_CAPTURE`, which contains the string "android.media.action. VIDEO_CAPTURE". This string is registered by the Camera application as an intent filter and will therefore be activated by an intent sent via the `Content.startActivity` or `Context.startActivityForResult` methods. Other applications may also register the same string, which would result in the user being prompted to choose which application he or she would like to use to perform the action.

```
Intent captureVideoIntent = new Intent(android.provider.MediaStore.
ACTION_VIDEO_CAPTURE);
startActivityForResult(captureVideoIntent, VIDEO_CAPTURED);
```

`VIDEO_CAPTURED` is a constant that should be defined as a class variable and is used to recognize when the Camera application returns a result to our activity via a call to our `onActivityResult` method:

```
public static int VIDEO_CAPTURED = 1;
```

The intent that is passed back to our activity in the `onActivityResult` method (data in the following code example) contains a Uri to the video file that was created by the Camera application.

```
protected void onActivityResult (int requestCode, int resultCode, Intent data) {
    if (resultCode == RESULT_OK && requestCode == VIDEO_CAPTURED) {
        Uri videoFileUri = data.getData();
    }
}
```

Here is a full example that uses an intent to trigger the built-in Camera application for video capture.

```
package com.apress.proandroidmedia.ch11.videocaptureintent;

import android.app.Activity;
import android.content.Intent;
import android.net.Uri;
import android.os.Bundle;
import android.view.View;
import android.view.View.OnClickListener;
import android.widget.Button;
import android.widget.VideoView;

public class VideoCaptureIntent extends Activity implements OnClickListener {
```

The VIDEO_CAPTURED constant is created to the activity that is returning via a call to onActivityResult.

```
    public static int VIDEO_CAPTURED = 1;
```

We'll use two buttons, one for triggering the sending of the intent, captureVideoButton, and another for playing the video once it is captured, playVideoButton.

```
    Button captureVideoButton;
    Button playVideoButton;
```

We will be using a standard VideoView object with a Uri to play back the video that has been captured.

```
    VideoView videoView;
    Uri videoFileUri;

    @Override
    public void onCreate(Bundle savedInstanceState) {
        super.onCreate(savedInstanceState);
        setContentView(R.layout.main);

        captureVideoButton = (Button) this.findViewById(R.id.CaptureVideoButton);
        playVideoButton = (Button) this.findViewById(R.id.PlayVideoButton);

        captureVideoButton.setOnClickListener(this);
        playVideoButton.setOnClickListener(this);
```

The playVideoButton will initially not be enabled, meaning it cannot be clicked. We'll set it to be enabled once we have captured the video.

```
        playVideoButton.setEnabled(false);

        videoView = (VideoView) this.findViewById(R.id.VideoView);
    }
```

Our activity implements `OnClickListener` and is registered as the `OnClickListener` for each of the Buttons. Therefore when a button is pressed or clicked, our `onClick` method will be called.

```
public void onClick(View v) {
        if (v == captureVideoButton) {
```

If the `captureVideoButton` was pressed, we create the intent and pass it along with our `VIDEO_CAPTURED` constant into the `startActivityForResult` method, which will kick off the built-in Camera application.

```
                Intent captureVideoIntent = new Intent(android.provider.
MediaStore.ACTION_VIDEO_CAPTURE);
                startActivityForResult(captureVideoIntent, VIDEO_CAPTURED);
        } else if (v == playVideoButton) {
```

If the `playVideoButton` is pressed, we'll set the Uri to play and start the playback.

```
                videoView.setVideoURI(videoFileUri);
                videoView.start();
        }
    }
```

When the Camera (or any triggered application/activity) returns, the following `onActivityResult` method will be called. We check that the `resultCode` is the constant `RESULT_OK` and the `requestCode` is what we passed into the `startActivityForResult`, `VIDEO_CAPTURED`, and then grab the Uri to the video file that was recorded. Following that, we'll enable the `playVideoButton` so the user can press it and trigger the video to play.

```
    protected void onActivityResult (int requestCode, int resultCode, Intent data) {
        if (resultCode == RESULT_OK && requestCode == VIDEO_CAPTURED) {
            videoFileUri = data.getData();
            playVideoButton.setEnabled(true);
        }
    }

}
```

Here is the layout XML contained in `res/layout/main.xml` referenced by the foregoing activity.

```
<?xml version="1.0" encoding="utf-8"?>
<LinearLayout xmlns:android="http://schemas.android.com/apk/res/android"
    android:orientation="vertical"
    android:layout_width="fill_parent"
    android:layout_height="fill_parent"
    >
      <Button android:text="Capture Video" android:id="@+id/CaptureVideoButton"
android:layout_width="wrap_content" android:layout_height="wrap_content"></Button>
      <Button android:text="Play Video" android:id="@+id/PlayVideoButton"
android:layout_width="wrap_content" android:layout_height="wrap_content"></Button>
      <VideoView android:id="@+id/VideoView" android:layout_width="wrap_content"
android:layout_height="wrap_content"></VideoView>
</LinearLayout>
```

As we have discovered, if we simply need to record video or want to offer the user all of the controls available in the Camera app, using an intent to trigger it is a great way to go.

Adding Video Metadata

As we discussed in Chapter 9, Android's `MediaStore` content provider has a portion, `MediaStore.Video`, dedicated to video in addition to the portions for image and audio files and metadata that we have previously looked at.

When triggering the Camera application via an intent, the Uri to the newly recorded video file that is returned is a `content://` style Uri, which is used in combination with a content provider—in this case, the `MediaStore`. In order to add additional metadata, we can use the Uri returned to update the video's record in the MediaStore.

As with any content provider, we use the `update` method on a `ContentResolver` object obtained from our Context. We pass in the `content://` style Uri and the new data in the form of a `ContentValues` object. Since we have a Uri to a specific record, we don't need to specify anything for the final two arguments, the SQL-style `WHERE` clause and `WHERE` clause arguments.

The `ContentValues` object contains name value pairs, with the names being `MediaStore.Video` specific column names. The possible names are listed as constants in `MediaStore.Video.Media`, with most of them being inherited from `android.provider.BaseColumns`, `MediaStore.MediaColumns`, and `MediaStore.Video.VideoColumns`.

```
ContentValues values = new ContentValues(1);
values.put(MediaStore.MediaColumns.TITLE, titleEditText.getText().toString());
int numRecordsUpdated = getContentResolver().update(videoFileUri, values, null, null);
```

Here is an update to the foregoing VideoCaptureIntent example that presents the user with the opportunity to associate a title with the newly captured video.

```
package  com.apress.proandroidmedia.ch11.videocaptureintent;

import android.app.Activity;
import android.content.ContentValues;
import android.content.Intent;
import android.net.Uri;
import android.os.Bundle;
import android.provider.MediaStore;
import android.view.View;
import android.view.View.OnClickListener;
import android.widget.Button;
import android.widget.EditText;
import android.widget.Toast;

public class VideoCaptureIntent extends Activity implements OnClickListener {

        public static int VIDEO_CAPTURED = 1;

        Button captureVideoButton;
        Button playVideoButton;
        Button saveVideoButton;
```

In this version, we'll have an EditText object, which will be used by the user to enter in the title for the video.

```
EditText titleEditText;

Uri videoFileUri;

    @Override
public void onCreate(Bundle savedInstanceState) {
    super.onCreate(savedInstanceState);
    setContentView(R.layout.main);

    captureVideoButton = (Button) this.findViewById(R.id.CaptureVideoButton);
    playVideoButton = (Button) this.findViewById(R.id.PlayVideoButton);
```

We'll also have a saveVideoButton, which, when pressed, will trigger the update of the record in the MediaStore.

```
saveVideoButton = (Button) this.findViewById(R.id.SaveVideoButton);

    titleEditText = (EditText) this.findViewById(R.id.TitleEditText);

    captureVideoButton.setOnClickListener(this);
    playVideoButton.setOnClickListener(this);
    saveVideoButton.setOnClickListener(this);

    playVideoButton.setEnabled(false);
    saveVideoButton.setEnabled(false);
    titleEditText.setEnabled(false);
}
```

The onClick method, triggered when any of the Buttons are pressed, performs most of the work. When the captureVideoButton is pressed, we trigger the built-in Camera application via an intent. When the playVideoButton is pressed, we trigger the built-in Media Player application via an intent (instead of using a VideoView as we did previously). Finally when we click the saveVideoButton, we update the MediaStore record for the video file.

```
public void onClick(View v) {
    if (v == captureVideoButton) {
            Intent captureVideoIntent = new Intent(android.provider.↵
MediaStore.ACTION_VIDEO_CAPTURE);
            startActivityForResult(captureVideoIntent, VIDEO_CAPTURED);
    } else if (v == playVideoButton) {
            Intent playVideoIntent = new Intent(Intent.ACTION_VIEW,↵
 videoFileUri);
            startActivity(playVideoIntent);
    } else if (v == saveVideoButton) {
```

First, we create a ContentValues object and populate it with the text the user has specified in the EditText object.

```
        ContentValues values = new ContentValues(1);
            values.put(MediaStore.MediaColumns.TITLE,↵
 titleEditText.getText().toString());
```

Then we call the update method on the ContentResolver object, passing in the Uri to the captured video and the ContentValues object.

```
        if (getContentResolver().update(videoFileUri, values, null,↵
null) == 1) {
```

If the result of the update method is 1, then we were successful; one row was updated, and we'll tell the user.

```
        Toast t = Toast.makeText(this, "Updated " +↵
titleEditText.getText().toString(), Toast.LENGTH_SHORT);
            t.show();
        }
        else {
```

If the result was anything other than 1, we'll tell the user that an error occurred.

```
        Toast t = Toast.makeText(this, "Error",↵
Toast.LENGTH_SHORT);
            t.show();
        }
      }
    }

    protected void onActivityResult (int requestCode, int resultCode, Intent data) {
        if (resultCode == RESULT_OK && requestCode == VIDEO_CAPTURED) {
            videoFileUri = data.getData();
            playVideoButton.setEnabled(true);
            saveVideoButton.setEnabled(true);
            titleEditText.setEnabled(true);
            }
        }
}
```

Here is the layout XML contained in res/layout/main.xml referenced by the foregoing activity.

```
<?xml version="1.0" encoding="utf-8"?>
<LinearLayout xmlns:android="http://schemas.android.com/apk/res/android"
    android:orientation="vertical"
    android:layout_width="fill_parent"
    android:layout_height="fill_parent"
    >
        <Button android:text="Capture Video" android:id="@+id/CaptureVideoButton"↵
android:layout_width="wrap_content" android:layout_height="wrap_content"></Button>
        <Button android:text="Play Video" android:id="@+id/PlayVideoButton"↵
android:layout_width="wrap_content" android:layout_height="wrap_content"></Button>

        <TextView android:text="Title:" android:id="@+id/TitleTextView"↵
android:layout_width="wrap_content" android:layout_height="wrap_content"></TextView>
        <EditText android:text="" android:id="@+id/TitleEditText"↵
android:layout_width="wrap_content" android:layout_height="wrap_content"></EditText>
        <Button android:text="Save Metadata" android:id="@+id/SaveVideoButton"↵
android:layout_width="wrap_content" android:layout_height="wrap_content"></Button>
</LinearLayout>
```

The preceding example shows how straightforward many aspects of using video within Android can be, especially so when using an intent to do the video capture and relying upon the MediaStore to handle metadata.

It should be noted that when updating the metadata in the MediaStore, the data is not updated within the video file itself; rather, it is stored only in the MediaStore record that pertains to the video. The Android SDK does not offer built-in classes to alter the media file's metadata directly.

Custom Video Capture

With images and audio there are multiple ways to do capture. Video capture is no exception; we don't have quite as many options as we do with audio, but we do have the ability to create a custom video capture example using the `MediaRecorder` class.

In many ways, building a custom video capture application is a lot like building a custom camera application combined with a custom audio recording application. We have to create a SurfaceView for the camera to draw preview or viewfinder images on, just like we did with our custom camera examples from Chapter 2, and we'll use a `MediaRecorder` for the actual recording, like we did in Chapter 7 for audio capture.

MediaRecorder for Video

To use the `MediaRecorder` for video capture, we have to follow all of the same steps for audio capture plus some video specific steps. In addition, the `MediaRecorder` is a state machine, and we therefore have to follow a specific sequence of steps to go from instantiation to recording.

First we'll instantiate it, and then go through the steps in sequence.

```
MediaRecorder recorder = new MediaRecorder();
```

Audio and Video Sources

Following instantiation, we can set the audio and video sources. To set the audio source, we use the `setAudioSource` method, passing in a constant representing the source we would like to use.

```
recorder.setAudioSource(MediaRecorder.AudioSource.DEFAULT);
```

The possible audio source values are constants defined in the `MediaRecorder.AudioSource` class:

- *CAMCORDER*: If the device has different microphones for use with different cameras (front-facing, rear-facing), using this value will specify that the appropriate microphone is used (Android 2.1/API level 7 or later).

- *DEFAULT*: This specifies that the default microphone on the device will be used.

- *MIC*: This specifies that the normal microphone meant for use with video recording is used.

- *VOICE_CALL*: This specifies that the audio should be taken from a call that is currently in progress. This is currently unsupported by most if not all handsets.

- *VOICE_DOWNLINK*: This specifies that the audio should be taken from a call, specifically the incoming audio (the other party). This is currently unsupported by most if not all handsets.

- *VOICE_UPLINK*: This specifies that the audio should be taken from a call, specifically the outgoing audio (the audio that the handset is sending). This is currently unsupported by most if not all handsets.

- *VOICE_RECOGNITION*: This specifies that the audio should be taken from a microphone that is set for the voice recognition functions on the phone. If no such microphone is specified, the DEFAULT microphone will be used.

The possible video source values are defined in the MediaRecorder.VideoSource class, which contains only two constants:

- CAMERA
- DEFAULT

Both indicate the same thing, that the device's main camera should be used for recording video.

To set the video source, we use the setVideoSource method:

```
recorder.setVideoSource(MediaRecorder.VideoSource.DEFAULT);
```

> **NOTE:** It would make sense that using the MediaRecorder.VideoSource.DEFAULT in the MediaRecorder's setVideoSource method or MediaRecorder.AudioSource.DEFAULT in the MediaRecorder's setAudioSource method would be the same as not calling the methods. After all, they are the *default* values. Unfortunately, on the contrary, each method is required to be called for that specific data to be captured. In other words, if the audio source isn't set, no audio will be recorded, and if the video source isn't set, no video will be recorded.

Output Format

Following the setting of the audio and video sources, we can set the output format using the MediaRecorder's setOutputFormat method, passing in the format to be used.

```
recorder.setOutputFormat(MediaRecorder.OutputFormat.DEFAULT);
```

The possible formats are listed as constants in the `MediaRecorder.OutputFormat` class.

- *DEFAULT*: Specifies that the default output format will be used. This *may* be different across devices. On a Nexus 1 running Android 2.2, it is MPEG-4, the same format used if the MPEG_4 constant is used.

- *MPEG_4*: Specifies that the audio and video will be captured to a file in the MPEG-4 file format. This file will be an `.mp4` file. MPEG-4 files typically contain H.264–, H.263–, or MPEG-4 Part 2–encoded video with AAC– or MP3–encoded audio (although other codecs may be used). MPEG-4 files are widely used in Flash with iPods and many other online video technologies and consumer electronics devices.

- *RAW_AMR*: This setting is for audio recording only and does not work with video.

- *THREE_GPP*: Specifies that the audio and video will be captured to a file in the 3GP file format. This file will be a `.3gp` file. 3GPP files typically contain video encoded with H.264, MPEG-4 Part 2, or H.263 codecs and audio encoded with AMR or AAC codecs.

Audio and Video Encoders

After we set the output format, we should specify the audio and video encoders that we would like used. Using the `MediaRecorder`'s `setVideoEncoder` method, we specify the video codecs that will be used:

```
recorder.setVideoEncoder(MediaRecorder.VideoEncoder.DEFAULT);
```

The possible values that can be passed into `setVideoEncoder` are defined as constants in `MediaRecorder.VideoEncoder`:

- *DEFAULT*: This is a device-dependent setting specifying that the codec used will be the default for the device. In many cases, this will be H.263 since it is the only codec that is required to be supported on Android.

- *H263*: This specifies that the codec used will be H.263. H.263 is a codec that was released in 1995 and was developed specifically for low bitrate video transmission. It became the basis for many early Internet video technologies such as those used early on in Flash and the RealPlayer. It is required to be supported for encoding on Android and therefore can be counted on to be available.

- *H264*: This specifies that the codec used will be H.264 (which also goes by the name MPEG-4 Part 10 or AVC, Advanced Video Coding). H.264 is a state-of-the-art codec used in a wide range of technologies from BluRay to Flash. It was released in 2003. Most Android devices support this codec for video playback. A smaller set of devices use it for video encoding.

- *MPEG_4_SP*: This specifies that the codec used will be the MPEG-4 SP (Simple Profile) codec. MPEG-4 SP is technically the MPEG-4 Part 2 Simple Profile. It was released in 1999 and was developed for use by technologies that require low bitrate video without requiring a lot of processor power.

Using the `MediaRecorder`'s `setAudioEncoder` method, we specify the audio codecs that will be used.

```
recorder.setAudioEncoder(MediaRecorder.AudioEncoder.DEFAULT);
```

The possible values that can be passed to `setAudioEncoder` are defined as constants in `MediaRecorder.AudioEncoder`.

`MediaRecorder.AudioEncoder` contains only two constants:

- *AMR_NB*: This specifies that the audio codec that will be used for audio encoding is AMR-NB, which stands for Adaptive Multi-Rate Narrow Band. AMR-NB is a codec tuned for voice and is widely used in mobile phones.

- *DEFAULT:* Since AMR-NB is the only other choice, the `DEFAULT` constant specifies that AMR-NB will be the audio codec used.

Audio and Video Bitrates

Video encoding bitrates can be set using the `setVideoEncodingBitrate` method on the `MediaRecorder` and passing in the bitrate requested in bits per second. A low bitrate setting for video would be in the range of 256,000 bits per second (256 kbps), while a high bitrate for video would be in the range of 3,000,000 bits per second (3 mbps).

```
recorder.setVideoEncodingBitRate(150000);
```

We can also specify the maximum bitrate that we would like used for the encoded audio data. We do so by passing the value as bits per second into the setAudioEncodingBitRate method on the MediaRecorder. For reference, 8,000 bits per second (8 kbps) is a very low bitrate that is appropriate for audio that needs to be delivered in real time over slow networks, while rates of 196,000 bits per second (196 kbps) and higher are not uncommon for music in MP3 files. Currently most Android devices support bitrates only on the low end of the spectrum, and the `MediaRecorder` will automatically select a bitrate within its supportable range should you choose one that is too high.

```
recorder.setAudioEncodingBitRate(8000);
```

Audio Sample Rate

Along with bitrate, the audio sample rate is important in determining the quality of the audio that is captured and encoded. The `MediaPlayer` has a method, `setAudioSampleRate`, which allows us to request a specific sample rate. The sample rate passed in is in Hz (hertz), which stands for the number of samples per second. The higher the sample rate, the larger the range of audio frequencies that can be represented in the captured file. A sample rate on the low end, 8,000 Hz, is suitable for capturing low-quality voice, and on the high end, 48,000 Hz is used in DVD and many other high-quality video formats. Most Android devices support sample rates only in the low range (8,000 Hz).

```
recorder.setAudioSamplingRate(8000);
```

Audio Channels

The number of audio channels to be captured can be specified by using the `setAudioChannels` method, passing in the number of channels. For the most part, incoming audio is currently limited to a single channel microphone on most Android devices, and therefore using more than one channel wouldn't be beneficial. Generally the choice of the number of channels to use will be between one channel for mono and two channels for stereo.

```
recorder.setAudioChannels(1);
```

Video Frame Rate

The number of frames of video captured per second can be controlled by using the `setVideoFrameRate` by passing in the requested frame rate. A value between 12 and 15 frames per second is generally adequate to represent motion. On the high end, television is 30 frames per second (29.97 in reality). The actual frame rate used will vary based on the capabilities of the device.

```
recorder.setVideoFrameRate(15);
```

Video Size

The width and height of the video as it is captured can be controlled with the `setVideoSize` method by passing in an integer for the width and the height in pixels. Standard sizes range from 176x144 to 640x480, with many devices supporting even higher resolutions.

> **NOTE:** Many Android devices also support 720×480, but it should noted that this isn't the same pixel aspect ratio that would be captured by a DV camera, which captures *rectangular* pixels at 720×480. On Android devices, the pixels are generally *square*, and therefore if 720×480 video from an Android device is brought into video editing software, the software might make the wrong assumption about the video due to its resolution, causing the output to be distorted. To correct this, the software needs to be told that the pixel aspect ratio is square or 1.0.
>
> ```
> recorder.setVideoSize(640,480);
> ```

Maximum File Size

The maximum size of a file captured by MediaRecorder can be specified by passing in the maximum size in bytes to the setMaxFileSize method.

```
recorder.setMaxFileSize(10000000); // 10 megabytes
```

To determine when maximum file size has been reached, we need to implement the MediaRecorder.OnInfoListener in our activity and register it with our MediaRecorder. The onInfo method will then be called and the what parameter can be checked against the MediaRecorder.MEDIA_RECORDER_INFO_FILESIZE_REACHED constant. If they match, the maximum file size was reached.

According to the documentation, the MediaRecorder is supposed to stop when the maximum file size is reached, but it seems that it does not do so reliably as of Android 2.2.1. Unfortunately no methods exist for us to check whether it has stopped. In order to actually stop the recording, we must explicitly call the stop method.

Here is some extremely abbreviated code to illustrate.

```
public class VideoCapture extends Activity implements MediaRecorder.OnInfoListener {
    public void onCreate(Bundle savedInstanceState) {
        recorder.setOnInfoListener(this);
    }
    public void onInfo(MediaRecorder mr, int what, int extra) {
        if (what == MediaRecorder.MEDIA_RECORDER_INFO_MAX_FILESIZE_REACHED) {
            Log.v("VIDEOCAPTURE","Maximum Filesize Reached");
        }
    }
}
```

Maximum Duration

The maximum duration of a file captured by the MediaRecorder can be set by passing in the maximum duration in milliseconds to the setMaxDuration method.

```
recorder.setMaxDuration(10000); // 10 seconds
```

To determine when the maxium duration has been reached, we need to implement the MediaRecorder.OnInfoListener and register it with our MediaRecorder. Then when the duration has been reached, our onInfo method will be triggered, with the what integer being set to the constant MediaRecorder.MEDIA_RECORDER_INFO_MAX_DURATION_REACHED.

According to the documentation, the MediaRecorder is supposed to stop when the maximum duration is reached, but it seems that it does not do so reliably as of Android 2.2.1. Unfortunately no methods exist for us to check whether it has stopped. In order to actually stop the recording, we must explicitly call the stop method.

Here is an abbreviated illustration.

```
public class VideoCapture extends Activity implements MediaRecorder.OnInfoListener {
    public void onCreate(Bundle savedInstanceState) {
        recorder.setOnInfoListener(this);
    }
```

```
    public void onInfo(MediaRecorder mr, int what, int extra) {
        if (what == MediaRecorder.MEDIA_RECORDER_INFO_MAX_DURATION_REACHED) {
            Log.v("VIDEOCAPTURE","Maximum Duration Reached");
            mr.stop();
        }
    }
}
```

Profile

Starting with Android 2.2 (API Level 8), `MediaRecorder` has a method, `setProfile`, which takes in an instance of `CamcorderProfile`. `CamcorderProfile` has a static method, `CamcorderProfile.get`, which takes in an integer with the possible values being defined as constants, `CamcorderProfile.QUALITY_HIGH` or `CamcorderProfile.QUALITY_LOW`. Using this method allows us to set an entire set of configuration variables according to preset values. Of course, `QUALITY_HIGH` refers to settings for high-quality video capture, and `QUALITY_LOW` refers to settings for low-quality video capture.

`QUALITY_HIGH` has the following settings:

- *Audio Bit Rate*: 12,200 bits per second
- Audio Channels: 1
- Audio Codec: AMR-NB
- Audio Sample Rate: 8000 Hz
- *Duration*: 60 seconds
- File Format: MP4
- *Video Bit Rate*: 3,000,000 bits per second
- Video Codec: H.264
- Video Frame Width: 720 pixels
- Video Frame Height: 480 pixels
- *Video Frame Rate*: 24 frames per second

Take note that as described previously, many of the settings are maximum or requested and the capabilities of the device will dictate the results. For instance, a sample video captured using the `QUALITY_HIGH` settings on a Nexus 1 running Android 2.2.1 yielded video at 12.6 frames per second and a total bitrate of 1,617.34 kb/second.

Here are the `QUALITY_LOW` settings:

- *Audio Bit Rate*: 12,200 bits per second
- Audio Channels: 1
- Audio Codec: AMR-NB
- Audio Sample Rate: 8000 Hz

- *Duration*: 30 seconds

- File Format: 3GPP

- *Video Bit Rate*: 256,000 bits per second

- Video Codec: 3

- Video Frame Width: 176 pixels

- Video Frame Height: 144 pixels

- *Video Frame Rate*: 15 frames per second

As with the `QUALITY_HIGH` version, these settings yield slightly different results as well. The resulting video was captured at 16.06 frames per second with a bitrate of 207.96 kb/second.

Output File

Following all of that, we can set the location of the output file. We can pass in either a `FileDescriptor` or a String representing the path to the file.

```
recorder.setOutputFile("/sdcard/recorded_video.mp4");
```

Preview Surface

Before we can move forward, we need to specify a Surface for the `MediaRecorder` preview (viewfinder) images to draw. We'll handle this in a similar manner to how we handled the preview images in our custom camera examples in Chapter 2.

Let's go through an abbreviated example. First, we'll create a Surface in our layout.

```
<?xml version="1.0" encoding="utf-8"?>
<LinearLayout xmlns:android="http://schemas.android.com/apk/res/android"
    android:orientation="vertical"
    android:layout_width="fill_parent"
    android:layout_height="fill_parent"
    >
    <SurfaceView android:id="@+id/CameraView" android:layout_width="640px"
      android:layout_height="480px"></SurfaceView>
</LinearLayout>
```

In our activity, we need to implement `SurfaceHolder.Callback` so that we can be notified when the Surface is created, changed, or destroyed.

```
...
public class VideoCapture extends Activity implements SurfaceHolder.Callback{
        MediaRecorder recorder;
        SurfaceHolder holder;

    @Override
    public void onCreate(Bundle savedInstanceState) {
                super.onCreate(savedInstanceState);
                recorder = new MediaRecorder();
```

At this point in the code, we would perform all of the normal setup of the `MediaRecorder` object, such as setting the audio and video sources, the output file location, and so on. We are leaving that out to illustrate just how to work with the Surface in this code snippet.

```
setContentView(R.layout.main);
```

Following the setting of the content view, we can obtain a reference to our SurfaceView and get a reference to its `SurfaceHolder`.

```
SurfaceView cameraView = (SurfaceView)↵
findViewById(R.id.CameraView);
        holder = cameraView.getHolder();
```

We'll add our activity as its `SurfaceHolder.Callback` implementer.

```
holder.addCallback(this);
```

As with the camera examples in Chapter 2, the preview Surface will have its buffers managed externally by the `Camera` object that is underlying the `MediaRecorder`; therefore we need to set the type to be SURFACE_TYPE_PUSH_BUFFERS.

```
holder.setType(SurfaceHolder.SURFACE_TYPE_PUSH_BUFFERS);
    }
```

Because our activity has implemented and is registered as the `SurfaceHolder.Callback`, our `surfaceCreated` method will be called when the Surface is actually created. When this occurs, we can set the Surface to be the preview display of the `MediaRecorder` object with the `setPreviewDisplay` method. We can't do this before the Surface is created.

```
public void surfaceCreated(SurfaceHolder holder) {
        recorder.setPreviewDisplay(holder.getSurface());
    }
```

As we are implementing `SurfaceHolder.Callback`, we also have to have methods for `surfaceChanged` and `surfaceDestroyed`, which are named for when they are called: `surfaceChanged` when a change occurs to the Surface, such as its height and width are changed; `surfaceDestroyed` when it is no longer used, such as when the activity is no longer visible.

When `surfaceDestroyed` is called, we should stop recording video, as recording works only when a Surface is available to draw preview images onto.

```
    public void surfaceChanged(SurfaceHolder holder, int format, int width,↵
int height) {
    }

    public void surfaceDestroyed(SurfaceHolder holder) {
        recorder.stop();
    }
}
```

Prepare to Record

Once all of the MediaRecorder settings are set, we are ready to use the prepare method. This method is required and performs all of the internal functions getting the MediaRecorder ready to record.

```
recorder.prepare();
```

Start Recording

After the MediaRecorder has been "prepared," we are ready to start the recording. The start method does just that—it starts the recording.

```
recorder.start();
```

Stop Recording

After recording has been started, it can be stopped by using the stop method.

```
recorder.stop();
```

Release Resources

Finally, once we are done with the MediaRecorder, we should call the release method to free up its resources. This is important as only one application at a time can use many of the underlying resources, such as the hardware camera and microphone.

```
recorder.release();
```

State Machine

As just described and as with the MediaPlayer object, the MediaRecorder has various states, and certain methods can be called only when in the appropriate state. Figure 11–1 is an illustration of the possible states and what state it moves to when specific methods are called (reproduced again here for reference).

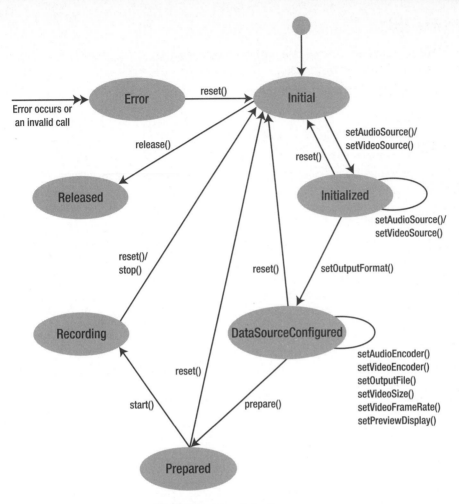

MediaRecorder state diagram

Figure 11–1. *MediaRecorder state diagram from Android API Reference*

Permissions

Using the MediaRecorder for both audio and video capture and saving to a file on the SD card requires the following permissions be set in the AndroidManifest.xml file.

```
<uses-permission android:name="android.permission.RECORD_AUDIO"></uses-permission>
<uses-permission android:name="android.permission.CAMERA"></uses-permission>
<uses-permission android:name="android.permission.WRITE_EXTERNAL_STORAGE">↩
</uses-permission>
```

Full Custom Video Capture Example

Here is a full example putting all of the foregoing steps together. It is using
CamcorderProfile, so it requires Android 2.2 or higher.

```
package  com.apress.proandroidmedia.ch11.videocapture;

import java.io.IOException;
import android.app.Activity;
import android.content.pm.ActivityInfo;
import android.media.CamcorderProfile;
import android.media.MediaRecorder;
import android.os.Bundle;
import android.util.Log;
import android.view.SurfaceHolder;
import android.view.SurfaceView;
import android.view.View;
import android.view.Window;
import android.view.WindowManager;
import android.view.View.OnClickListener;
```

In this example, our activity will implement OnClickListener, so that the user can click to
start and stop recording, and SurfaceHolder.Callback to handle Surface-related events.

```
public class VideoCapture extends Activity implements OnClickListener,↵
SurfaceHolder.Callback {
        MediaRecorder recorder;
        SurfaceHolder holder;
```

Here we have a Boolean that represents whether we are currently recording. It will be
false when we are not recording and true when we are.

```
        boolean recording = false;
        public static final String TAG = "VIDEOCAPTURE";

        @Override
    public void onCreate(Bundle savedInstanceState) {
                super.onCreate(savedInstanceState);
```

This activity will run full-screen and in landscape, so we'll set that up with the following
methods.

```
                requestWindowFeature(Window.FEATURE_NO_TITLE);
getWindow().setFlags(WindowManager.LayoutParams.FLAG_FULLSCREEN,↵
WindowManager.LayoutParams.FLAG_FULLSCREEN);
                setRequestedOrientation(ActivityInfo.SCREEN_ORIENTATION_LANDSCAPE);
```

Next, we'll instantiate our MediaRecorder object.

```
                recorder = new MediaRecorder();
```

The initRecorder method, defined further on, will handle all of the MediaRecorder
settings.

```
                initRecorder();

                setContentView(R.layout.main);
```

Continuing on, we'll get a reference to the `SurfaceView` and the `SurfaceHolder` as well as register our activity as the `SurfaceHolder.Callback`.

```
SurfaceView cameraView = (SurfaceView)
findViewById(R.id.CameraView);
            holder = cameraView.getHolder();
            holder.addCallback(this);
            holder.setType(SurfaceHolder.SURFACE_TYPE_PUSH_BUFFERS);
```

We'll make our `SurfaceView` clickable and register our activity as the `OnClickListener` for it. This way our `onClick` method will be called when the `SurfaceView` is touched.

```
            cameraView.setClickable(true);
            cameraView.setOnClickListener(this);
    }
```

The `initRecorder` method, defined here, takes care of all of the `MediaRecorder` settings.

```
    private void initRecorder() {
```

We'll use the default audio and video sources.

```
        recorder.setAudioSource(MediaRecorder.AudioSource.DEFAULT);
        recorder.setVideoSource(MediaRecorder.VideoSource.DEFAULT);
```

Rather than go through all of the individual settings, we'll use one of the built-in `CamcorderProfile`'s—in this case, the one specified by the `QUALITY_HIGH` constant.

```
        CamcorderProfile cpHigh =
CamcorderProfile.get(CamcorderProfile.QUALITY_HIGH);
        recorder.setProfile(cpHigh);
```

We'll specify the path to a file to record to. In this case, it is a file directly on the SD card.

```
        recorder.setOutputFile("/sdcard/videocapture_example.mp4");
```

Then we'll specify a maximum duration in milliseconds.

```
        recorder.setMaxDuration(50000); // 50 seconds
```

Finally we'll specify a maximum file size in bytes.

```
        recorder.setMaxFileSize(5000000); // Approximately 5 megabytes
    }
```

The following `prepareRecorder` method exists to separate the `setPreviewDisplay` method from the rest of the `MediaRecorder` methods. We need to do this as this step needs to be performed after the Surface has been created, whereas the other steps can be performed at any time after the `MediaRecorder` is instantiated or after it has been stopped.

```
    private void prepareRecorder() {
        recorder.setPreviewDisplay(holder.getSurface());
```

After the preview display has been set, we can call the `prepare` method on the `MediaRecorder` object. This step gets everything ready for capture. We have to wrap it in a try/catch block as it throws some exceptions. If we get any, we'll just finish. In your applications, you will probably want to handle them more gracefully.

```
        try {
```

```
                            recorder.prepare();
              } catch (IllegalStateException e) {
                            e.printStackTrace();
                            finish();
              } catch (IOException e) {
                            e.printStackTrace();
                            finish();
              }
      }
```

When the SurfaceView is clicked, our activity's onClick method will be called.

```
    public void onClick(View v) {
```

If the recording Boolean is true, we'll call the stop method on the recorder and set the recording Boolean to false. Additionally, if we are done with the MediaRecorder, we should call the release method to free up its resources, as only one application can use it at a time.

```
        if (recording) {
                recorder.stop();
                //recorder.release();
                recording = false;
                Log.v(TAG,"Recording Stopped");
```

In this example, we are going to allow the user to record again, so we'll call initRecorder and prepareRecorder to set everything back up. We need to do this because after recording is stopped with the stop method, its state is as if it were just initialized, and it therefore isn't ready to record again.

```
            // Let's initRecorder so we can record again
            initRecorder();
            prepareRecorder();
        } else {
```

If the recording Boolean is false, we'll call the start method on the MediaRecorder and update the Boolean.

```
                recording = true;
                recorder.start();
                Log.v(TAG,"Recording Started");
        }
    }
```

As explained previously, we'll call prepareRecorder once the Surface is created.

```
        public void surfaceCreated(SurfaceHolder holder) {
                Log.v(TAG,"surfaceCreated");
                prepareRecorder();
        }

        public void surfaceChanged(SurfaceHolder holder, int format, int width,↵
    int height) {
        }
```

We'll stop the recording if we are recording when the Surface is destroyed. This will likely happen when the activity is no longer visible. Since the MediaRecorder uses shared resources, such as the camera and microphone, we'll call the release method so that other applications may use them. In addition, there is no reason to keep this application running; we'll call finish so that next time it is started, everything is initialized again.

```
public void surfaceDestroyed(SurfaceHolder holder) {
        Log.v(TAG,"surfaceDestroyed");
        if (recording) {
                recorder.stop();
                recording = false;
        }
        recorder.release();
        finish();
    }
}
```

Here is the layout XML that we are using.

```
<?xml version="1.0" encoding="utf-8"?>
<LinearLayout xmlns:android="http://schemas.android.com/apk/res/android"
    android:orientation="vertical"
    android:layout_width="fill_parent"
    android:layout_height="fill_parent"
    >
    <SurfaceView android:id="@+id/CameraView" android:layout_width="640px"↵
    android:layout_height="480px"></SurfaceView>
</LinearLayout>
```

Here are the contents of AndroidManifest.xml for this example. Of note are the three uses-permission tags that are required.

```
<?xml version="1.0" encoding="utf-8"?>
<manifest xmlns:android="http://schemas.android.com/apk/res/android"
      package="com.apress.proandroidmedia.ch11.videocapture"
      android:versionCode="1"
      android:versionName="1.0">
    <application android:icon="@drawable/icon" android:label="@string/app_name">
        <activity android:name=".VideoCapture"
                  android:label="@string/app_name">
            <intent-filter>
                <action android:name="android.intent.action.MAIN" />
                <category android:name="android.intent.category.LAUNCHER" />
            </intent-filter>
        </activity>
    </application>
    <uses-sdk android:minSdkVersion="8" />
    <uses-permission android:name="android.permission.RECORD_AUDIO">
    </uses-permission>
    <uses-permission android:name="android.permission.CAMERA"></uses-permission>
    <uses-permission android:name="android.permission.WRITE_EXTERNAL_STORAGE">
    </uses-permission>
</manifest>
```

As we see, writing an application to perform custom video capture isn't terribly difficult, but it can be a bit painful if we don't pay attention to the Surface creation and the order of the steps. Creating our own application gives us a lot of flexibility in changing the settings, such as the codec, bitrate, and format used to record. Figure 11–2 shows the foregoing example as it looks on a device.

Figure 11–2. *Custom Video Capture activity*

Summary

This concludes our exploration of video capabilities on Android. In previous chapters, we looked at playback, storage, and networked video. In this chapter, we brought capture into the mix and saw that just like the other media capture capabilities that exist on Android, we can either use the built-in capabilities through an intent or create our own capture application. Both ways are valid; the first offers a rich set of capabilities but less control, while the second allows for a more controlled experience.

Chapter 12

Media Consumption and Publishing Using Web Services

It would be negligent to put out a book that didn't cover the wide range of possibilities available for online media consumption from sites such as Flickr, which offers photos and videos, and YouTube, famous for its wide range of user-generated video.

It also makes sense that since so much of this book has been about means and methods for building applications that allow users to create or produce media, we should cover methods for publishing that media to the same or similar places, such as Blip.TV for video and Flickr for images.

Additionally, in the process of this media consuming and publishing, we'll be doing two things: we'll be learning about and using web services and web service protocols such as REST and JSON, and we'll look at utilizing location. We'll learn how we can query platforms such as Flickr for content that was created around the user.

Web Services

We are all familiar with web pages and the sites that encompass them, such as Yahoo, Google, Hulu, and Apress.com. What you may not be as familiar with is the concept of a "web service." Simply put, a web service is a means to access the content and services offered by a web site in a programmatic fashion.

Sites will enable their content to be accessed in this manner to allow third-party developers such as ourselves the ability to embed their content and functionality into applications. For instance, Android phones typically come with a YouTube application pre-installed. This application receives its data from YouTube's site through a web service protocol and displays it within the application. This is different from accessing YouTube's mobile web site, which we could do in a browser. In this case, we aren't getting the layout and formatting data from YouTube's web site; we are getting just the data—for instance, the list of most viewed and top-rated videos, which are then displayed within the application's layout.

There are several web service technologies that are used to do this kind of behind-the-scenes data delivery. We are going to cover two of them, JSON and REST. First, though, we need to cover one of the basics of working with web services, which is making a web or HTTP request in the first place.

HTTP Requests

A web service wouldn't be a "web" service if we didn't use HTTP to access it. Making an HTTP request on Android is straightforward using the Apache-provided `HttpClient` classes that are included with Android in the `org.apache.http` package.

First we need to create an `HttpClient` object, which will actually be a `DefaultHttpClient` object.

```
HttpClient httpclient = new DefaultHttpClient();
```

Following that, we can construct the request. In this case, we'll be making an HTTP GET request, which puts any parameters on the URL in the form of a query string. This is as opposed to an HTTP POST request, which sends additional data as the body of the request message, which is not part of the URL.

To create an HTTP GET request, we'll instantiate an `HttpGet` object, passing in a URL to the page that we would like to retrieve. In this case, we are passing in a URL to the page about this book on Apress's site.

```
HttpGet httpget = new HttpGet("http://www.apress.com/book/view/9781430232674");
```

We'll then execute the request by passing the `HttpGet` object to the `HttpClient` object via the execute method. This will return an `HttpResponse` object.

```
HttpResponse response = httpclient.execute(httpget);
```

The `HttpResponse` will contain an `HttpEntity`, which is basically an HTTP message. Both requests and responses contain entities.

```
HttpEntity entity = response.getEntity();
```

The getContent method on the `HttpEntity` returns an `InputStream` that we can use to read the actual content that was sent in response.

```
InputStream inputstream = entity.getContent();
```

Let's go through a short example to illustrate.

```
package com.apress.proandroidmedia.ch12.simplehttprequest;

import java.io.BufferedReader;
import java.io.IOException;
import java.io.InputStream;
import java.io.InputStreamReader;
```

```
import org.apache.http.HttpEntity;
import org.apache.http.HttpResponse;
import org.apache.http.client.HttpClient;
import org.apache.http.client.methods.HttpGet;
import org.apache.http.impl.client.DefaultHttpClient;

import android.app.Activity;
import android.os.Bundle;
import android.util.Log;

public class SimpleHTTPRequest extends Activity {

    @Override
    public void onCreate(Bundle savedInstanceState) {
        super.onCreate(savedInstanceState);
        setContentView(R.layout.main);
```

First we'll instantiate our `HttpClient` and `HttpGet` objects.

```
        HttpClient httpclient = new DefaultHttpClient();
        HttpGet httpget = new HttpGet("http://www.apress.com/book/view/9781430232674");
```

The execute method on our `HttpClient` may throw an exception, so we need to wrap it in a try catch block.

```
        try {
            HttpResponse response = httpclient.execute(httpget);
            HttpEntity entity = response.getEntity();

            if (entity != null) {
```

If the `HttpEntity` exists, we can get access to the `InputStream`, which can be used to read the response.

```
                InputStream inputstream = entity.getContent();
```

We'll wrap the `InputStream` in a `BufferedReader` and utilize a `StringBuilder` object to turn it into a normal `String` that we can work with in the end.

```
                BufferedReader bufferedreader =
                    new BufferedReader(new InputStreamReader(inputstream));
                StringBuilder stringbuilder = new StringBuilder();

                String currentline = null;
                try {
                    while ((currentline = bufferedreader.readLine()) != null) {
                        stringbuilder.append(currentline + "\n");
                    }
                } catch (IOException e) {
                    e.printStackTrace();
                }
```

After fully reading the content, we use the toString method on our `StringBuilder` object to get the resulting `String`, which will then print out via the Log.

```
                String result = stringbuilder.toString();
                Log.v("HTTP REQUEST",result);
                inputstream.close();
            }
```

```
            } catch (Exception e) {
                e.printStackTrace();
            }
        }
    }
```

Of course, we'll need to have permission to access the Internet, so we'll need to specify that in our AndroidManifest.xml.

```
<uses-permission android:name="android.permission.INTERNET"></uses-permission>
```

Now that we know how to make an HTTP request for a generic web resource, let's look at how we can deal with the type of data that may be returned after a request to a web service. We'll start with JSON-formatted data.

JSON

JSON stands for JavaScript Object Notation. While originally designed for use in JavaScript, as a data-interchange format, it is language-independent. Additionally, for a variety of reasons, one being that it is relatively easy to implement, many web services offer it as an alternative to other formats that are based on XML for data transmission. It is also more lightweight, more compact, and easier for machines to parse than XML.

Android is bundled with a JSON parser within the org.json package.

We won't get too far into the exact syntax of JSON data, but here is a prototypical JSON object representation.

```
{"result":{"aname":"value", "anumber":1234, "aboolean":false}}
```

As you can see in the JSON representation, the entire representation is surrounded by brackets, "{" and "}", and the name of the object is first, in quotes, followed by a colon: "result":. The next set of brackets signifies all of the data that is part of that object. Each piece of data is similarly labeled, with its name in quotes, followed by a colon and then the actual data. Quotes are used to signify strings; a number without quotes is simply a number; Boolean values are represented by true or false; and finally an array of data would be a series of objects within square brackets "[" and "]", separated by commas.

Here is an array called anarray:

```
{"anarray":[{"arrayelement":"Array Element 1"}, {"arrayelement":"Array Element 2"}]}
```

This array has two elements, each one an object surrounded by "{" and "}", with a comma between them. Each element is an object containing a string called "arrayelement."

Let's look at how we can parse JSON data using Android's built-in JSON parser.

We'll start by working with this simple JSON data:

```
{"results":{"aname":"value", "anumber":1234, "aboolean":false, "anarray":⏎
[{"arrayelement":"Array Element 1"}, {"arrayelement":"Array Element 2"}]}}
```

It will have to be in a String in order to work with the JSON parser. To do that, we'll have to escape the double quotes.

```
String JSONData = "" +
        "{\"results\":{\"aname\":\"value\", \"anumber\":1234, \"aboolean\":false, " +
        "\"anarray\":[{\"arrayelement\":\"Array Element 1\"}, {\"arrayelement\":↵
\"Array Element 2\"}]}}";
```

The JSON package available in Android contains a JSONObject class, which can be constructed by passing in JSON-formatted data such as we have in the JSONData String.

```
JSONObject overallJSONObject = new JSONObject(JSONData);
```

Once we have a JSONObject, we can pull out any JSON objects, JSON arrays, or regular fields that it may contain. Since results is the JSON object that is directly inside the outer object, we can get a reference to that by using the getJSONObject method, passing in the name of the object we are attempting to pull out.

```
JSONObject resultsObject = overallJSONObject.getJSONObject("results");
```

Once we have that JSONObject, we can pull out any of the data that it contains. There are different methods for each data type.

To pull out a String, we use the getString method, passing in the name as specified in the JSON data.

```
String aname = resultsObject.getString("aname");
```

To pull out an integer, we use the getInt method, passing in the name specified in the JSON data. Correspondingly we can pull out JSON numbers as a double, using getDouble, or as a long, using getLong.

```
int anumber = resultsObject.getInt("anumber");
```

To pull out a Boolean, we use the getBoolean method, passing in the name specified in the JSON data.

```
boolean aboolean = resultsObject.getBoolean("aboolean");
```

Our example data also has an array of JSON objects within the resultsObject called anarray. We can get a reference to that using the getJSONArray method, passing in the name of the array.

```
JSONArray anarray = resultsObject.getJSONArray("anarray");
```

We can loop through the JSONArray object and pull out the individual JSON object elements, using the getJSONObject method available for use on JSONArray and passing in the index number of the element.

```
for (int i = 0; i < anarray.length(); i++) {
    JSONObject arrayElementObject = anarray.getJSONObject(i);
    String arrayelement = arrayElementObject.getString("arrayelement");
}
```

Here is a full example putting all of the foregoing together.

```
package com.apress.proandroidmedia.ch12.simplejson;
import org.json.JSONArray;
```

```
import org.json.JSONException;
import org.json.JSONObject;

import android.app.Activity;
import android.os.Bundle;
import android.util.Log;

public class SimpleJSON extends Activity {
    @Override
    public void onCreate(Bundle savedInstanceState) {
        super.onCreate(savedInstanceState);
        setContentView(R.layout.main);

        String JSONData = "" +
        "{\"results\":{\"aname\":\"value\", \"anumber\":1234, \"aboolean\":false, " +
        "\"anarray\":[{\"arrayelement\":\"Array Element 1\"}, {\"arrayelement\":\"Array⏎
Element 2\"}]}}";
```

We need to wrap many of the JSONObject and JSONArray methods in a try catch block, as many of them throw exceptions. This includes the JSONObject and JSONArray constructors.

```
        try {
            JSONObject overallJSONObject = new JSONObject(JSONData);
            Log.v("SIMPLEJSON", overallJSONObject.toString());

            JSONObject resultsObject = overallJSONObject.getJSONObject("results");
            Log.v("SIMPLEJSON", resultsObject.toString());

            String aname = resultsObject.getString("aname");
            Log.v("SIMPLEJSON", aname);

            int anumber = resultsObject.getInt("anumber");
            Log.v("SIMPLEJSON", ""+anumber);

            boolean aboolean = resultsObject.getBoolean("aboolean");
            Log.v("SIMPLEJSON", ""+aboolean);

            JSONArray anarray = resultsObject.getJSONArray("anarray");
            for (int i = 0; i < anarray.length(); i++) {
                JSONObject arrayElementObject = anarray.getJSONObject(i);
                String arrayelement = arrayElementObject.getString("arrayelement");
                Log.v("SIMPLEJSON", arrayelement);
            }
        } catch (JSONException e) {
```

For the most part, the exception that we'll need to catch is an instance of JSONException. This will signify that an error has occurred in the parsing. Here we are printing a stack trace. In your applications, you will probably want to do something a bit more intelligent, such as showing the user an error message or attempting the parsing without the step that generated the error.

```
            e.printStackTrace();
        }
    }
}
```

As illustrated, the basics of parsing JSON data are very straightforward. Let's now go through how we can put together an HTTP request for JSON data in a real-world example.

Pulling Flickr Images Using JSON

Flickr, a popular online photo and video sharing site, has a very full-featured web service API that offers JSON as one of the output formats.

As with many sites that offer their functionality via web service APIs, Flickr requires developers to register and request an API key. An API key uniquely identifies the application to the Flickr system so that it may be tracked, and if it is causing problems it can be otherwise dealt with (such as being disabled).

To request an API key from Flickr, you must log in and visit the page `www.flickr.com/services/apps/create/apply/?` to answer their questions. Following this, they will display your API key and an additional "Secret" string, which is required for some functions, such as logging users in.

In the following example, we'll be using the Flickr API to search for images that have been tagged with "waterfront." To do this, we'll use the `flickr.photos.search` method. You can find documentation of all of the methods available in the Flickr API online at `www.flickr.com/services/api/`.

To call this method, we simply need to construct a URL that passes in the parameters that we need to specify. We'll specify `flickr.photos.search` as the `method`, `waterfront` as the `tags`, `json` as the `format,` and `5` as the number of pictures returned per page (we'll be looking at only one page, the first page by default). We also need to pass in a `1` for `nojsoncallback`, which tells Flickr to return plain JSON rather than JSON wrapped with a JavaScript method call. Finally, you'll need to specify your API Key (shown as `YOUR_API_KEY` in the example here).

```
http://api.flickr.com/services/rest/?method=flickr.photos.search&tags=↵
waterfront&format=json&api_key=YOUR_API_KEY&per_page=5&nojsoncallback=1
```

To see what this API call returns, we can simply put it in our desktop browser and look at the response. Here is what is returned now. The data will be different if you try it, as it shows the last five images tagged with "waterfront." The structure, on the other hand, will remain the same, which is important as we'll need it to be consistent to build an app around it.

```
{"photos":{"page":1, "pages":69200, "perpage":5, "total":"345999",↵
 "photo":[{"id":"5224082852", "owner":"43034272@N03", "secret":"9c694fa5f",↵
 "server":"4130", "farm":5, "title":"_G8J1792", "ispublic":1, "isfriend":0,↵
 "isfamily":0}, {"id":"5124084164", "owner":"43034272@N03", "secret":"64c867f86",↵
 "server":"4051", "farm":5, "title":"_G8J1798", "ispublic":1, "isfriend":0,↵
 "isfamily":0}, {"id":"5123480013", "owner":"43034272@N03", "secret":"b571b786e",↵
 "server":"4061", "farm":5, "title":"_G8J1781", "ispublic":1, "isfriend":0,↵
 "isfamily":0}, {"id":"5124083470", "owner":"43034272@N03", "secret":"537b42326",↵
 "server":"4070", "farm":5, "title":"_G8J1783", "ispublic":1, "isfriend":0,↵
 "isfamily":0}, {"id":"5124082142", "owner":"43034272@N03", "secret":"288b74481",↵
```

```
"server":"1381", "farm":2, "title":"_G8J1774", "ispublic":1, "isfriend":0,↵
"isfamily":0}]}, "stat":"ok"}
```

Looking over the JSON data that is returned, we can determine what steps we'll need to take using the JSON parser to get the information we need. Breaking it down, we can see that there is an overall object called photos, which contains an array of JSON objects called photo.

Each item in the photo array has a series of other values, id, owner, secret, server, farm, title, and so on. The Flickr API documentation has a section about how to use these values to construct the URL to the actual image file: www.flickr.com/services/api/misc.urls.html.

Let's go through a full example, putting it all together.

```
package com.apress.proandroidmedia.ch12.flickrjson;

import java.io.BufferedReader;
import java.io.IOException;
import java.io.InputStream;
import java.io.InputStreamReader;
import java.net.HttpURLConnection;
import java.net.MalformedURLException;
import java.net.URL;

import org.apache.http.HttpEntity;
import org.apache.http.HttpResponse;
import org.apache.http.client.HttpClient;
import org.apache.http.client.methods.HttpGet;
import org.apache.http.impl.client.DefaultHttpClient;
import org.json.JSONArray;
import org.json.JSONObject;

import android.app.Activity;
import android.content.Context;
import android.graphics.Bitmap;
import android.graphics.BitmapFactory;
import android.os.Bundle;
import android.util.Log;
import android.view.LayoutInflater;
import android.view.View;
import android.view.ViewGroup;
import android.widget.BaseAdapter;
import android.widget.ImageView;
import android.widget.ListView;
import android.widget.TextView;

public class FlickrJSON extends Activity {
```

In the line here, the text "YOUR_API_KEY" needs to be replaced with the API Key provided by Flickr after a request for one is made.

```
    public static final String API_KEY =  "YOUR_API_KEY";
```

Further down in this example, we have defined a class called FlickrPhoto. One FlickrPhoto object will be created for each photo element found in the JSON data. We'll put all of the FlickrPhoto objects into an array called photos, defined here.

```
FlickrPhoto[] photos;

@Override
public void onCreate(Bundle savedInstanceState) {
    super.onCreate(savedInstanceState);
    setContentView(R.layout.main);
```

When our activity first starts, we'll make our request to the Flickr API using the
HttpClient.

```
HttpClient httpclient = new DefaultHttpClient();
HttpGet httpget = new HttpGet(
            "http://api.flickr.com/services/rest/?method=flickr.photos.search&↵
tags=waterfront&format=json&api_key=" + API_KEY + "&per_page=5&nojsoncallback=1");

HttpResponse response;
try {
    response = httpclient.execute(httpget);
    HttpEntity entity = response.getEntity();

    if (entity != null) {
        InputStream inputstream = entity.getContent();
```

Once we have the InputStream to the content, we'll read it in and create a single String
that we can pass into the JSON parser.

```
BufferedReader bufferedreader = new BufferedReader(
        new InputStreamReader(inputstream));
StringBuilder stringbuilder = new StringBuilder();

String currentline = null;
try {
    while ((currentline = bufferedreader.readLine()) != null) {
        stringbuilder.append(currentline + "\n");
    }
} catch (IOException e) {
    e.printStackTrace();
}
String result = stringbuilder.toString();
```

Now that we have the results of the HTTP request, we can go about parsing the returned
JSON data. First we'll create a JSONObject with the overall JSON data, then another
using the first object, getting the main JSON photos object by name.

```
JSONObject thedata = new JSONObject(result);
JSONObject thephotosdata = thedata.getJSONObject("photos");
```

Once we have that, we can get at the JSONArray, which is named photo.

```
JSONArray thephotodata = thephotosdata.getJSONArray("photo");
```

Now that we have the array of JSON photo objects, we set the length of the array of
FlickrPhoto objects. Following that, we'll loop through the JSON objects, pull out all of
the relevant data, and create a FlickrPhoto object in the FlickrPhoto photos array.

```
photos = new FlickrPhoto[thephotodata.length()];
for (int i = 0; i < thephotodata.length(); i++) {
    JSONObject photodata = thephotodata.getJSONObject(i);
```

```
            Log.v("JSON", photodata.getString("id"));

            photos[i] = new FlickrPhoto(photodata.getString("id"),
                                        photodata.getString("owner"),
                                        photodata.getString("secret"),
                                        photodata.getString("server"),
                                        photodata.getString("title"),
                                        photodata.getString("farm")
                                        );
        }
        inputstream.close();
    }
} catch (Exception e) {
    e.printStackTrace();
}
```

Finally, last in the onCreate method, we'll get access to the ListView we have set up in our layout and set its adapter. We'll be using a class defined here called FlickrGalleryAdapter to construct an adapter, passing in the array of FlickrPhotos.

```
    ListView listView = (ListView) this.findViewById(R.id.ListView);
    listView.setAdapter(new FlickrGalleryAdapter(this, photos));
}
```

What follows is the FlickrGalleryAdapter class, whose responsibility it is to determine the content that will appear in a ListView. In this case, it will be used to populate the ListView defined in the layout displaying the photo and title from the Flickr search.

```
class FlickrGalleryAdapter extends BaseAdapter {
    private Context context;
    private FlickrPhoto[] photos;

    LayoutInflater inflater;

    public FlickrGalleryAdapter(Context _context, FlickrPhoto[] _items) {
        context = _context;
        photos = _items;

        inflater =
          (LayoutInflater)context.getSystemService(Context.LAYOUT_INFLATER_SERVICE);
    }

    public int getCount() {
        return photos.length;
    }

    public Object getItem(int position) {
        return photos[position];
    }

    public long getItemId(int position) {
        return position;
    }
```

The getView method is the meat of the class. It determines what will display in an individual cell in the ListView.

```
    public View getView(int position, View convertView, ViewGroup parent) {
```

First we'll get a reference to the View that exists for each row. In this case, we'll do that by inflating the list_item layout, which is defined in list_item.xml.

```
    View photoRow = inflater.inflate(R.layout.list_item, null);
```

After we have access to the main View for the cell, we can get the individual elements and set what should be in them. First we'll deal with the ImageView and set the Bitmap to be the image returned from the URL we construct within the FlickrPhoto object, using the data returned from the JSON data.

```
    ImageView image = (ImageView) photoRow.findViewById(R.id.ImageView);
    image.setImageBitmap(imageFromUrl(photos[position].makeURL()));
```

Then we'll do the same for the TextView and set its text to be the title of the image.

```
    TextView imageTitle = (TextView) photoRow
            .findViewById(R.id.TextView);
    imageTitle.setText(photos[position].title);
    return photoRow;
}
```

Here is a method used to create a Bitmap for use in the foregoing ImageView from a URL to an image available online. It uses HttpURLConnection to open an InputStream to that image file and passes that to BitmapFactory for the creation of the Bitmap.

```
    public Bitmap imageFromUrl(String url) {
        Bitmap bitmapImage;

        URL imageUrl = null;
        try {
            imageUrl = new URL(url);
        } catch (MalformedURLException e) {
            e.printStackTrace();
        }
        try {
            HttpURLConnection httpConnection =
                (HttpURLConnection) imageUrl.openConnection();
            httpConnection.setDoInput(true);
            httpConnection.connect();
            InputStream is = httpConnection.getInputStream();

            bitmapImage = BitmapFactory.decodeStream(is);
        } catch (IOException e) {
            e.printStackTrace();
            bitmapImage = Bitmap.createBitmap(10, 10, Bitmap.Config.ARGB_8888);
        }
        return bitmapImage;
    }
}
```

Finally, here is the FlickrPhoto class. It is a Java representation of the data we need from each photo represented in the JSON data.

```
class FlickrPhoto {
    String id;
    String owner;
```

```
            String secret;
            String server;
            String title;
            String farm;

            public FlickrPhoto(String _id, String _owner, String _secret,
                    String _server, String _title, String _farm) {
                id = _id;
                owner = _owner;
                secret = _secret;
                server = _server;
                title = _title;
                farm = _farm;
            }
```

The following makeURL method will turn this data into a URL to the image as per Flickr's API documentation.

```
            public String makeURL() {
                return "http://farm" + farm + ".static.flickr.com/" + server + "/"
                        + id + "_" + secret + "_m.jpg";
                // http://farm{farm-id}.static.flickr.com/{server-id}/{id}_↵
{secret}_[mstzb].jpg
                // From: http://www.flickr.com/services/api/misc.urls.html
            }
        }
    }
```

Here is the main.xml file, which contains the layout used in the foregoing code.

```
<?xml version="1.0" encoding="utf-8"?>
<LinearLayout xmlns:android="http://schemas.android.com/apk/res/android"
    android:orientation="vertical"
    android:layout_width="fill_parent"
    android:layout_height="fill_parent"
    >
<ListView android:layout_width="wrap_content" android:layout_height="wrap_content"↵
  android:id="@+id/ListView"></ListView>
</LinearLayout>
```

Here is the list_item.xml file, which defines the layout used for the ListView.

```
<?xml version="1.0" encoding="utf-8"?>
<LinearLayout
  xmlns:android="http://schemas.android.com/apk/res/android"
  android:layout_width="wrap_content"
  android:layout_height="wrap_content">
    <ImageView android:id="@+id/ImageView" android:layout_width="wrap_content"↵
  android:layout_height="wrap_content"></ImageView>
    <TextView android:text="@+id/TextView01" android:layout_width="wrap_content"↵
  android:layout_height="wrap_content" android:id="@+id/TextView"></TextView>
</LinearLayout>
```

Finally, here is AndroidManifest.xml, which contains the INTERNET permission that is required to pull data from Flickr.

```
<?xml version="1.0" encoding="utf-8"?>
<manifest xmlns:android="http://schemas.android.com/apk/res/android"
      package="com.apress.proandroidmedia.ch12.flickrjson"
```

```
            android:versionCode="1"
            android:versionName="1.0">
    <application android:icon="@drawable/icon" android:label="@string/app_name">
        <activity android:name=".FlickrJSON"
                    android:label="@string/app_name">
            <intent-filter>
                <action android:name="android.intent.action.MAIN" />
                <category android:name="android.intent.category.LAUNCHER" />
            </intent-filter>
        </activity>
    </application>
    <uses-sdk android:minSdkVersion="4" />
    <uses-permission android:name="android.permission.INTERNET"></uses-permission>
</manifest>
```

Figure 12–1 shows the results of the foregoing example.

As we have seen, using JSON to interact with a web service such as Flickr is very straightforward and potentially very powerful.

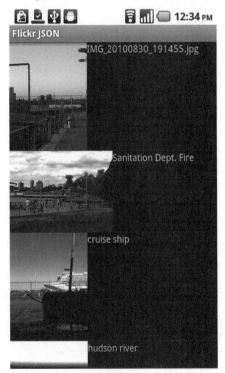

Figure 12–1. *ListView displaying images tagged with "waterfront" from Flickr*

Location

Since we are accessing these services on mobile devices whose location may change, it may be interesting to utilize location as part of the request. Searching for "waterfront" on Flickr in one place will then yield different results from searching in another place.

Android provides us with a `LocationManager` class, which we can use to look up and track location changes in our applications.

Here is a quick snippet of code illustrating how we can harness `LocationManager` and listen for location updates.

```
package com.apress.proandroidmedia.ch12.locationtracking;
```

```
import android.app.Activity;
import android.content.Context;
import android.location.Location;
import android.location.LocationListener;
import android.location.LocationManager;
import android.location.LocationProvider;
import android.os.Bundle;
import android.util.Log;
import android.widget.TextView;
```

To receive location updates from the `LocationManager`, we'll have our activity implement `LocationListener`.

```
public class LocationTracking extends Activity implements LocationListener {

    LocationManager lm;
    TextView tv;

    public void onCreate(Bundle savedInstanceState) {
        super.onCreate(savedInstanceState);
        setContentView(R.layout.main);

        tv = (TextView) this.findViewById(R.id.location);
```

We get an instance of `LocationManager` by using the getSystemService method available in Context, which Activity is a subclass of—therefore it is available to us.

```
        lm = (LocationManager) getSystemService(Context.LOCATION_SERVICE);
```

`LocationManager` offers us the ability to specify that we want our `LocationListener`, in this case, our activity, to be notified of location-related changes. We register our activity as the `LocationListener` by passing it in as the last argument to the requestLocationUpdates method.

The first argument in the method is the location provider that we would like to use. The two location providers available are specified as constants in the `LocationManager` class. The one we are using here, NETWORK_PROVIDER, utilizes network services such as cell tower location or WiFi access point location to determine location. The other one available is GPS_PROVIDER, which provides location information utilizing GPS (Global Positioning Satellites). NETWORK_PROVIDER is generally a much faster but potentially less accurate location lookup than GPS. GPS may take a significant amount of time to acquire signals from satellites and may not work at all indoors or in areas where the sky is not clearly visible (midtown Manhattan, for instance).

The second argument is the minimum amount of time the system will wait between "location changed" notifications. It is specified as a `long` representing milliseconds. Here we are using 60,000 milliseconds or 1 minute.

The third argument is the amount of distance that the location needs to have changed before a "location changed" notification is given. This is specified as a `float` representing meters. Here we are using 5 meters.

```
        lm.requestLocationUpdates(LocationManager.NETWORK_PROVIDER, 600001,↵
5.0f, this);
    }
```

When using the `LocationManager`, particularly when using GPS as the provider, it may be prudent to stop the location updates when the application is no longer in the foreground. This will conserve battery power. To do so, we can override the normal `onPause` or `onStop` method in our activity and call the `removeUpdates` method on the `LocationManager` object.

```
    public void onPause()
    {
        super.onPause();
        lm.removeUpdates(this);
    }
```

The `onLocationChanged` method will be called on the registered `LocationListener` and passed a `Location` object whenever the location has changed and the change is greater than the distance and time parameters specified in the `requestLocationUpdates` method.

The `Location` object that is passed in has methods available for getting latitude (`getLatitude`), longitude (`getLongitude`), altitude (`getAltitude`), and many more, detailed in the documentation:
http://developer.android.com/reference/android/location/Location.html.

```
    public void onLocationChanged(Location location) {
        tv.setText(location.getLatitude() + " " + location.getLongitude());
        Log.v("LOCATION", "onLocationChanged: lat=" + location.getLatitude() + ", lon=↵
" + location.getLongitude());
    }
```

The `onProviderDisabled` method within the registered `LocationListener` will get called should the provider that is being monitored be disabled by the user.

```
    public void onProviderDisabled(String provider) {
        Log.v("LOCATION", "onProviderDisabled: " + provider);
    }
```

The `onProviderEnabled` method within the registered `LocationListener` will get called should the provider that is being monitored be enabled by the user.

```
    public void onProviderEnabled(String provider) {
        Log.v("LOCATION", "onProviderEnabled: " + provider);
    }
```

Finally, the `onStatusChanged` method in the registered `LocationListener` will be called if the location provider's status changes. There are three constants in `LocationProvider` that can be tested against the `status` variable which can be usedto determine what the change that happened is. They are `AVAILABLE`, which will get called should the provider become available after a period of time being unavailable, `TEMPORARILY_UNAVAILABLE`, which is just as its name implies, the provider is temporarily unable to be used as it was unable to fetch the current location and lastly, OUT_OF_SERVICE, which means that the provider is unable to be used probably due to losing connectivity or signal.

```
public void onStatusChanged(String provider, int status, Bundle extras) {
    Log.v("LOCATION", "onStatusChanged: " + provider + " status:" + status);
    if (status == LocationProvider.AVAILABLE) {
        Log.v("LOCATION","Provider Available");
    } else if (status == LocationProvider.TEMPORARILY_UNAVAILABLE) {
        Log.v("LOCATION","Provider Temporarily Unavailable");
    } else if (status == LocationProvider.OUT_OF_SERVICE) {
        Log.v("LOCATION","Provider Out of Service");
    }
  }
}
```

Here is the layout XML that is required by the foregoing activity.

```
<?xml version="1.0" encoding="utf-8"?>
<LinearLayout xmlns:android="http://schemas.android.com/apk/res/android"
    android:orientation="vertical"
    android:layout_width="fill_parent"
    android:layout_height="fill_parent"
    >
<TextView
    android:layout_width="fill_parent"
    android:layout_height="wrap_content"
    android:text="@string/hello"
    android:id="@+id/location"
    />
</LinearLayout>
```

Accessing location requires that permission be requested, so we need to add the following uses-permission tag into our AndroidManifest.xml file. Note that the following tag is for the LocationManager.NETWORK_PROVIDER provider, which gives us a coarse location.

```
<uses-permission android:name="android.permission.ACCESS_COARSE_LOCATION">↵
</uses-permission>
```

If we are interested in using more precise location with GPS, we'll need to use the ACCESS_FINE_LOCATION permission.

```
<uses-permission android:name="android.permission.ACCESS_FINE_LOCATION">↵
</uses-permission>
```

Pulling Flickr Images Using JSON and Location

We can update our Flickr JSON example, adding location into the mix by requesting location changes from the LocationManager and then executing our request when we are notified of a location. Of course, we'll have to add location to the request, which Flickr supports as part of the query string in the request.

```
package com.apress.proandroidmedia.ch12.flickrjsonlocation;

import java.io.BufferedReader;
import java.io.IOException;
```

```
import java.io.InputStream;
import java.io.InputStreamReader;
import java.net.HttpURLConnection;
import java.net.MalformedURLException;
import java.net.URL;

import org.apache.http.HttpEntity;
import org.apache.http.HttpResponse;
import org.apache.http.client.HttpClient;
import org.apache.http.client.methods.HttpGet;
import org.apache.http.impl.client.DefaultHttpClient;
import org.json.JSONArray;
import org.json.JSONObject;

import android.app.Activity;
import android.content.Context;
import android.graphics.Bitmap;
import android.graphics.BitmapFactory;
import android.location.Location;
import android.location.LocationListener;
import android.location.LocationManager;
import android.os.Bundle;
import android.util.Log;
import android.view.LayoutInflater;
import android.view.View;
import android.view.ViewGroup;
import android.widget.BaseAdapter;
import android.widget.ImageView;
import android.widget.ListView;
import android.widget.TextView;
```

We'll have our `FlickrJSONLocation` activity implement `LocationListener` so that we can be notified to changes in location.

```
public class FlickrJSONLocation extends Activity implements LocationListener {

    public static final String API_KEY = "YOUR_API_KEY";

    FlickrPhoto[] photos;
    TextView tv;
    LocationManager lm;

    @Override
    public void onCreate(Bundle savedInstanceState) {
        super.onCreate(savedInstanceState);
        setContentView(R.layout.main);

        tv = (TextView) findViewById(R.id.TextView);
        tv.setText("Looking Up Location");
```

Instead of directly making a request to Flickr, we'll first specify that we want location by creating an instance of the `LocationManager` and calling the `requestLocationUpdates` method, registering our activity as the `LocationListener`. We are specifying that we want updates at most every 60 seconds and after at least 500 meters moved.

```
        lm = (LocationManager) getSystemService(Context.LOCATION_SERVICE);
        lm.requestLocationUpdates(LocationManager.NETWORK_PROVIDER, 60000l, 500.0f,↵
```

```
this);
    }

  public void onPause()
  {
      super.onPause();
      lm.removeUpdates(this);
  }
```

Now, when our onLocationChanged method is called, we'll make the request to Flickr, taking into account the location as passed in via the Location object.

```
  public void onLocationChanged(Location location) {
      tv.setText(location.getLatitude() + " " + location.getLongitude());
      Log.v("LOCATION", "onLocationChanged: lat=" + location.getLatitude() + ", lon=↵
" + location.getLongitude());

      HttpClient httpclient = new DefaultHttpClient();
```

We'll construct the URL to hit with a few additional parameters: lat for the latitude, lon for the longitude, and accuracy, which is a number that represents the range of latitude and longitude to return results from. According to the Flickr API documentation, a value of 1 is the entire world, 6 is a "region," 11 is approximately a city, and 16 is approximately a street. Additionally, we are specifying two tags, "halloween" and "dog," separated by a comma as per the Flickr API documentation.

```
      String url = "http://api.flickr.com/services/rest/?method=↵
flickr.photos.search&tags= dog,halloween&format=json&api_key=" + API_KEY +↵
 "&per_page=5&nojsoncallback=1&accuracy=6&lat="+location.getLatitude()+"&lon=↵
"+location.getLongitude();
      HttpGet httpget = new HttpGet(url);

      HttpResponse response;
      try {
          response = httpclient.execute(httpget);
          HttpEntity entity = response.getEntity();

          if (entity != null) {

              InputStream inputstream = entity.getContent();

              BufferedReader bufferedreader = new BufferedReader(
                      new InputStreamReader(inputstream));
              StringBuilder stringbuilder = new StringBuilder();

              String currentline = null;
              try {
                  while ((currentline = bufferedreader.readLine()) != null) {
                      stringbuilder.append(currentline + "\n");
                  }
              } catch (IOException e) {
                  e.printStackTrace();
              }
              String result = stringbuilder.toString();

              JSONObject thedata = new JSONObject(result);
              JSONObject thephotosdata = thedata.getJSONObject("photos");
```

```
            JSONArray thephotodata = thephotosdata.getJSONArray("photo");

            photos = new FlickrPhoto[thephotodata.length()];
            for (int i = 0; i < thephotodata.length(); i++) {
                JSONObject photodata = thephotodata.getJSONObject(i);
                photos[i] = new FlickrPhoto(photodata.getString("id"),
                        photodata.getString("owner"), photodata
                                .getString("secret"), photodata
                                .getString("server"), photodata
                                .getString("title"), photodata
                                .getString("farm"));
                Log.v("URL", photos[i].makeURL());
            }

            inputstream.close();
        }
    } catch (Exception e) {
        e.printStackTrace();
    }

    ListView listView = (ListView) this.findViewById(R.id.ListView);
    listView.setAdapter(new FlickrGalleryAdapter(this, photos));
}
```

Of course, since we are implementing LocationListener, we need to provide the
onProviderDisabled and onProviderEnabled methods. Here they are empty methods. In
your application, you would probably want to notify the user of their occurrence to
explain why location updates have either stopped or started working.

```
public void onProviderDisabled(String provider) {
}

public void onProviderEnabled(String provider) {
}

public void onStatusChanged(String provider, int status, Bundle extras) {
}
```

The remainder of the code in the example is as it was previously presented. We'll be
using a class, FlickrGalleryAdapter, to handle the population of the ListView with the
results from Flickr.

```
class FlickrGalleryAdapter extends BaseAdapter {
    private Context context;
    private FlickrPhoto[] photos;

    LayoutInflater inflater;

    public FlickrGalleryAdapter(Context _context, FlickrPhoto[] _items) {
        context = _context;
        photos = _items;

        inflater = (LayoutInflater) context
                .getSystemService(Context.LAYOUT_INFLATER_SERVICE);
    }

    public int getCount() {
```

```java
        return photos.length;
    }

    public Object getItem(int position) {
        return photos[position];
    }

    public long getItemId(int position) {
        return position;
    }

    public View getView(int position, View convertView, ViewGroup parent) {
        View videoRow = inflater.inflate(R.layout.list_item, null);

        ImageView image = (ImageView) videoRow.findViewById(R.id.ImageView);
        image.setImageBitmap(imageFromUrl(photos[position].makeURL()));

        TextView videoTitle = (TextView) videoRow
                .findViewById(R.id.TextView);
        videoTitle.setText(photos[position].title);
        return videoRow;
    }

    public Bitmap imageFromUrl(String url) {
        Bitmap bitmapImage;

        URL imageUrl = null;
        try {
            imageUrl = new URL(url);
        } catch (MalformedURLException e) {
            e.printStackTrace();
        }
        try {
            HttpURLConnection httpConnection =
                (HttpURLConnection) imageUrl.openConnection();
            httpConnection.setDoInput(true);
            httpConnection.connect();
            int length = httpConnection.getContentLength();
            InputStream is = httpConnection.getInputStream();

            bitmapImage = BitmapFactory.decodeStream(is);
        } catch (IOException e) {
            e.printStackTrace();
            bitmapImage = Bitmap.createBitmap(10, 10, Bitmap.Config.ARGB_8888);
        }
        return bitmapImage;
    }
}
```

Finally, as in the previous example, we have a FlickrPhoto class, which is used to hold the data for each individual photo that was sent to us from Flickr via JSON.

```java
class FlickrPhoto {
    String id;
    String owner;
    String secret;
    String server;
    String title;
```

```
        String farm;

        public FlickrPhoto(String _id, String _owner, String _secret,
                String _server, String _title, String _farm) {
            id = _id;
            owner = _owner;
            secret = _secret;
            server = _server;
            title = _title;
            farm = _farm;
        }

        public String makeURL() {
            return "http://farm" + farm + ".static.flickr.com/" + server + "/"
                    + id + "_" + secret + "_m.jpg";
            // http://farm{farm-id}.static.flickr.com/{server-id}/{id}_{secret}_↵
[mstzb].jpg
        }
    }
}
```

Here is the `main.xml` layout for use by the example.

```xml
<?xml version="1.0" encoding="utf-8"?>
<LinearLayout xmlns:android="http://schemas.android.com/apk/res/android"
    android:orientation="vertical"
    android:layout_width="fill_parent"
    android:layout_height="fill_parent"
    >
    <TextView android:layout_width="wrap_content" android:layout_height="wrap_content"↵
     android:id="@+id/TextView"></TextView>
    <ListView android:layout_width="wrap_content" android:layout_height="wrap_content"↵
     android:id="@+id/ListView"></ListView>
</LinearLayout>
```

And here is the `list_item.xml` file for the `ListView` layout used in the example.

```xml
<?xml version="1.0" encoding="utf-8"?>
<LinearLayout
  xmlns:android="http://schemas.android.com/apk/res/android"
  android:layout_width="wrap_content"
  android:layout_height="wrap_content">
    <ImageView android:id="@+id/ImageView" android:layout_width="wrap_content"↵
 android:layout_height="wrap_content"></ImageView>
    <TextView android:text="@+id/TextView01" android:layout_width="wrap_content"↵
 android:layout_height="wrap_content" android:id="@+id/TextView"></TextView>
</LinearLayout>
```

Of course, we'll need to specify that we need permission to access the Internet and use location in this example. After adding the appropriate "uses-permission" tags, the `AndroidManifest.xml` file for this example will be as follows.

```xml
<?xml version="1.0" encoding="utf-8"?>
<manifest xmlns:android="http://schemas.android.com/apk/res/android"
      package="com.apress.proandroidmedia.ch12.flickrjsonlocation"
      android:versionCode="1"
      android:versionName="1.0">
    <application android:icon="@drawable/icon" android:label="@string/app_name">
```

```
<activity android:name=".FlickrJSONLocation"
          android:label="@string/app_name">
    <intent-filter>
        <action android:name="android.intent.action.MAIN" />
        <category android:name="android.intent.category.LAUNCHER" />
    </intent-filter>
</activity>
</application>
<uses-sdk android:minSdkVersion="4" />
<uses-permission android:name="android.permission.ACCESS_COARSE_LOCATION">↵
</uses-permission>
<uses-permission android:name="android.permission.INTERNET"></uses-permission>
</manifest>
```

As we can see, simply paying attention to location in our applications offers us the ability to create a very dynamic experience. In this case, as the user moves around, he or she is presented with a whole new set of "dog,halloween" photographs delivered via Flickr, as illustrated in Figure 12–2.

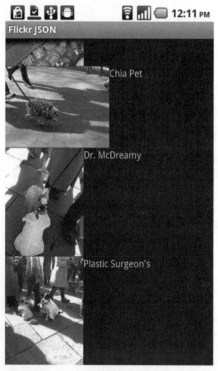

Figure 12–2. *Displaying images tagged with "dog" and "halloween" that were taken near my current location from Flickr*

Now let's turn our attention back to web service protocols and talk about REST.

REST

REST stands for Representational State Transfer. It is a set of architecture principles for design of client-server services. In general, a web service is considered "RESTful," meaning it follows REST principles, under the following conditions:

- When it uses HTTP methods (GET, POST)

- When it is stateless, meaning that each transaction is independent from other transactions

- When it uses directory-style URLs to pass data rather than query string variables (`www.afakeurl.com/shawn/van_every` instead of `www.afakeurl.com/?firstname=shawn&lastname=van_every`)

- When it uses XML (or JSON) for the transfer of data.

A good place to learn more about REST-based web service architecture is an article entitled "RESTful Web Services: The Basics," by Alex Rodriguez, from IBM developerWorks: `www.ibm.com/developerworks/webservices/library/ws-restful/`.

The reason we are discussing REST here is that it is very commonly used in combination with XML for the transfer of web service data. While we didn't use the XML options in the Flickr example, choosing JSON instead, we could have. The structure of the XML representation of the data to be transferred doesn't have to follow any strict Document Type Definitions (DTD) or XML Schemas and is often created and documented as needed by those services that are building the web service.

Representing Data in XML

Here is an example of an XML document that defines a "user" on a theoretical web service. This document would be the response to a query for information about a user given the `user-id`.

```
<?xml version="1.0"?>
<user>
    <user-id>15</user-id>
    <username>vanevery</username>
    <firstname>Shawn</firstname>
    <lastname>Van Every</lastname>
</user>
```

There are several different flavors of XML parsing available on Android by default. These include the two main methods, SAX (Simple API for XML) and DOM (Document Object Model), as well as others. On mobile devices, SAX is often chosen over DOM, as it reads in the XML sequentially, allowing actions on the XML to occur as it is being read, whereas DOM creates a representation of the XML in memory as objects, which, if the XML is large, can take a long time and use up a significant amount of memory.

SAX Parsing

To use the built-in SAX parser on Android, we first need to create a class that extends DefaultHandler. This will be the class that contains the methods that will get notified when a XML element starts and stops and content is read. Here is a bare-bones version that just logs output.

```
private class XMLHandler extends DefaultHandler {
    @Override
    public void startDocument() throws SAXException {
        Log.v("SimpleXMLParser","startDocument");
    }

    @Override
    public void endDocument() throws SAXException {
        Log.v("SimpleXMLParser","endDocument");
    }

    @Override
    public void startElement(String uri, String localName, String qName, Attributes↵
attributes) throws SAXException {
        Log.v("SimpleXMLParser","startElement " + localName);
    }

    @Override
    public void endElement(String uri, String localName, String qName) throws↵
SAXException {
        Log.v("SimpleXMLParser","endElement " + localName);
    }

    @Override
    public void characters(char[] ch, int start, int length) throws SAXException {
        String stringChars = new String(ch, start, length);
        Log.v("SimpleXMLParser",stringChars);
    }
}
```

Once we have that, we can create an instance of a SAXParserFactory and then create an instance of a SAXParser.

```
SAXParserFactory aSAXParserFactory = SAXParserFactory.newInstance();
SAXParser aSAXParser = aSAXParserFactory.newSAXParser();
```

From the SAXParser object, we can get an XMLReader, which we'll use to determine what happens during the parsing and to perform the actual parsing.

```
XMLReader anXMLReader = aSAXParser.getXMLReader();
```

We then instantiate our XMLHandler and pass it to the setContentHandler method on our XMLReader.

```
XMLHandler anXMLHandler = new XMLHandler();
anXMLReader.setContentHandler(anXMLHandler);
```

Finally we call the parse method on our XMLReader. In this case, we are assuming we have an InputStream called xmlInputStream, which contains the XML that we'll be parsing.

```
anXMLReader.parse(new InputSource(xmlInputStream));
```

Let's go through a full example that shows how to parse the foregoing "user" XML.

```
package com.apress.proandroidmedia.ch12.simplexmlparser;

import java.io.ByteArrayInputStream;
import java.io.IOException;

import javax.xml.parsers.ParserConfigurationException;
import javax.xml.parsers.SAXParser;
import javax.xml.parsers.SAXParserFactory;

import org.xml.sax.Attributes;
import org.xml.sax.InputSource;
import org.xml.sax.SAXException;
import org.xml.sax.XMLReader;
import org.xml.sax.helpers.DefaultHandler;

import android.app.Activity;
import android.os.Bundle;
import android.util.Log;

public class SimpleXMLParser extends Activity {
```

We'll be turning the XML into an instance of a class called XMLUser that is towards the end of the code. This will be our Java representation of the data defined in the XML.

```
    XMLUser aUser;

    @Override
    public void onCreate(Bundle savedInstanceState) {
        super.onCreate(savedInstanceState);
        setContentView(R.layout.main);
```

In this example, the XML that we'll be parsing is included as a String called xml.

```
        String xml = "<?xml version=\"1.0\"?>\n"
                    + "<user>\n"
                    + "<user-id>15</user-id>\n"
                    + "<username>vanevery</username>\n"
                    + "<firstname>Shawn</firstname>\n"
                    + "<lastname>Van Every</lastname>\n"
                    + "</user>\n";
```

Here we'll follow the steps previously described, and create a SAXParserFactory, a SAXParser, and an XMLReader.

```
        SAXParserFactory aSAXParserFactory = SAXParserFactory.newInstance();
        try {

            SAXParser aSAXParser = aSAXParserFactory.newSAXParser();
            XMLReader anXMLReader = aSAXParser.getXMLReader();
```

We'll be using an instance of UserXMLHandler, defined here, as our Handler that will determine what happens as the parsing occurs.

```
            UserXMLHandler aUserXMLHandler = new UserXMLHandler();
            anXMLReader.setContentHandler(aUserXMLHandler);
```

Finally, we'll perform the actual parsing. We have to do a bit of additional work turning the XML located in the xml String into an InputStream and an InputSource that can be used by the XMLReader.

```
anXMLReader.parse(
    new InputSource(new ByteArrayInputStream(xml.getBytes())));

    } catch (ParserConfigurationException e) {
        e.printStackTrace();
    } catch (SAXException e) {
        e.printStackTrace();
    } catch (IOException e) {
        e.printStackTrace();
    }
}
```

The meat of our example is the UserXMLHandler. This extends DefaultHandler and will be given the data from the XML as it is parsed.

```
private class UserXMLHandler extends DefaultHandler {
```

We'll use the following constants in combination with the state variable to keep track of what elements have been read in.

```
static final int NONE = 0;
static final int ID = 1;
static final int FIRSTNAME = 2;
static final int LASTNAME = 3;

int state = NONE;
```

We'll use the following constants to match against the element names that may occur in the XML.

```
static final String ID_ELEMENT = "user-id";
static final String FIRSTNAME_ELEMENT = "firstname";
static final String LASTNAME_ELEMENT = "lsatname";
```

The startDocument method is called when the parser identifies that an XML document has started. In this method, we'll instantiate our XMLUser object that we'll use to hold the data represented in the XML.

```
@Override
public void startDocument() throws SAXException {
    Log.v("SimpleXMLParser","startDocument");
    aUser = new XMLUser();
}
```

The endDocument method will be called when the parser identifies that the XML document has finished. We'll simply print out the contents of our XMLUser object.

```
@Override
public void endDocument() throws SAXException {
    Log.v("SimpleXMLParser","endDocument");
    Log.v("SimpleXMLParser","User Info: " + aUser.user_id + " " +↵
aUser.firstname + " " + aUser.lastname);
}
```

The startElement method will be called when a new element has been identified as starting. In other words, an opening tag in the XML is found. The name of the element is passed in via the localName variable. In this method, we'll simply compare that name with the constants defined earlier and use that to change the state variable.

```
        @Override
        public void startElement(String uri, String localName, String qName,↵
Attributes attributes) throws SAXException {
            Log.v("SimpleXMLParser","startElement");
            if (localName.equalsIgnoreCase(ID_ELEMENT)) {
                state = ID;
            } else if (localName.equalsIgnoreCase(FIRSTNAME_ELEMENT)) {
                state = FIRSTNAME;
            } else if (localName.equalsIgnoreCase(LASTNAME_ELEMENT)) {
                state = LASTNAME;
            } else {
                state = NONE;
            }
        }
```

The endElement method will be called when any closing XML tag is found.

```
        @Override
        public void endElement(String uri, String localName, String qName)↵
throws SAXException {
            Log.v("SimpleXMLParser","endElement");

        }
```

The characters method is called whenever text is found between an opening and closing tag. In our implementation, we'll take the data and place it in our XMLUser object based upon where we are in the document as represented by our state variable.

```
        @Override
        public void characters(char[] ch, int start, int length) throws SAXException {
            String stringChars = new String(ch, start, length);
            Log.v("SimpleXMLParser",stringChars);
            if (state == ID) {
                aUser.user_id += stringChars.trim();
                Log.v("SimpleXMLParser","user_id:"+aUser.user_id);
            } else if (state == FIRSTNAME) {
                aUser.firstname += stringChars.trim();
                Log.v("SimpleXMLParser","firstname:"+aUser.firstname);
            } else if (state == LASTNAME) {
                aUser.lastname += stringChars.trim();
                Log.v("SimpleXMLParser","lastname:"+aUser.lastname);
            }
        }
    }
```

Here is the XMLUser class, which we are using to hold onto the data that is given to us within the XML.

```
    class XMLUser {
        String user_id;
        String firstname;
        String lastname;
```

```
        public XMLUser() {
            user_id = "";
            firstname = "";
            lastname = "";
        }
    }
}
```

Having gone through this quick example, we can use it as a template for any XML parsing we might need to do on Android, including dealing with data that we may receive in response to a request to a web service.

HTTP File Uploads

One way that we may wish to allow the user to distribute media that is created by applications we develop is to allow them to be posted to online video sharing sites, such as YouTube, Vimeo, or Blip.TV.

In order to post files to services such as these, we need to do an HTTP file upload. There are several ways we might accomplish an HTTP file upload on Android. The way that gives us the most flexibility is to involve importing and using libraries from Apache's HTTP Components (http://hc.apache.org/) that were not fully included with Android.

We'll need `httpmime-4.0.x.jar`, which is provided within the `HttpClient` 4.0.x (GA) download available at `http://hc.apache.org/downloads.cgi`. (The "x" in the version numbers is currently at 3; it may be higher when you go to download it.)

We'll also need Apache Mime4J version 0.6 (`apache-mime4j-0.6.jar`) or higher, which is downloadable from `http://james.apache.org/download.cgi`.

When you build an application, you will simply bring these files into your Eclipse project by dragging them onto the project folder in the Eclipse Package Explorer. We then have to edit the Java Build Path in the Project Properties. To include them in the build path, go to the Libraries tab in the Java Build Path dialog, select "Add JARs," and finally select them.

What we gained from importing the foregoing libraries is a `MultipartEntity` that can be used within an `HttpPost` request as used by `HttpClient`. `MultipartEntity` allows for the making of multipart/form-data style posts to servers. This is the same mechanism used by browsers to do uploads from forms that allow the user to select a file.

Making an HTTP Request

Here is a quick sketch of how to use it.

First we'll create an `HttpClient` object by instantiating `DefaultHttpClient`.

```
HttpClient httpclient = new DefaultHttpClient();
```

Following that, we'll create an HttpPost object that represents a POST request to a specific URL that we'll pass in.

```
HttpPost httppost = new HttpPost("http://webserver/file-upload-app");
```

Following that, we can instantiate our `MultipartEntity`. As just described, we can have multiple parts in this type of entity.

```
MultipartEntity multipartentity = new MultipartEntity();
```

The main part that we'll need is the actual file that will be uploaded. To do this, we'll use the `addPart` method and pass in the name as a `String` and a `FileBody` object as the value. This `FileBody` object takes in a `File` object that represents the actual file we want uploaded—in this case, a video file on the root of the SD card.

```
multipartentity.addPart("file", new FileBody(new File↵
("/sdcard/video_h264_640x480.mp4")));
```

If we need to add other elements such as username, password, and the like, we use the same `addPart` method, passing in the name and value. In this case, the value should be a `StringBody` object that contains the actual value as a `String`.

```
multipartentity.addPart("username", new StringBody("myusername"));
multipartentity.addPart("password", new StringBody("mypassword"));
multipartentity.addPart("title", new StringBody("A Title"));
```

Once our `MultipartEntity` is all set, we pass it to the `HttpPost` object by calling the `setEntity` method.

```
httppost.setEntity(multipartentity);
```

Now we can execute the request and get the response.

```
HttpResponse httpresponse = httpclient.execute(httppost);
HttpEntity responseentity = httpresponse.getEntity();
```

We can read the response by getting an `InputStream` through a call to `getContent` on the `HttpEntity` we were given.

```
InputStream inputstream = responseentity.getContent();
```

To read from `InputStream`, we'll wrap it in an `InputStreamReader` and a `BufferedReader` and go through the normal reading process.

```
BufferedReader bufferedreader = new BufferedReader(new InputStreamReader(inputstream));
```

We'll use a `StringBuilder` to hold all of the data we read in.

```
StringBuilder stringbuilder = new StringBuilder();
```

And we will read line by line from the `BufferedReader` until it returns null.

```
String currentline = null;
while ((currentline = bufferedreader.readLine()) != null) {
    stringbuilder.append(currentline + "\n");
}
```

When we are done reading, we'll convert the `StringBuilder` object to a normal `String` and output it to the log.

```
String result = stringbuilder.toString();
Log.v("HTTP UPLOAD REQUEST",result);
```

Finally, we'll close the InputStream.

```
inputstream.close();
```

Of course, we'll need to have permission to access the Internet in our application. Therefore we need to add the following uses-permission line to our AndroidManifest.xml file.

```
<uses-permission android:name="android.permission.INTERNET"></uses-permission>
```

Once we have the required libraries downloaded and imported, doing file uploads is not much more difficult than doing a normal HTTP request using the HttpClient class.

Uploading Video to Blip.TV

Blip.TV is a popular video sharing site that offers a REST-based file upload API that we can use to build a video sharing mechanism onto a capture application or even as a stand-alone application.

The Blip.TV upload API is documented online at http://wiki.blip.tv/index.php/REST_Upload_API. It details the various elements that may be included with the request. In particular, we'll need the uploaded file element to be named "file". To run the sample code, you will need a regular Blip.TV user login (username) and password (which, in an real-world application, should be supplied by the user). We'll need a title, and we'll need to include post with a value of "1" and skin with a value of api to get back a response in XML.

Once a video is uploaded to Blip.TV through the API, they respond with XML something like the following:

```
<response>
    <current_time>2010-10-30T00:13:00Z</current_time>
    <timestamp>1288397581081</timestamp>
    <status>OK</status>
     <payload>
        <asset>
            <timestamp>1288397580</timestamp>
            <id>4332695</id>
            <item_type>file</item_type>
            <item_id>4314031</item_id>
            <links>
                <link rel="alternate" type="text/html"↵
href="http://blip.tv/file/4314031/" />
                <link rel="alternate" type="application/rss+xml"↵
href="http://blip.tv/rss/4332695" />
                <link rel="alternate" type="application/atom+xml"↵
href="http://blip.tv/file/4314031/?skin=atom" />
                <link rel="service.edit" type="text/html"↵
href="http://blip.tv/file/post/4314031/" />
                <link rel="service.edit" type="text/xml"↵
href="http://blip.tv/file/post/4314031/?skin=api" />
            </links>
            <files>
                <file src="Username-AVideo562.3gp"↵
```

```
            submitted_as="VID_20101029_200900.3gp" role='Source' />
                </files>
            </asset>
        </payload>
</response>
```

Of note, the XML gives a status of OK if the upload was successful and gives a link to the original file in the file element. We can parse this XML using a SAX parser, looking for those items and presenting the video back to the user for verification that the upload worked.

If the upload fails, the XML gives a status of ERROR and an error tag that includes a code and a message. Here is an example where the username/password combination was incorrectly entered.

```
<response>
     <current_time>2010-10-30T00:38:32Z</current_time>
     <timestamp>1288399112662</timestamp>
     <status>ERROR</status>
     <error>
         <code>AUTHENTICATION_REQUIRED</code>
         <message>The operation you attempted to perform require authentication,↵
but your authentication information is invalid, missing or insufficient for the↵
action you are attempting to perform.</message>
     </error>
</response>
```

Let's go through the full code for capturing a video and uploading to Blip.TV:

```java
package com.apress.proandroidmedia.ch12.blipuploader;

import java.io.BufferedReader;
import java.io.ByteArrayInputStream;
import java.io.File;
import java.io.FilterOutputStream;
import java.io.IOException;
import java.io.InputStream;
import java.io.InputStreamReader;
import java.io.OutputStream;

import javax.xml.parsers.ParserConfigurationException;
import javax.xml.parsers.SAXParser;
import javax.xml.parsers.SAXParserFactory;

import org.apache.http.HttpEntity;
import org.apache.http.HttpResponse;
import org.apache.http.client.ClientProtocolException;
import org.apache.http.client.HttpClient;
import org.apache.http.client.methods.HttpPost;
import org.apache.http.entity.mime.MultipartEntity;
import org.apache.http.entity.mime.content.FileBody;
import org.apache.http.entity.mime.content.StringBody;
import org.apache.http.impl.client.DefaultHttpClient;
import org.xml.sax.Attributes;
import org.xml.sax.InputSource;
import org.xml.sax.SAXException;
import org.xml.sax.XMLReader;
```

```
import org.xml.sax.helpers.DefaultHandler;

import android.app.Activity;
import android.content.Intent;
import android.database.Cursor;
import android.net.Uri;
import android.os.AsyncTask;
import android.os.Bundle;
import android.util.Log;
import android.widget.TextView;

public class BlipTVUploader extends Activity {
```

Our activity will use an intent to trigger the Camera activity for video recording and the default activity for video playback, so we'll need to set two constants to know which activity is returning.

```
final static int VIDEO_CAPTURED = 0;
final static int VIDEO_PLAYED = 1;
```

We have a couple of variables: a File to represent the captured video on the SD card, a String title that will be the title for it when uploaded to Blip.TV, as well as a username and password for Blip.TV. In a real-world application, the title, username, and password should be gotten from the user.

```
File videoFile;
String title = "A Video";
String username = "BLIPTV_USERNAME";
String password = "BLIPTV_PASSWORD";
```

The postingResult variable will contain the results given in the XML response from Blip.TV after the upload.

```
String postingResult = "";
```

The fileLength variable will be set after the video is recorded so that we can track the progress of the upload.

```
long fileLength = 0;
```

We'll use a TextView to display to the user the upload progress and other information.

```
TextView textview;

@Override
public void onCreate(Bundle savedInstanceState) {
    super.onCreate(savedInstanceState);
    setContentView(R.layout.main);

    textview = (TextView) findViewById(R.id.textview);
```

When we first start up, we'll use an intent to trigger the default video capture application, generally the built-in Camera activity to launch and allow the user to capture video. We're passing in the VIDEO_CAPTURED constant along with the intent to startActivityForResult so we know in onActivityResult what is being returned to us.

```
Intent captureVideoIntent =
  new Intent(android.provider.MediaStore.ACTION_VIDEO_CAPTURE);
```

```
        startActivityForResult(captureVideoIntent, VIDEO_CAPTURED);
    }

    protected void onActivityResult (int requestCode, int resultCode, Intent data) {
```

When the Camera activity returns, we can get the Uri to the video file as it was captured in the manner described in Chapter 11.

```
        if (resultCode == RESULT_OK && requestCode == VIDEO_CAPTURED) {
            Uri videoFileUri = data.getData();
```

In order to get the actual video file on the SD card, we need to query the MediaStore, asking for the DATA column that represents the file.

```
            String[] columns = { android.provider.MediaStore.Video.Media.DATA };
            Cursor cursor = managedQuery(videoFileUri, columns, null, null, null);
            int fileColumn =
             cursor.getColumnIndexOrThrow(android.provider.MediaStore.Video.Media.DATA);
            if (cursor.moveToFirst()) {
                String videoFilePath = cursor.getString(fileColumn);
                Log.v("VIDEO FILE PATH",videoFilePath);
```

Once we have the path to the file, we'll construct the File object, get its length, and instantiate a BlipTVFilePoster object. BlipTVFilePoster extends AsyncTask, so to start it doing work, we'll call its execute method.

```
                videoFile = new File(videoFilePath);
                fileLength = videoFile.length();
                BlipTVFilePoster btvfp = new BlipTVFilePoster();
                btvfp.execute();
            }
```

If it is the video player activity returning to us, we'll simply finish. Our work is done.

```
        } else if (requestCode == VIDEO_PLAYED) {
            finish();
        }
    }
```

As mentioned, the BlipTVFilePoster class extends AsyncTask. This way it can do work in a background thread without tying up the interface. It will also implement ProgressListener, which is an interface we designed here to handle progress callbacks from the uploading class, and BlipXMLParserListener so it can handle callbacks from the XML parsing class.

```
    class BlipTVFilePoster extends AsyncTask<Void, String, Void> implements⏎
ProgressListener, BlipXMLParserListener {
```

The videoUrl variable will contain the URL to the video file after it has been uploaded to Blip.TV.

```
        String videoUrl;

        @Override
        protected Void doInBackground(Void... params) {
```

As previously described, we can use HttpClient with a MultipartEntity to perform an HTTP file upload.

```
HttpClient httpclient = new DefaultHttpClient();
HttpPost httppost = new HttpPost("http://blip.tv/file/post");
```

For this example, we are using a class, ProgressMultipartEntity, which extends MultipartEntity but lets us track the upload progress. We pass ourselves in as the listener, which we can do since we implement ProgressListener.

```
ProgressMultipartEntity multipartentity = new ProgressMultipartEntity(this);
```

We need to add several parts to the post as required by Blip.TV. Of course, we need the file, but we also need the user login (username), password, title, post with a value of "1" so that it actually gets posted, and skin with a value of api so that we get XML in response instead of a normal web page.

```
try {
    multipartentity.addPart("file", new FileBody(videoFile));

    multipartentity.addPart("userlogin", new StringBody(username));
    multipartentity.addPart("password", new StringBody(password));
    multipartentity.addPart("title", new StringBody(title));
    multipartentity.addPart("post", new StringBody("1"));
    multipartentity.addPart("skin", new StringBody("api"));

    httppost.setEntity(multipartentity);
    HttpResponse httpresponse = httpclient.execute(httppost);

    HttpEntity responseentity = httpresponse.getEntity();
    if (responseentity != null) {
```

Once we execute the HTTP file upload, we can get an InputStream to read the response from the server. In our case, we want to simply hand that InputStream to an implementation of a SAX parser so we can determine if the upload succeeded.

```
        InputStream inputstream = responseentity.getContent();

        SAXParserFactory aSAXParserFactory = SAXParserFactory.newInstance();
        try {

            SAXParser aSAXParser = aSAXParserFactory.newSAXParser();
            XMLReader anXMLReader = aSAXParser.getXMLReader();
```

We'll be using a BlipResponseXMLHandler, defined here to deal specifically with the XML responses from Blip.TV after a file upload.

```
            BlipResponseXMLHandler xmlHandler =
                new BlipResponseXMLHandler(this);
            anXMLReader.setContentHandler(xmlHandler);
            anXMLReader.parse(new InputSource(inputstream));

        } catch (ParserConfigurationException e) {
            e.printStackTrace();
        } catch (SAXException e) {
            e.printStackTrace();
        } catch (IOException e) {
            e.printStackTrace();
        }

        inputstream.close();
```

```
        }
    } catch (ClientProtocolException e) {
        e.printStackTrace();
    } catch (IOException e) {
        e.printStackTrace();
    }

    return null;
}
```

As is normal in an `AsyncTask`, the `onProgressUpdate` method is eventually triggered when `publishProgress` is called. This method can interact directly with the UI thread, unlike the `doInBackground` method.

```
protected void onProgressUpdate(String... textToDisplay) {
    textview.setText(textToDisplay[0]);
}
```

The `onPostExecute` method is triggered when the `doInBackground` method has completed. When this occurs, and if our `videoUrl` variable has been populated by the XML parser, we simply create an intent to play the uploaded file back using the default video player activity.

```
protected void onPostExecute(Void result) {
    if (videoUrl != null) {
        Intent viewVideoIntent = new Intent(Intent.ACTION_VIEW);
        Uri uri = Uri.parse("http://blip.tv/file/get/" + videoUrl);
        viewVideoIntent.setDataAndType(uri, "video/3gpp");
        startActivityForResult(viewVideoIntent, VIDEO_PLAYED);
    }
}
```

The transferred method, defined here, is required as part of the implementation of the `ProgressListener` interface. It will be called by the `ProgressMultipartEntity` while the file is being uploaded. It will call the `publishProgress` method, which triggers the `onProgressUpdate` method to update the UI.

```
public void transferred(long num) {
    double percent = (double)num/(double)fileLength;
    int percentInt = (int) (percent * 100);

    publishProgress("" + percentInt + "% Transferred");
}
```

The `parseResult` method is required as part of the implementation of the `BlipXMLParserListener`. This method will be called when there is progress in parsing the XML that should be reported to the user. It simply calls `publishProgress`, which triggers `onProgressUpdate` to display the results to the user.

```
public void parseResult(String result) {
    publishProgress(result);
}
```

setVideoUrl is also required as part of the implementation of the
BlipXMLParserListener. It simply populates the videoUrl variable with the URL to the
video after it has been uploaded.

```java
public void setVideoUrl(String url) {
    videoUrl = url;
}
}
```

Here is ProgressMultipartEntity, which extends MultipartEntity. This class hosts the
ProgressListener so it can report progress and overrides the writeTo methods to use
an OutputStream that can count the outgoing bytes.

```java
class ProgressMultipartEntity extends MultipartEntity {
    ProgressListener progressListener;

    public ProgressMultipartEntity(ProgressListener pListener) {
        super();
        this.progressListener = pListener;
    }

    @Override
    public void writeTo(OutputStream outstream) throws IOException {
        super.writeTo(new ProgressOutputStream(outstream, this.progressListener));
    }
}
```

The ProgressListener interface is very simple—it just specifies that we need to have a
method, transferred in the implementing class.

```java
interface ProgressListener {
    void transferred(long num);
}
```

Here is ProgressOutputStream, which overrides the write methods in
FilterOutputStream and tracks the number of bytes that have been transferred.

```java
static class ProgressOutputStream extends FilterOutputStream {

    ProgressListener listener;
    int transferred;

    public ProgressOutputStream(final OutputStream out, ProgressListener listener) {
        super(out);
        this.listener = listener;
        this.transferred = 0;
    }

    public void write(byte[] b, int off, int len) throws IOException {
        out.write(b, off, len);
        this.transferred += len;
        this.listener.transferred(this.transferred);
    }

    public void write(int b) throws IOException {
        out.write(b);
        this.transferred++;
        this.listener.transferred(this.transferred);
```

```
        }
    }
```

Finally we have the `BlipXMLParserListener` interface and `BlipResponseXMLHandler`, which deal with the XML as delivered from Blip.TV in response to our file upload.

```
interface BlipXMLParserListener {
    void parseResult(String result);
    void setVideoUrl(String url);
}
```

```
class BlipResponseXMLHandler extends DefaultHandler {
```

The following constants are used in combination with the `state` variable to keep track of where we are within the XML.

```
int NONE = 0;
int ONSTATUS = 1;
int ONFILE = 2;
int ONERRORMESSAGE = 3;

int state = NONE;
```

The next set of constants defines the possible `status` values that may be returned in the XML. We'll use these to keep track of the status in the `status` integer defined directly here.

```
int STATUS_UNKNOWN = 0;
int STATUS_OK = 1;
int STATUS_ERROR = 2;

int status = STATUS_UNKNOWN;
```

The `message` variable will be used to contain either the error message returned from the XML or URL of the video if it was a successful upload.

```
String message = "";
```

Of course, we'll need to hold onto the `BlipXMLParserListener` that is passed in via the constructor.

```
BlipXMLParserListener listener;

public BlipResponseXMLHandler(BlipXMLParserListener bxpl) {
    super();
    listener = bxpl;
}

@Override
public void startDocument() throws SAXException {
}

@Override
public void endDocument() throws SAXException {
}
```

Much of the work will be done within the `startElement` tag. The `localName` variable that contains the name of the XML tag will be checked to see if it matches anything that we need to pay attention to, and if it does, we'll set the state variable to the appropriate constant.

```
@Override
public void startElement(String uri, String localName, String qName, ↵
Attributes attributes) throws SAXException {
      if (localName.equalsIgnoreCase("status")) {
            state = ONSTATUS;
      } else if (localName.equalsIgnoreCase("file")) {
            state = ONFILE;
```

If it is the file element, we tell the listener, and we'll pull out the src attribute, which will equal the file name that Blip.TV gave it after it was uploaded.

```
            listener.parseResult("onFile");
            message = attributes.getValue("src");
            listener.parseResult("filemessage:" + message);
```

We'll then pass that to BlipXMLParserListener via the setVideoUrl method.

```
            listener.setVideoUrl(message);
      } else if (localName.equalsIgnoreCase("message")) {
            state = ONERRORMESSAGE;
            listener.parseResult("onErrorMessage");
      }
}

@Override
public void endElement(String uri, String localName, String qName) ↵
throws SAXException {
      if (localName.equalsIgnoreCase("status")) {
            state = NONE;
      } else if (localName.equalsIgnoreCase("file")) {
            state = NONE;
      } else if (localName.equalsIgnoreCase("message")) {
            state = NONE;
      }
}
```

Our characters method will be triggered when any content is found within an element. If our state variable indicates that we are reading an element that we need to be concerned with, we'll take action.

```
@Override
public void characters(char[] ch, int start, int length) throws SAXException {
      String stringChars = new String(ch, start, length);
```

If we are reading the status element, we'll set the status variable to the appropriate constant.

```
      if (state == ONSTATUS) {
            if (stringChars.equalsIgnoreCase("OK")) {
                  status = STATUS_OK;
            } else if (stringChars.equalsIgnoreCase("ERROR")) {
                  status = STATUS_ERROR;
            } else {
                  status = STATUS_UNKNOWN;
            }
```

If we are on the error message element, we'll get the text, set it to be our message variable, and send it off to the listener.

```
                } else if (state == ONERRORMESSAGE) {
                    message += stringChars.trim();
                    listener.parseResult(message);
                }
            }
        }
}
```

The method utilized in the foregoing example for tracking the progress of the upload is based on the answer provided by "tuler," including edits by ColinD on the Stack Overflow question asked by SoaperGEM on this page: http://stackoverflow.com/questions/254719/file-upload-with-java-with-progress-bar/470047#470047.

Here is the layout XML in use by the foregoing activity.

```
<?xml version="1.0" encoding="utf-8"?>
<LinearLayout xmlns:android="http://schemas.android.com/apk/res/android"
    android:orientation="vertical"
    android:layout_width="fill_parent"
    android:layout_height="fill_parent"
    >
    <TextView
        android:id="@+id/textview"
        android:layout_width="fill_parent"
        android:layout_height="wrap_content"
        android:text=""
        />
</LinearLayout>
```

Finally, here is AndroidManifest.xml, which includes the uses-permission tag specifying that we need to be able to access the Internet.

```
<?xml version="1.0" encoding="utf-8"?>
<manifest xmlns:android="http://schemas.android.com/apk/res/android"
      package="com.apress.proandroidmedia.ch12.blipuploader"
      android:versionCode="1"
      android:versionName="1.0">
    <application android:icon="@drawable/icon" android:label="@string/app_name">
        <activity android:name=".BlipTVUploader"
                    android:label="@string/app_name">
            <intent-filter>
                <action android:name="android.intent.action.MAIN" />
                <category android:name="android.intent.category.LAUNCHER" />
            </intent-filter>
        </activity>
    </application>
    <uses-sdk android:minSdkVersion="4" />
    <uses-permission android:name="android.permission.INTERNET"></uses-permission>
</manifest>
```

This example illustrates the means to allow our users to directly publish their creations to an online video sharing platform. Similar code could be used to publish to other sharing platforms and, of course, isn't limited to video. We could upload images to Flickr or Picasa. We could upload audio files to audio sharing sites.

Summary

As we have seen throughout this chapter, leveraging online services for both obtaining media and allowing users to publish media opens a wide range of possibilities. We found that utilizing HTTP, REST, JSON, and XML with Android isn't terribly difficult and brings us the ability to access almost any web service. Furthermore, adding location into the mix allows us to add yet another dynamic to our applications.

Index

■A

AAC format, 106
ACCESS_FINE_LOCATION permission, 266
accuracy parameter, 268
ACTION_DOWN event, 96
ACTION_IMAGE_CAPTURE constant, 2
ACTION_MOVE event, 114
ACTION_PICK intent, 47, 50, 72
ACTION_VIDEO_CAPTURE constant, 229
Activity class, 4, 211
addPart method, 279
Advanced Video Coding (AVC), 195
album browsing app example, 118–123
ALBUM column, 118
ALBUM constant, 118–119
ALPHA_8 constant, 80
AMR format, 106
AMR_NB constant, 239
analyzing audio, 187–193
    capturing sound for, 188
    visualizing frequencies, 189
Android API, 55
Android SDK, 70
android.app.Service class, 127
android.content.Intent.ACTION_VIEW intent,
    107–108
android.graphics.PorterDuff.Mode.DARKEN
    rule, 71, 77
android.graphics.PorterDuff.Mode.DST rule,
    70, 75
android.graphics.PorterDuff.Mode.DST_ATO
    P rule, 70
android.graphics.PorterDuff.Mode.DST_IN
    rule, 70
android.graphics.PorterDuff.Mode.DST_OU
    T rule, 70
android.graphics.PorterDuff.Mode.DST_OVE
    R rule, 70
android.graphics.PorterDuff.Mode.LIGHTEN
    rule, 71, 77

android.graphics.PorterDuff.Mode.MULTIPL
    Y rule, 71, 76
android.graphics.PorterDuff.Mode.SCREEN
    rule, 71, 78
android.graphics.PorterDuff.Mode.SRC rule,
    70, 76
android.graphics.PorterDuff.Mode.SRC_AT
    OP rule, 70
android.graphics.PorterDuff.Mode.SRC_IN
    rule, 70
android.graphics.PorterDuff.Mode.SRC_OU
    T rule, 70
android.graphics.PorterDuff.Mode.SRC_OV
    ER rule, 70
android.graphics.PorterDuff.Mode.XOR rule,
    71
AndroidManifest.xml file, 2, 24, 42, 45, 136,
    161, 254, 262, 271, 280
android.provider.BaseColumns class, 118
android.provider.MediaStore class, 229
android.provider.MediaStore.Audio
    package, 115
android.provider.MediaStore.Audio.AlbumC
    olumns class, 118
android.provider.MediaStore.Audio.Albums
    class, 118
android.provider.MediaStore.Audio.Media
    class, 115
android.provider.MediaStore.Audio.Media.D
    ATA constant, 116
android.provider.MediaStore.Images.Media
    class, 11
android.provider.MediaStore.MediaColumns
    interface, 11
android.R.id.text1 view, 119
android.R.layout.simple_list_item_1 layout,
    119
apache-mime4j-0.6.jar file, 278
ARGB_4444 constant, 80
ARGB_8888 constant, 80
Artist tag, 21

AsyncTask class, 180, 190, 283, 285
audio, 105–150
    analyzing, 187–193
        capturing sound for, 188
        visualizing frequencies, 189
    background playback, 125–137
        Local Service example, 126–129
        Local vs. Remote Services, 126
    MediaPlayer class, 109–115
        controlling playback, 111–115
        creating object, 110
    MediaStore for, 115–123
        accessing audio from, 115–117
        album browsing app example,
            118–123
        browsing audio in, 118
    networked, 137–150
        HTTP playback, 137–143
        RTSP streaming, 150
        streaming audio via HTTP, 143–149
    supported formats, 106–107
    synthesizing, 179–187
        generating samples, 182–187
        playing synthesized sound, 180–182
    using Music app via intent, 107–108
audio and video bitrates, 238
audio and video encoders, 237–238
audio capture, 151–177
    AudioRecord class for, 167–170
        example of, 172
    and AudioTrack class
        example of, 172
        playback with, 170–171
    inserting audio into MediaStore, 167
    MediaRecorder class for, 154–166
        example of, 157–161
        setAudioEncoder method, 156
        setAudioSource method, 155
        setOutputFile method, 156
        setOutputFormat method, 155
        state of, 156
    using intent, 151–154
audio sample rate, 238–239
AudioFormat class, 168, 170
AudioManager class, 170
AudioProcessing activity, 192–193
AudioRecord class, 151, 167–170, 172, 177,
    179–180, 188
AudioSource class, 155
AudioSynthesisTask class, 180

AudioTrack class, 170–172, 177, 179–180,
    187
AVAILABLE constant, 265
AVC (Advanced Video Coding), 195

■ B

background audio playback, 125–137
    Local Service example, 126–129
        binding with MediaPlayer class,
            132–137
        implementing MediaPlayer class,
            129–132
        Local vs. Remote Services, 126
BaseAdapter class, 215
bestHeight variable, 31
bestWidth variable, 31
bindService method, 133–134
Bitmap
    applying Matrix class while creating,
        64–65
    configurations for, 80
    drawing Bitmap onto, 52–53
Bitmap.Config class, 79
Bitmap.Config.ARGB_8888 constant, 79
BitmapFactory class, 6–7, 12
BitmapFactory.Options class, 6–7
BitmapFactory.Options.inJustDecodeBound
    s variable, 7
BitmapFactory.Options.inSampleSize
    variable, 7
BitmapFactory.Options.outHeight variable, 7
BitmapFactory.Options.outWidth variable, 7
bitrates, audio and video, 238
BlipResponseXMLHandler class, 284, 287
Blip.TV, uploading video to, 280
BlipTVFilePoster class, 283
BlipXMLParserListener interface, 283,
    285–288
brightness, changing with ColorMatrix class,
    67–69
BufferedReader class, 279

■ C

callback methods, for Camera class, 34–35
CAMCORDER constant, 155, 235
CamcorderProfile.get method, 241
CamcorderProfile.QUALITY_HIGH constant,
    241

CamcorderProfile.QUALITY_LOW constant, 241
Camera application, capturing images using, 1–9
   displaying large images from, 6–9
   returning data from, 3–5
   and size restrictions, 5
Camera class, 23–45
   example using, 35–38
   extending, 38–45
      time-lapse photography app, 43–45
      timer-based camera app, 38–42
   implementing, 25–35
      callback methods for, 34–35
      capturing and saving image, 32–33
      parameters for, 27–30
      preview size for, 30–32
   and permissions, 24
   SurfaceView class for, 24–25
CAMERA permission, 24, 37, 42
Camera.AutoFocusCallback method, 34
Camera.ErrorCallback method, 35
Camera.OnZoomChangeListener method, 35
Camera.Parameters class, 23, 27, 30–31
Camera.Parameters setRotation method, 28
Camera.PictureCallback.onPictureTaken method, 32
Camera.PreviewCallback method, 34
Camera.ShutterCallback method, 35
Camera.takePicture method, 33
cancel method, 163
Canvas class, 79–92
   circles with, 86
   creating, 81
   creating Bitmap, 79
   drawLine method, 84
   drawPoint method, 83
   drawText method, 87–92
      built-in fonts, 88–89
      drawTextOnPath method, 92
      external fonts, 91
      font styles, 90
   ovals with, 86
   Paint class, 82–83
      setColor method, 82
      setStrokeWidth method, 83
      setStyle method, 83
   paths with, 87
   rectangles with, 85
capture. See video capture

captureVideoButton button, 230–231, 233
channels, audio, 239
characters method, 277, 288
choosePicture button, 49, 102
ChopinScript.ttf file, 91
circles, with Canvas class, 86
click events, 48
Color class, 82
Color.argb method, 82
Color.BLACK constant, 82
Color.BLUE constant, 82
ColorMatrix class, 65–69
   changing brightness with, 67–69
   changing contrast with, 67–69
   changing saturation with, 69
   overview, 65–67
Color.RED constant, 82
compositing, of images, 69–78
compress method, 102
ContentProvider class, 211
Content.startActivity method, 229
Context class, 127
Context.getResources( ).getConfiguration( ) method, 28
Context.startActivityForResult method, 229
contrast, changing with ColorMatrix class, 67–69
controlling playback, 111
Copyright tag, 21
create method, 90, 110–111
createBitmap method, Bitmap class, 53, 64
createRecording Button, 153
currentState variable, 119–120, 122
Cursor class, 18, 116
custom video capture, 235–250. See also MediaRecorder for video
CustomRecorder activity, 158

D

DAC (digital-to-analog conversion), 179
DATA column, 116, 283
DATE_ADDED column, 116
DATE_MODIFIED column, 116
decodeStream method, BitmapFactory class, 52
DEFAULT constant, 236–238
DefaultHandler class, 274, 276
DefaultHttpClient class, 278
DFT (discrete Fourier transform), 189
digital-to-analog conversion (DAC), 179

discrete Fourier transform (DFT), 189
do while loop, 214
Document Object Model (DOM), 273
Document Type Definitions (DTD), 273
doInBackground method, 165, 176, 180,
    191, 285
DOM (Document Object Model), 273
downx variable, 95–96
downy variable, 95–96
drawBitmap method, 53, 55
drawing graphics, 79–104
    Canvas class, 79–92
        circles with, 86
        creating, 81
        creating Bitmap, 79
        drawLine method, 84
        drawPoint method, 83
        drawText method, 87–92
        ovals with, 86
        Paint class, 82–83
        paths with, 87
        rectangles with, 85
    with finger, 93–104
        on existing images, 97–100
        saving drawing, 101–104
        touch events for, 93–96
drawLine method, for Canvas class, 84
drawPoint method, for Canvas class, 83
drawText method, for Canvas class, 87–92
    built-in fonts, 88–89
    and drawTextOnPath method, 92
    external fonts, 91
    font styles, 90
drawTextOnPath method, for Canvas class,
    92
DTD (Document Type Definitions), 273

■E

Eclipse Package Explorer, 278
EditText elements, 15
EFFECT_AQUA constant,
    Camera.Parameters class, 30
EFFECT_BLACKBOARD constant,
    Camera.Parameters class, 30
EFFECT_MONO constant,
    Camera.Parameters class, 30
EFFECT_NEGATIVE constant,
    Camera.Parameters class, 30
EFFECT_NONE constant,
    Camera.Parameters class, 30

EFFECT_POSTERIZE constant,
    Camera.Parameters class, 30
EFFECT_SEPIA constant,
    Camera.Parameters class, 30
EFFECT_SOLARIZE constant,
    Camera.Parameters class, 30
EFFECT_WHITEBOARD constant,
    Camera.Parameters class, 30
encoders, audio and video, 237–238
endDocument method, 276
endElement method, 277
error tag, 281
execute method, 164, 167, 173, 252–253,
    283
ExifInterface class, 21
EXTERNAL_CONTENT_URI constant, 11,
    167
EXTRA_OUTPUT constant, 5

■F

FFT (fast Fourier transform), 189
FFT class, 191
FFTPACK library, 189
fftpack package, 189
file element, 281, 288
file uploads, HTTP
    overview, 278–290
    uploading video to Blip.TV, 280
File variable, 282
File.createTempFile method, 156
fileLength variable, 282
FilterOutputStream class, 286
findViewById function, 113
findViewById method, 4, 13
finger painting, 93–104
    on existing images, 97–100
    saving drawing, 101–104
    touch events for, 93–96
finish method, 249
flags parameter, 128
flash mode, 29
Flickr, pulling images using JSON, 257–272
FlickrGalleryAdapter class, 260, 269
FlickrPhoto class, 261, 270
flickr.photos.search method, 257
flipping images, with Matrix class, 63
fonts, for drawText method
    built-in, 88–89
    external fonts, 91
    styles for, 90

format parameter, 257
formats
    supported for audio, 106–107
    for video, 195–196
frame rate, video, 239
frequencies, visualizing, 189
full custom example, 246

G

Gallery application, selecting images using, 47–52
gen folder, 110
GET request, 252
getAction method, 94
getAltitude method, 265
getAssets method, 91
getBitmap method, 20
getBoolean method, 255
getColorEffect method, 29
getColumnIndex method, 116, 121
getContent method, 252, 279
getCount method, 215
getData method, 154
getDouble method, 255
getFlashMode( ) method, 29
getHolder method, 24
getInt method, 18
getItem method, 215
getJSONArray method, 255
getJSONObject method, 255
getLatitude method, 265
getLong method, 255
getLongitude method, 265
getMaxAmplitude method, 162, 165–166
getMinBufferSize method, 168, 171
getService method, 134
getString method, 18, 121, 255
getSupportedColorEffects method, 29
getSystemService method, 264
getVideoHeight method, 206
getVideoWidth method, 206
getView method, 215–216, 260
Global Positioning Satellites (GPS), 264
goodmorningandroid_m4a.m4a file, 111
goodmorningandroid_mp3.mp3 file, 111
goodmorningandroid.m4a file, 111
goodmorningandroid.mp3 file, 111, 113, 130
GPS (Global Positioning Satellites), 264
GPS_PROVIDER constant, 264

H

H263 constant, 237
H264 constant, 237
haveFun method, 136
haveFunButton button, 134–135
HTTP (Hypertext Transfer Protocol)
    audio playback via, 137–143
    file uploads
        overview, 278–290
        uploading video to Blip.TV, 280
    networked video, 218–219
    requests
        making, 278–280
        overview, 252–254
    streaming audio via, 143–149
HttpClient class, 252, 278, 280
HttpEntity class, 279
httpmime-4.0.x.jar file, 278
HttpPost request, 278
Hypertext Transfer Protocol. See HTTP

I

_ID column, 118
_ID constant, 119
ImageDescription tag, 21
images, 1–22, 47–78
    capture using Camera app, 1–9
        displaying large images from, 6–9
        returning data from, 3–5
        and size restrictions, 5
    capturing and saving, with Camera class, 32–33
    ColorMatrix class, 65–69
        changing brightness with, 67–69
        changing contrast with, 67–69
        changing saturation with, 69
        overview, 65–67
    compositing of, 69–78
    creating viewing application for, 18–20
    drawing Bitmap onto Bitmap, 52–53
    drawing with finger on, 97–100
    Matrix class
        applying while creating Bitmap, 64–65
        flipping with, 63
        mirroring with, 62
        overview, 55–58
        pre and post methods for, 61
        setRotation method, 58–59

setScale method, 60
setTranslate method, 61
and metadata, 10–22
adding later, 12
associating to image, 12–16
is part of file, 21–22
obtaining URI for image, 11
prepopulating, 11–12
retrieving saved, 12
retrieving using MediaStore, 16–18
selecting using Gallery app, 47–52
initRecorder method, 246–248
InputStream class, 279–280
InputStreamReader class, 279
inSampleSize parameter, 6
insert method, 167
Intent.ACTION_VIEW constant, 196
intents
audio capture using, 151–154
playing video with, 196–197
recording video using, 229–232
INTERNAL_CONTENT_URI constant, 11
INTERNET permission, 262
invalidate method, 95
IOException, 25, 138

J, K

javasource directory, 189
jfftpack.tgz file, 189
JSON (JavaScript Object Notation), 254–272
pulling Flickr images using, 257–272
using location as part of request,
263–272
JSONArray constructor, 256
JSONException, 256
JSONObject class, 255
JSONObject constructor, 256

L

LARGEST_HEIGHT constant,
Camera.Parameters class, 31
LARGEST_WIDTH constant,
Camera.Parameters class, 31
lat parameter, 268
layout/main.xml file, 13, 51
list_item.xml file, 216–217, 261–262
ListActivity class, 120
ListView layout, 119

Local Service
example of, 126–129
binding with MediaPlayer class,
132–137
implementing MediaPlayer class,
129–132
vs. Remote Service, 126
localName variable, 277, 287
LocationManager class, 264–265, 267
LocationManager.NETWORK_PROVIDER
constant, 266
Log command, 12
lon parameter, 268

M

main.xml file, 16, 127, 131, 149, 161, 207,
216, 262, 271
makeURL method, 262
managedQuery method, 17, 19, 116,
118–119, 121, 212
Matrix class
applying while creating Bitmap, 64–65
flipping with, 63
mirroring with, 62
overview, 55–58
pre and post methods for, 61
setRotation method, 58–59
setScale method, 60
setTranslate method, 61
MediaController class, adding controls with
playing video with MediaPlayer class,
208
playing video with VideoView, 199–200
MediaController view, 208
MediaPlayer class, 109–115
controlling playback, 111–115
creating object, 110
and Local Service
binding with, 132–137
implementing in, 129–132
networked video playback with, 221
playing video with, 200–210
adding controls with MediaController
class, 208
example of, 202–208
states of, 200–201
MediaPlayer constructor, 137
MediaRecorder class, 154–166
example of, 157–161
setAudioEncoder method, 156

setAudioSource method, 155
setOutputFile method, 156
setOutputFormat method, 155
state of, 156
MediaRecorder for video, 235–245
  audio and video bitrates, 238
  audio and video encoders, 237–238
  audio and video sources, 235–236
  audio channels, 239
  audio sample rate, 238–239
  maximum duration, 240
  maximum file size, 240
  output file, 242
  output format, 236–237
  permissions, 245
  preparing to record, 244
  preview Surface, 242–243
  profile, 241–242
  releasing resources, 244
  starting recording, 244
  state machine, 244–245
  stopping recording, 244
  video frame rate, 239
  video size, 239
MediaRecorder.AudioEncoder class, 156
MediaRecorder.AudioSource class, 235
MediaRecorder.MEDIA_RECORDER_INFO_
  FILESIZE_REACHED constant, 240
MediaRecorder.MEDIA_RECORDER_INFO_
  MAX_DURATION_REACHED
  constant, 240
MediaRecorder.OutputFormat class, 155,
  237
MediaRecorder.OutputFormat.MPEG_4
  constant, 155
MediaRecorder.OutputFormat.RAW_AMR
  constant, 155
MediaRecorder.OutputFormat.THREE_GPP
  constant, 156
MediaRecorder.VideoSource class, 236
MediaScanner service, 217
MediaStore
  for audio, 115–123
    accessing audio from, 115–117
    album browsing app example,
     118–123
    browsing audio in, 118
  inserting audio into, 167
  for video, 211–218
    example of, 212–218
    thumbnails from, 212

MediaStore class, 2, 12, 15, 18, 33, 283
MediaStore query, 215
MediaStore.Audio package, 115
MediaStore.Audio.Albums class, 119
MediaStore.Audio.Albums.ALBUM constant,
  119
MediaStore.Audio.Media class, 151, 167
MediaStore.Audio.Media.DATA constant,
  167
MediaStore.Audio.Media.RECORD_SOUND
  _ACTION action, 153
MediaStore.Images.Media class, 17
MediaStore.MediaColumns class, 211
MediaStore.Video class, 211
MediaStore.Video.Media class, 211
MediaStore.Video.Media query, 213
MediaStore.Video.Media._ID field, 211–212
MediaStore.Video.Media.DATA variable, 211
MediaStore.Video.Media.EXTERNAL_CONT
  ENT_URI constant, 211–212
MediaStore.Video.Thumbnails class, 211
MediaStore.Video.Thumbnails queries, 213
message variable, 287, 289
metadata
  for images, 10–22
    adding later, 12
    associating to image, 12–16
    is part of file, 21–22
    obtaining URI for image, 11
    prepopulating, 11–12
  for video, 232–235
method parameter, 257
MIC constant, 236
mirroring images, with Matrix class, 62
MotionEvent class, 94
MotionEvent.ACTION_CANCEL constant, 94
MotionEvent.ACTION_DOWN constant, 94
MotionEvent.ACTION_MOVE constant, 94
MotionEvent.ACTION_UP constant, 94
moveToFirst method, 18–19, 117
moveToNext method, 19, 118
moveToPosition method, 120, 122
MP3 format, 106
MPEG_4 constant, 237
MPEG_4_SP constant, 238
MultipartEntity class, 278–279, 284, 286
MULTIPLY mode, 73
Music app, using via intent, 107–108
Music directory, 108
myfavoritepicture.jpg file, 5

N

NETWORK_PROVIDER constant, 264
networked audio, 137–150
    HTTP playback, 137–143
    RTSP streaming, 150
    streaming audio via HTTP, 143–149
networked video, 218–228
    HTTP, 218–219
    playback with MediaPlayer, 221
    playback with VideoView, 221
    RTSP, 219–221
nojsoncallback parameter, 257
Nyquist, Harry, 188

O

of MediaRecorder class, 156
Ogg format, 106
onActivityResult method, 16, 48, 50, 73, 98,
    153–154, 229–231
onBind method, 127–128
onBufferingUpdate method, 142, 222
onClick method, 33, 40, 49, 98, 114, 141,
    153, 159, 231, 247
OnClickListener method, 14–15, 19, 231
onCompletion method, 111, 113, 130,
    141–142, 153–154, 161, 204–205
OnCompletionListener interface, 140
onCreate method, 13–14, 27, 44, 48, 119,
    140, 159, 203, 209
onDestroy method, 128, 130
onError method, 141, 205
onInfo method, MediaRecorder class, 240,
    242
onItemClick method, 214
onListItemClick method, ListActivity class,
    120
onLocationChanged method, 265, 268
onPause method, 265
onPictureTaken method, 32–33, 36
onPostExecute method, 176, 285
onPrepare method, 226
onPrepareAsync method, 226
onPrepared method, 142, 148, 204, 206,
    209
OnPreparedListener interface, 140, 206
onProgressUpdate method, 165, 176, 192,
    285
onProviderDisabled method, 265, 269
onProviderEnabled method, 265, 269

onServiceConnected method, 134
onServiceDisconnected method, 135
onStart method, 111, 128, 130
onStartCommand method, 128, 130
onStatusChanged method, 265
onStop method, 111, 265
onTouch method, 93, 95, 98–99, 185–186
OnTouchListener activity, 185
OnTouchListener interface, 93
ORDER BY clause, 17, 116
ORDER BY variable, 121
org.apache.http package, 252
org.json package, 254
OUT_OF_SERVICE constant, 266
OutputStream class, 286
ovals, with Canvas class, 86

P

Paint class, 82–83
    setColor method, 82
    setStrokeWidth method, 83
    setStyle method, 83
Paint.setTypeface method, 90–91
Paint.Style class, 83
Paint.Style.FILL constant, 83
Paint.Style.FILL_AND_STROKE constant, 83
Paint.Style.STROKE constant, 83
parameters, for Camera class, 27–30
Parameters.set method, 27, 29
parse method, 274
parseButton button, 145
parsePlaylistFile method, 145–146
parseResult method, 285
paths, with Canvas class, 87
pause method, 141, 148, 199
PCM format, 107
Pelletier, Claude, 91
permissions, and Camera class, 24
photo element, 258
PlayAudio class, 174
playButton button, 145, 147
playing video, 195–210
    with intent, 196–197
    with MediaPlayer class, 200–210
        adding controls with MediaController
            class, 208
        example of, 202–208
        states of, 200–201
    supported formats, 195–196
    with VideoView, 197–200

PlaylistFile class, 149
playlistItems Vector, 145–148
playPlaylistItems method, 145, 147
playRecording Button, 153–154, 159–161
playVideoButton button, 230–231, 233
PorterDuff.Mode class, 70
PorterDuffXfermode class, 70, 75–78
post methods, for Matrix class, 61
POST request, 252, 278
postingResult variable, 282
postTranslate method, Matrix class, 62
pre methods, for Matrix class, 61
prepare method, 138, 159, 162, 166, 204, 244, 247
prepareAsync method, 138–139, 141–142, 148, 204, 224
prepareRecorder method, 247–248
preview size, for Camera class, 30–32
ProgressListener interface, 285–286
ProgressMultipartEntity class, 284–286
ProgressOutputStream class, 286
publishProgress method, 165, 175–176, 192, 285

Q

qt-faststart application, 219
QUALITY_HIGH constant, CamcorderProfile class, 241–242, 247
QUALITY_LOW constant, CamcorderProfile class, 241

R

R class, 130
raw folder, res folder, 110
RAW_AMR constant, 237
Real Time Streaming Protocol. See RTSP
RealDoubleFFT class, 189–190
Real-time Transport Protocol (RTP), 220
RECORD_REQUEST constant, 153–154
RECORD_SOUND_ACTION constant, 151
RecordAmplitude class, 162–163
RecordAudio class, 175, 190
recording video, using intents, 229–232
rectangles, with Canvas class, 85
RectF class, 85
release method, 167, 244, 248
Remote Service, vs. Local Service, 126
removeCallbacks method, 44

removeUpdates method, 265
Representational State Transfer. See REST
requestLocationUpdates method, 264–265, 267
res folder, 110–111
reset method, 205
res/layout/main.xml file, 20, 37, 231, 234
res/layout/main.xml interface, 45
REST (Representational State Transfer), 273–278
    representing data in XML, 273
    SAX parsing, 274–278
RESULT_OK constant, 154, 231
RGB_565 constant, 80
R.java file, gen folder, 109
Rodriguez, Alex, 273
R.raw.goodmorningandroid constant, 130
RTP (Real-time Transport Protocol), 220
RTSP (Real Time Streaming Protocol)
    audio streaming, 150
    networked video, 219–221

S

sample rate, audio, 238–239
samples, for audio, 182–187
saturation, changing with ColorMatrix class, 69
Save Button, 103
savePicture button, 101–102
saveVideoButton button, 233
SAX parsing, 274–278
SAXParser class, 274–275
SAXParserFactory class, 274–275
SECONDS_BETWEEN_PHOTOS constant, 44–45
seek command, 207
setAudioChannels method, 166, 239
setAudioEncoder method, 155–156, 160, 238–239
setAudioEncodingBitRate method, 166
setAudioSampleRate method, MediaPlayer class, 238
setAudioSamplingRate method, 166
setAudioSource method, 155, 160, 235
setColor method, 82
setColorEffect method, 29
setContentHandler method, 274
setContentView method, 13, 199
setDataAndType method, 196

setDataSource method, 138, 141, 147, 159, 203, 223

setDisplay method, 204

setDisplayOrientation(int degrees) method, Camera class, 29

setEntity method, 279

setFlashMode(Camera.Parameters.FLASH_ MODE_AUTO) method, 29

setListAdapter method, 119

setLooping(true) method, 112

setMaxDuration method, 162, 240

setMaxFileSize method, 162, 240

setMediaPlayer method, 209

setOneShotPreviewCallback(Camera.Previe wCallback) method, 34

setOnTouchListener method, 93

setOutputFile method, 155–156, 160

setOutputFormat method, 155–156, 160, 162, 236

setPreviewCallback(Camera.PreviewCallbac k) method, 34

setPreviewCallbackWithBuffer(Camera.Previ ewCallback) method, 34

setPreviewDisplay method, 243, 247

setProfile method, MediaRecorder class, 241

setRotation method, for Matrix class, 58–59

setScale method, Matrix class, 60, 62

setStrokeWidth method, for Paint class, 83

setStyle method, for Paint class, 83

setTextSize method, 88

setTranslate method, Matrix class, 61

setTypeface method, 88

setValues method, Matrix class, 55

setVideoEncoder method, MediaRecorder class, 155, 237

setVideoEncodingBitrate method, MediaRecorder class, 238

setVideoFrameRate method, 239

setVideoSize method, 240

setVideoSource method, 155, 236

setVideoUrl method, 286, 288

setVisibility method, 14

Short.MAX_VALUE constant, 191

SIZE column, 116

size restrictions, and capturing images using Camera app, 5

SizedCameraIntent activity, 10

Software tag, 21

src attribute, 288

src directory, 189

start method, 141, 156, 198–199, 244, 248

startActivity method, 3, 108

startActivityForResult method, 3, 14, 73, 153–154, 231

startButton button, 40, 140, 142

startDocument method, 276

startElement method, 277, 287

startId parameter, 128

startPlaybackButton button, 134

startRecording Button, 160

startRecording method, 169

StartService button, 127

startService command, 130

startService method, 127–128

startServiceButton button, 127

startStopButton button, 43

state variable, 276–277, 288

states
of MediaPlayer class, 200–201
of MediaRecorder class, 156

status element, 288

status variable, 265, 288

stop method, 148, 242, 244, 248

stopButton button, 140, 145, 148

stopPlaybackButton button, 134

stopRecording Button, 159–161

stopService method, 127–128

stopServiceButton button, 127

StringBuilder class, 279

supported formats
for audio, 106–107
for video, 195–196

SURFACE_TYPE_PUSH_BUFFERS constant, 243

surfaceChanged method, 243

surfaceCreated method, 28, 32, 204, 243

surfaceDestroyed method, 204, 243

SurfaceHolder class, 24, 222, 245

SurfaceHolder.Callback interface, 202–204, 243–244, 246–247

SurfaceHolder.Callback methods, 36

<SurfaceView /> element, 24

SurfaceView class, 24–25

synth_frequency variable, 186–187

synthesizing audio, 179–187
generating samples, 182–187
playing synthesized sound, 180–182

System.currenTimeMillis( ) method, 17

T

tags parameter, 257
takePicture method, Camera class, 32–33
TEMPORARILY_UNAVAILABLE constant, 265
Test_Movie_iPhone.m4v file, 196
TextView class, 222, 261, 282
Thread.sleep(500) method, 165
THREE_GPP constant, 237
thumbnails, from MediaStore for video, 212
time-lapse photography app, with Camera class, 43–45
timer-based camera app, with Camera class, 38–42
title variable, 282
toString method, 253
touch events, for finger painting, 93–96
true (while) loop, 170
try catch block, 247, 253, 256
Typeface class, 88, 90
Typeface.create method, 90
Typeface.createFromAsset method, 91
Typeface.DEFAULT constant, 89
Typeface.DEFAULT_BOLD constant, 89
Typeface.MONOSPACE constant, 88
Typeface.SANS_SERIF constant, 88
Typeface.SERIF constant, 88

U

update method, 232, 234
upx variable, 95
upy variable, 95
URI, obtaining for images, 11
Uri.fromFile method, 117
URL field, 144
UserComment tag, 21
UserXMLHandler class, 275–276
uses-permission tag, 249, 266
using Music app via intent, 107

V

video, 195–228
    MediaStore for, 211–218
        example of, 212–218
        thumbnails from, 212
    networked, 218–228
        HTTP, 218–219
        playback with MediaPlayer, 221

playback with VideoView, 221
RTSP, 219–221
    playback of, 195–210
        with intent, 196–197
        with MediaPlayer class, 200–202, 208–210
        supported formats, 195–196
        with VideoView, 197–200
video capture, 229–250
    adding video metadata, 232–235
    custom. See also MediaRecorder for video
        full custom example, 246–250
    recording video using intents, 229–232
video frame rate, 239
VIDEO_CAPTURED constant, 229–231, 282
VideoGalleryAdapter class, 214–215
videoHeight property, 206
videoUrl variable, 283, 285
VideoView
    networked video playback with, 221
    playing video with, 197–200
VideoView class, 214, 221
VideoViewInfo class, 215
videoWidth property, 206
View class, 93
View.GONE constant, 14
View.INVISIBLE constant, 14
visualizing frequencies, 189
VOICE_CALL constant, 155, 236
VOICE_DOWNLINK constant, 155, 236
VOICE_RECOGNITION constant, 155, 236
VOICE_UPLINK constant, 155, 236

W

web services, media consumption and publishing using, 251–290
    HTTP file uploads
        overview, 278–290
        uploading video to Blip.TV, 280
    HTTP requests
        making, 278–280
        overview, 252–254
    JSON, 254–272
        pulling Flickr images using, 257–272
        using location as part of request, 263–272
    overview, 251–252
    REST, 273–278
        representing data in XML, 273

SAX parsing, 274–278
what parameter, 240
WHERE clause, 17, 116, 121
while (true) loop, 170
while clause, 214
write method, 180, 182, 286
writeTo method, 286

■X, Y, Z

Xfermode class, 70
XML, representing data in, 273
XMLHandler class, 274
XMLReader class, 274–276
XMLUser class, 275, 277

You Need the Companion eBook